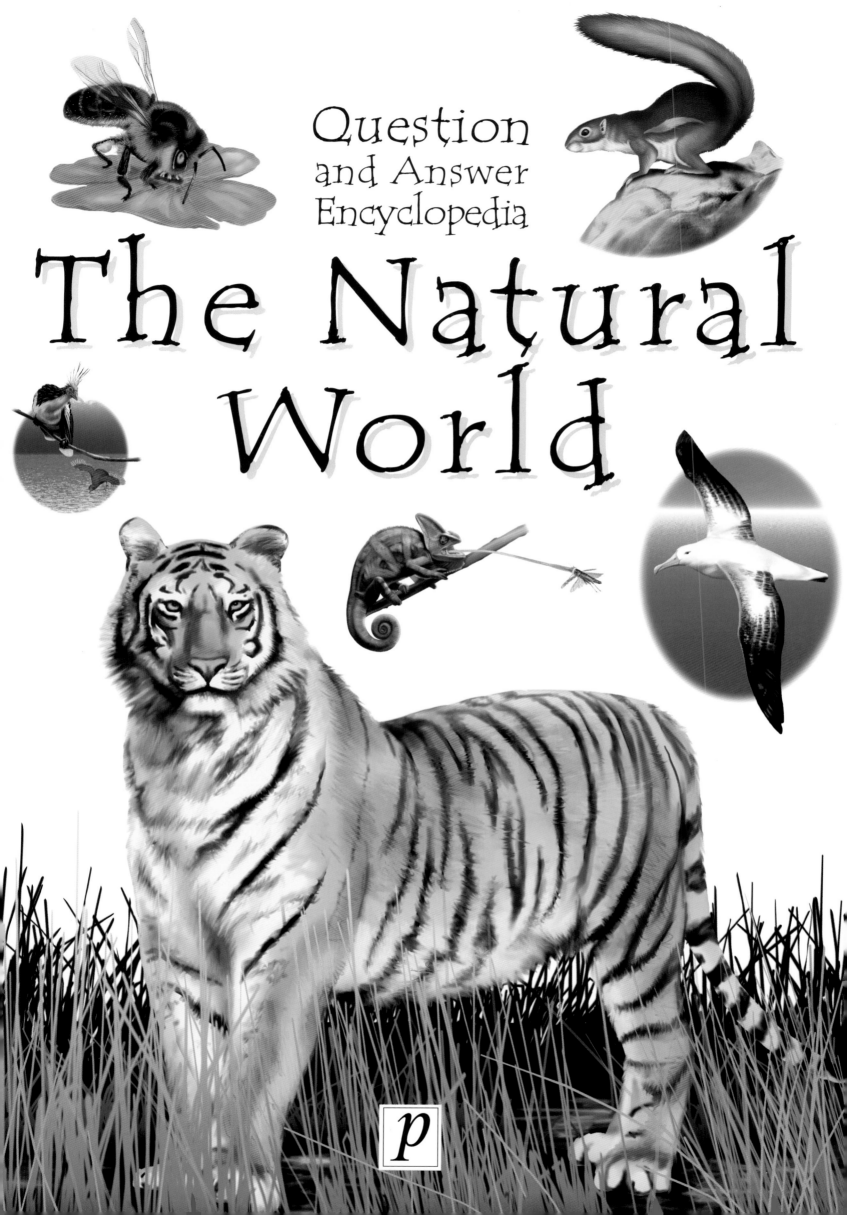

Question
and Answer
Encyclopedia

The Natural World

p

Question and Answer Encyclopedia
The Natural World

This is a Parragon Publishing Book
First published in 2000

Parragon Publishing
Queen Street House
4 Queen Street
Bath BA1 1HE, UK

ISBN 0-75253-843-8

Printed in Hong Kong

Produced by
Monkey Puzzle Media Ltd
Gissing's Farm
Fressingfield
Suffolk IP21 5SH
UK

Written by Anita Ganeri, Jen Green, Lucinda Hawksley,
Malcolm Penny, Joyce Pope and John Stidworthy
Illustrated by Michael Posen
Edited by Linda Sonntag and Stephen Setford
Designed by Simon Borrough, Sarah Crouch and Victoria Webb
Artwork commissioning: Roger Goddard-Coote
Project manager: Alex Edmonds

Contents

Sea Creatures

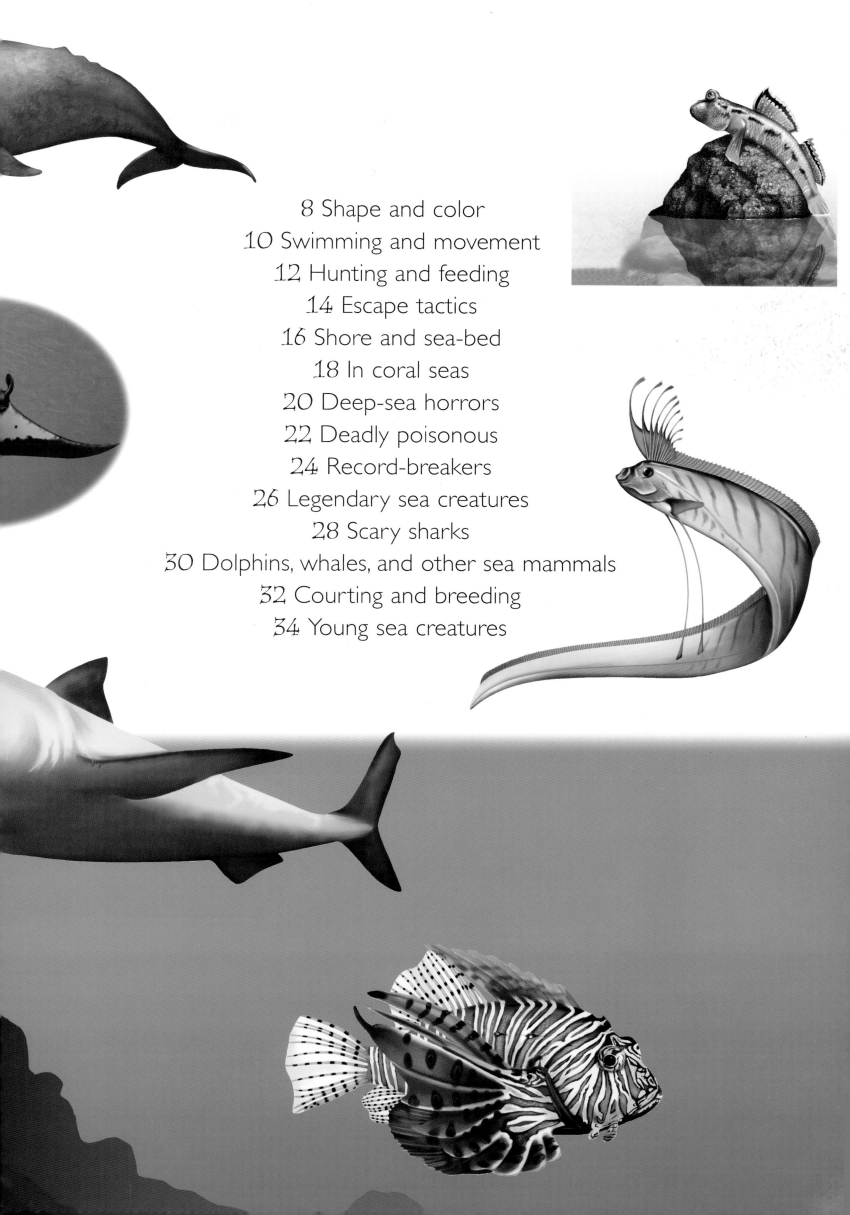

Why do most fish have slim, tapering bodies?

MOST CREATURES THAT SPEND THEIR WHOLE LIVES IN WATER HAVE A

sleek, streamlined shape that helps them to swim. Fish come in many different shapes and sizes. Eels are long and slender, plaice and rays are flat. Angelfish are tall and thin, so they are hard to see from the front, as they approach their prey. Other fish are rounded, but almost all have a tapering shape, that allows them to slip easily through the water.

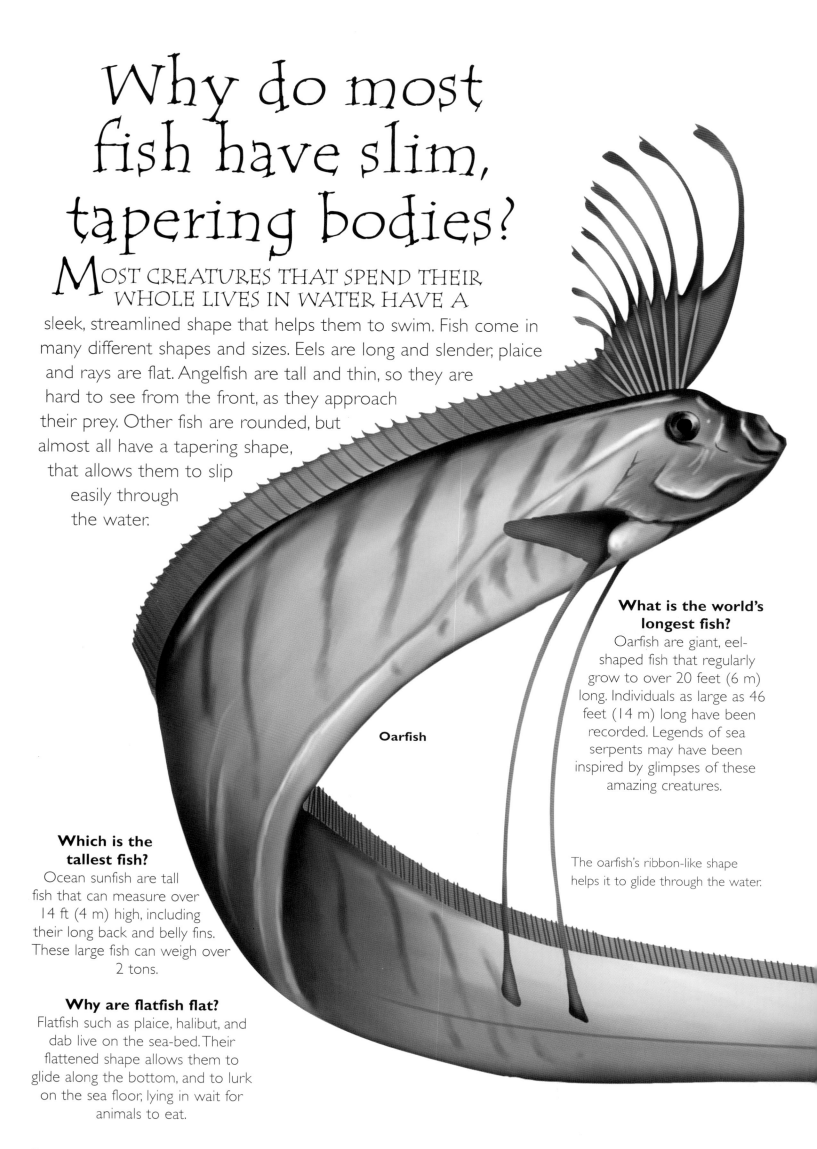

Oarfish

What is the world's longest fish?
Oarfish are giant, eel-shaped fish that regularly grow to over 20 feet (6 m) long. Individuals as large as 46 feet (14 m) long have been recorded. Legends of sea serpents may have been inspired by glimpses of these amazing creatures.

The oarfish's ribbon-like shape helps it to glide through the water.

Which is the tallest fish?
Ocean sunfish are tall fish that can measure over 14 ft (4 m) high, including their long back and belly fins. These large fish can weigh over 2 tons.

Why are flatfish flat?
Flatfish such as plaice, halibut, and dab live on the sea-bed. Their flattened shape allows them to glide along the bottom, and to lurk on the sea floor, lying in wait for animals to eat.

How do fish hide in the open sea?

Herring, mackerel and many other fish, that swim near the surface of the great oceans, have dark backs and pale bellies. This coloring, called countershading, works to cancel out the effect of sunlight shining on their bodies from above, and so helps these fish to hide even in open water.

What creatures plant a garden on their backs?

Spider crabs make their own disguises, from materials they find in the sea around them. They clip living sponges, or fronds of seaweed with their strong pincers, and plant them on their backs. When the seaweed dies, they replace it with a fresh piece!

Why do some fish have bright colors?

Many fish that live in tropical seas are brightly colored, or marked with bold spots and patterns. This coloring helps them to hide among the brightly colored coral and dark shadows, but also helps them to stand out clearly in open water. In the breeding season, when these fish are seeking mates and want to be noticed, they swim out into the open and become very obvious.

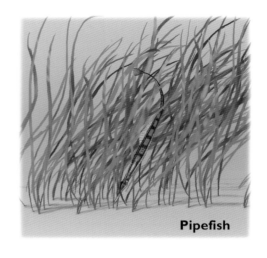

Pipefish

Predators find it very difficult to spot pipefish hiding among strands of seaweed.

What fish looks like seaweed?

Pipefish are long, slim, dark green fish that look just like strands of seaweed. In shallow, weedy waters, they swim upright among the seaweed fronds, and resemble their surroundings so closely, that they are almost impossible to see.

Carpet shark

The carpet shark's camouflage helps to conceal it from its prey.

How does the carpet shark stay hidden?

MANY SEA CREATURES HAVE BODIES WITH COLORS, shapes and patterns that blend in with their surroundings. This natural disguise, or camouflage, helps them to hide from enemies or sneak up on their prey. Carpet sharks live and hunt on the sea-bed. Their pale, blotchy colors help hide them from their prey – small fish and crabs – as they lie motionless on the bottom.

Flying fish leap up to 6 feet
(2 m) in the air, and glide
along with outstretched fins.

Flying fish

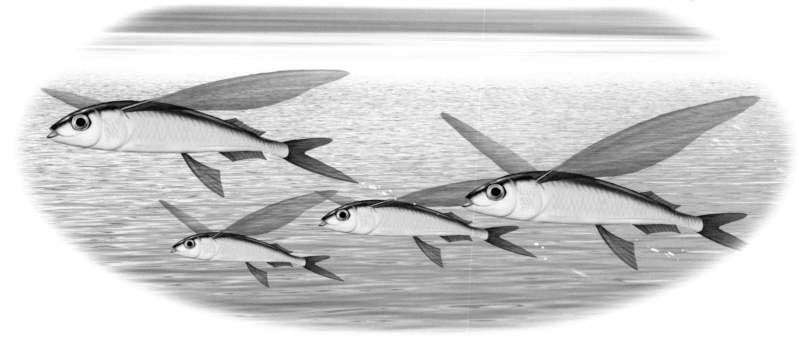

What sea creature looks like a pair of false teeth?
Scallops have a hard, hinged shell to protect their soft bodies. Some kinds of scallop swim along by clapping the two halves of their shell together, so water shoots out of the back. The swimming scallop looks like a pair of false teeth chattering as it zips along!

Which fish is the fastest swimmer?
Sailfish are large hunting fish that live in the open ocean. With their long, streamlined snouts, torpedo-shaped bodies and powerful tails, they can speed along at up to 67 mph (109 kph).

Which sea creature is the deepest diver?
Sperm whales are expert divers. Like all whales, they breathe at the surface, but swim down to depths of 1,600 feet (500 m) to hunt deep-sea creatures, such as giant squid. The snouts of sperm whales often bear the scars of battles with the squid.

How do fish swim?
Most fish swim by arching their bodies, and swishing their tails from side to side. The fish's body and tail push against the water to propel it forward. The chest, back, and belly fins help with steering and braking. A gas-filled organ, called the swim bladder, keeps the fish buoyant in the water.

Which sea creature uses jet-propulsion?
The octopus has a funnel-shaped siphon sticking out from its body. It shoots a jet of water from the funnel, to propel itself along, and can point its siphon in different directions to steer.

Which fish "flies" underwater?
Rays are flattened fish that live near the sea-bed. They swim along by flapping their wide, flat chest fins like wings, so they look as if they are flying underwater.

Which fish flies through the air?

Flying fish take to the air to escape from hungry predators such as sailfish and marlin. The flying fish gets up speed, then leaps right out of the water. In the air, it spreads its chest fins so they act like wings, keeping the fish airborne for up to 325 feet (100 m).

Mudskippers survive on land by filling their large gill-chambers with water.

How do jellyfish get about?

Jellyfish are soft creatures with bodies shaped like bells or saucers. To get about, they contract their bag-like bodies so water shoots out behind, pushing the creature along.

Which fish can walk on land?

Mudskippers are fish that live in swamps and muddy estuaries on tropical coasts. They come right out of the water and scurry about on land, using their muscular chest fins as crutches.

Why do dolphins leap out of the water?

DOLPHINS AND WHALES HAVE TAILS THAT ARE FLATTENED HORIZONTALLY, not vertically like fish-tails. They swim by sweeping their tails up and down. When swimming at speed, dolphins leap out of the water to save energy, because is is quicker and easier to move through air than water. Like all water-dwelling mammals, dolphins must also surface to breathe.

Mudskipper

How do barracuda surprise their prey?

The barracuda is a fierce hunting fish of tropical seas. It has keen eyesight and is armed with razor-sharp teeth. Its blue-grey coloring blends in well with the ocean, allowing it to sneak up on a shoal of small fish. The hunter speeds into the middle of the shoal with its jaws snapping, and seizes its prey in its deadly teeth.

How does the anemone catch its dinner?

Sea anemones are armed with a crown of stinging tentacles. When small fish brush against them, the stings fire and release a paralyzing poison. Then the tentacles push the weakened prey into the anemone's mouth.

Which fish has a fishing rod?

THE ANGLERFISH HAS A BUILT-IN FISHING ROD ON ITS HEAD – A LONG, THIN spine with a fleshy lobe on the end that looks like a wiggling worm. The angler lurks on the sea-bed, squat-bodied and well-camouflaged. When a small crab comes up to eat the "worm" the anglerfish lunges forward and grabs its prey in its enormous mouth.

Which fish has a secret weapon?

The torpedo ray. It can generate electricity using special muscles in its head. The ray lurks on the sea-bed, waiting for small fish to pounce on. It wraps its fins around its victims and blasts them with a charge of 200 volts.

The anglerfish lures its prey with its built-in fishing rod, complete with bait.

Archerfish start to shoot water when they are young, but only the adults can aim well enough to hit their target.

Archerfish

Which fish runs a cleaning service?

S MALL FISH, CALLED CLEANER WRASSE, feed on parasites that infest larger fish. The big fish welcome this cleaning service, so do not harm the wrasse, even when it swims right inside a big fish's mouth to clean it. Sometimes queues of fish form at the wrasse's cleaning station, patiently waiting their turn for a "wash and brush-up."

Which fish shoots to kill?

On tropical sea coasts, skilled archerfish can catch prey, such as spiders, that are perched on plants overhanging the water. With their powerful lips, they squirt a jet of water at their target and knock their prey into the water.

Anglerfish

How do parrotfish eat their meals?

Parrotfish have hard mouths shaped like parrots' beaks. With their tough mouths, they scrape algae and coral from the rocks. This food is then ground to a powder by horny plates inside the fish's mouth.

What fish is a thirsty bloodsucker?

Lampreys are strange fish with eel-shaped bodies. Instead of jaws, they have round mouths, filled with rows of horny teeth. The lamprey uses its mouth as a sucker, to fasten on to another fish's body. Its teeth scrape away the fish's skin, then the lamprey drinks its blood!

What creature gives a nasty nip?

Porcupine fish

CRABS AND THEIR RELATIVES, LOBSTERS, BELONG TO A GROUP OF shelled creatures called crustaceans. The crab's soft body parts are protected by a hard outer case that forms a snug suit of armor. The creature is also armed with powerful claws, that can give a nasty nip if an enemy comes too close.

How do herring avoid being eaten?

Fish, such as herring and mackerel, swim in groups called shoals. Living in a large group provides safety in numbers, because it is difficult for predators to single out a likely target among a shifting, shimmering mass of fish.

What is slimy and hides in anemones?

In tropical seas, clownfish hide from their enemies among the stinging tentacles of sea anemones. The tentacles do not harm the clownfish, because its body is covered with a thick layer of slimy mucus, but no predator dares to come close!

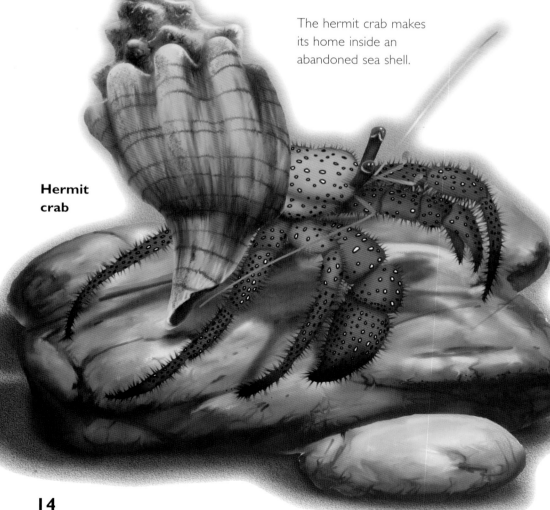

The hermit crab makes its home inside an abandoned sea shell.

Hermit crab

Which fish makes eyes at its enemies?

The twinspot wrasse has two dark patches on its back. Hunting fish may mistake the spots for the eyes of a large and possibly dangerous creature, and swim away. If this trick fails, the wrasse has another. It dives down to the sea-bed and quickly buries itself in the sand.

Why does the hermit crab need a home?

Unlike other crabs, the hermit crab has no hard case to protect it. Instead, it shelters its soft rear end inside an empty sea shell. As the crab grows bigger, its shell becomes too tight, so it moves into a larger new home.

Few predators will tackle a porcupine fish once it has inflated itself into a spiny ball.

Which creature can grow four new arms?

The starfish is a five-limbed sea creature. If a hungry predator bites off one of its arms, the starfish can grow a new one to replace it. In fact, it can replace up to four of its arms, provided the central body of the animal is unharmed.

Which creature throws ink at its enemies?

Cuttlefish are relatives of squid and octopus. Like their cousins, they can produce a cloud of ink to confuse their enemies. The cuttlefish jets away under cover of this "smokescreen."

What makes a pistol shrimp go bang?

Pistol shrimps are named after the cracking noise they make by snapping their claws. Enemies are frightened off by these unexpected "pistol shots."

Which fish blows itself up into a prickly ball?

THE PORCUPINE FISH IS NAMED FOR THE SHARP SPINES, LIKE A PORCUPINE'S, that cover its body. Usually the spines lie flat against the fish's body, but if danger threatens, it can raise them. If an enemy comes too close, the fish takes in water, so that its body swells to twice its normal size. It becomes a prickly ball too large and uncomfortable for predators to swallow. When the danger passes, the porcupine slowly returns to its normal shape and size.

Spiny lobsters cover up to 9 miles (15 km) a day as they migrate along the sea-bed in a line.

Spiny lobsters

What buries itself in the sand?

MANY CREATURES THAT DWELL ON THE OCEAN BOTTOM ESCAPE from their enemies, by burying themselves in the sand or mud. Crabs dig down and lie low with just their sensitive antennae showing. Weeverfish, which hide in the same way, have eyes on top of their heads. Their eyes stick out above the sand, so the fish can still see while the rest of its body is buried.

Which fish "walks" on three legs?

The tripod fish is a strange fish that lives in deep, dark waters. Its two chest fins and tail fin have long, stiff spines. Together, the three spines form a tripod which the fish uses to rest and move along the sea-bed.

The tripod fish uses its stiff spines like stilts to walk along the sea-bed.

Tripod fish

How did the butterfish get its name?

Butterfish are long, slender fish that live in pools on rocky sea-shores. The slimy, slippery feel of their bodies has earned them their name.

How does a limpet grip its rock?

The limpet clamps its muscular foot on to a seaside rock, and grips by suction. Even the pounding waves cannot dislodge it. Its hold is so tight it can be prised away only if an enemy attacks without warning.

Which creature has five sets of jaws?

Underneath its round, spiny body, the sea urchin has a mouth with five sets of jaws. It feeds by crawling along the sea floor, scraping up seaweed and tiny creatures from the rocks.

Why do crabs walk sideways?

All crabs have ten legs – eight for walking and two with powerful pincers for picking up food. Crabs scuttle sideways along the shore and sea-bed. The sideways movement helps to prevent them tripping over their own legs! Large species of crab move only slowly, but small ghost crabs can scurry along the shore at a fast clip.

What queues up for its winter vacation?

Spiny lobsters live mainly solitary lives. But each year in the fall they gather to move to deeper waters, where they will be safe from violent storms. The lobsters form a long line, and march off along the sea-bed. When they reach their winter destination they separate, and only meet up again to begin the long trip back.

Which fish would disappear on a chess board?

Plaice are flatfish that live on the sea-bed. In a matter of minutes, they can change their body color, from pale and sandy, to dark or blotchy, to match their surroundings as they drift over the sea-bed in search of food. They can even adjust their coloring to become checkered, if a chess board is placed under them! Only the upper part of the fish, visible to enemies, is colored. The underside is white.

What needs a new suit of armor every year?

A crab's shell gives good protection. The disadvantage is that there is no space inside for the crab to grow! Each year, the crab sheds its old, tight skin and grows a new, slightly larger one. While the new soft skin is still hardening the creature is very easy to attack, so it hides away from enemies under rocks.

What is coral made of?

CORAL REEFS ARE MADE BY TINY CREATURES CALLED POLYPS

that live in colonies in tropical seas. Polyps are shaped like little sea anemones, but have a hard, chalky cup-shaped shell to protect their bodies. When they die, the shells remain, and new polyps grow on top of them. Over time, billions of shells build up to form a coral reef.

Surgeon fish

Where is the world's biggest coral reef?
The Great Barrier Reef off the north-east coast of Australia is the world's largest coral reef. Stretching for 1,200 miles (2,000 km), it is the largest structure made by living creatures. The reef is home to many spectacular animals, including 1,500 different kinds of fish.

What are dead man's fingers?
Dead man's fingers is a species of soft coral that grows on rocks. Each coral colony is made up of thousands of polyps that form a fleshy mass, like a rubbery hand. When a piece of this coral washes up on the sea-shore, it may give swimmers a fright!

Why does a crown-of-thorns threaten coral reefs?
The crown-of-thorns starfish is a reef-killer. It fastens on to the living coral, sticks its stomach out, and releases juices that digest the coral polyps. When only the coral shells are left, the starfish moves on. It can kill a big patch of coral in a day, and has destroyed large areas of the Great Barrier Reef.

Leafy seadragon

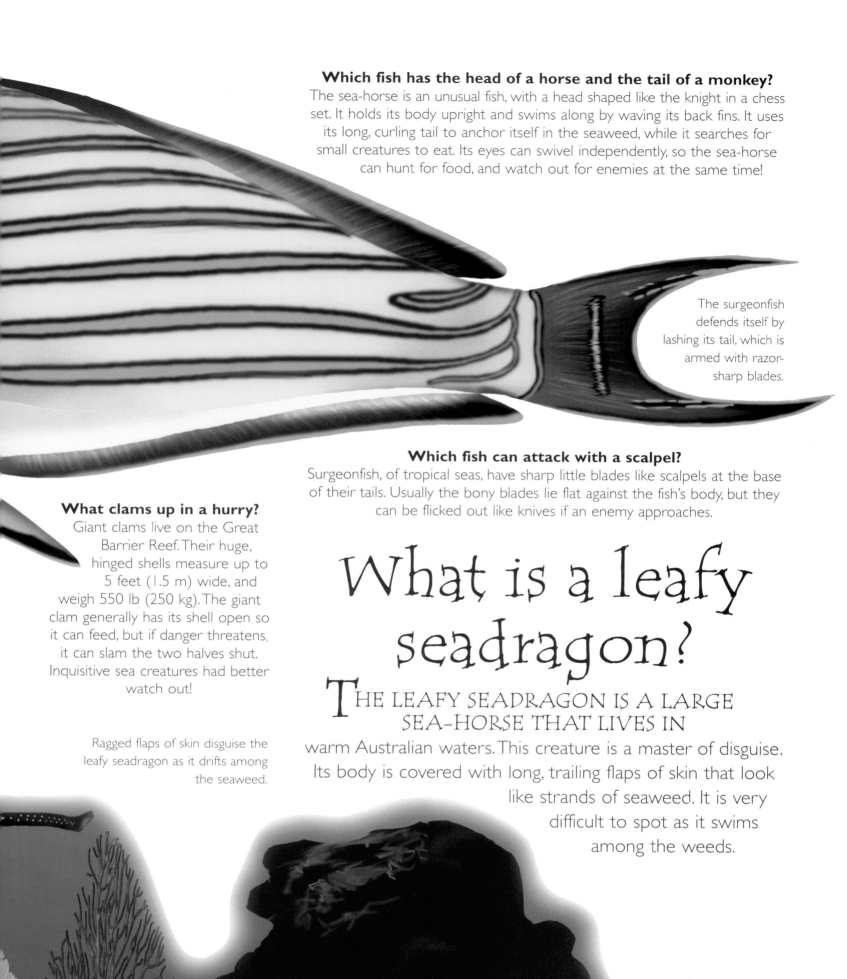

Which fish has the head of a horse and the tail of a monkey?

The sea-horse is an unusual fish, with a head shaped like the knight in a chess set. It holds its body upright and swims along by waving its back fins. It uses its long, curling tail to anchor itself in the seaweed, while it searches for small creatures to eat. Its eyes can swivel independently, so the sea-horse can hunt for food, and watch out for enemies at the same time!

The surgeonfish defends itself by lashing its tail, which is armed with razor-sharp blades.

Which fish can attack with a scalpel?

Surgeonfish, of tropical seas, have sharp little blades like scalpels at the base of their tails. Usually the bony blades lie flat against the fish's body, but they can be flicked out like knives if an enemy approaches.

What clams up in a hurry?

Giant clams live on the Great Barrier Reef. Their huge, hinged shells measure up to 5 feet (1.5 m) wide, and weigh 550 lb (250 kg). The giant clam generally has its shell open so it can feed, but if danger threatens, it can slam the two halves shut. Inquisitive sea creatures had better watch out!

Ragged flaps of skin disguise the leafy seadragon as it drifts among the seaweed.

What is a leafy seadragon?

THE LEAFY SEADRAGON IS A LARGE SEA-HORSE THAT LIVES IN warm Australian waters. This creature is a master of disguise. Its body is covered with long, trailing flaps of skin that look like strands of seaweed. It is very difficult to spot as it swims among the weeds.

Hatchetfish

How do fish hide in dark seas?

Deep-sea fish are camouflaged to blend in with their surroundings. Many have black or dark bodies to match the inky waters. Others are transparent. Hatchetfish have silvery bodies that reflect any small gleams of light.

The hatchetfish has a line of tiny lights running down its belly that hides its shadow in the water.

What creatures can survive at great ocean depths?

Viperfish

A CENTURY AGO, SCIENTISTS BELIEVED THAT NO LIFE COULD EXIST in the very deep oceans. Now we know that creatures do survive there, but conditions are very harsh. 3,330 feet (one thousand metres) below the sunlit surface, the water is pitch-black and very cold. Deep-sea fish must be able to stand the great pressure caused by the weight of water on top of them, which would kill surface creatures. Many deep-sea fish look like monsters from a horror film, with large heads, huge mouths with fierce teeth, and long, thin bodies. Yet most of these deep-sea horrors are very small — less than 1 ft (30 cm) long.

Why are deep-sea fish mysterious?

SCIENTISTS STILL KNOW VERY LITTLE ABOUT DEEP-SEA FISH, BECAUSE of the difficulties of descending to the ocean bottom to study them. Most deep-sea fish don't survive if they are brought to the surface. Some even explode, because their bodies are built to withstand the great pressure of the ocean depths!

How do deep-sea creatures find their food in the dark?

In the black depths, many deep-sea fish sense their prey by smell, taste, and touch. A line of nerves running down the fish's body picks up vibrations in the water caused by other swimming creatures. Some deep-sea hunters have long touch- and taste-sensitive tentacles trailing from their jaws.

Can deep-sea fish see in the dark?

For many deep-sea fish, vision is little use in the inky darkness. They have tiny eyes, or no eyes at all, and cannot see. Other fish have large eyes that pick up any faint glimmers of light, or tube-shaped eyes that work like binoculars. Still other species make their own light to hunt their prey.

Why don't gulper eels get hungry?

Food is scarce in the ocean depths, for no water plants and few creatures live there. So fishes' meals are few and far between. Gulper eels and viperfish have large, stretchy stomachs that can expand to fit any victim that passes. Another deep-sea fish, the black swallower, can swallow and digest a fish twice its own size.

With its giant mouth, the viperfish is a fierce deep-ocean predator. The long teeth point backwards to make sure no prey escapes from its jaws.

What hunts with a luminous "worm"?

Like other anglerfish, the deep-sea angler has a long, thin spine that forms a "fishing rod" to catch prey creatures. On the end of the spine, a luminous lure dangles like a glowing worm to attract the fish's victims.

How do deep-sea creatures light up the dark?

As many as 1,000 different fish make light in the deep oceans. Some have luminous bacteria living under their skin. Others have special light-producing organs, or can cause a chemical reaction that gives off light.

Blue-ringed octopus

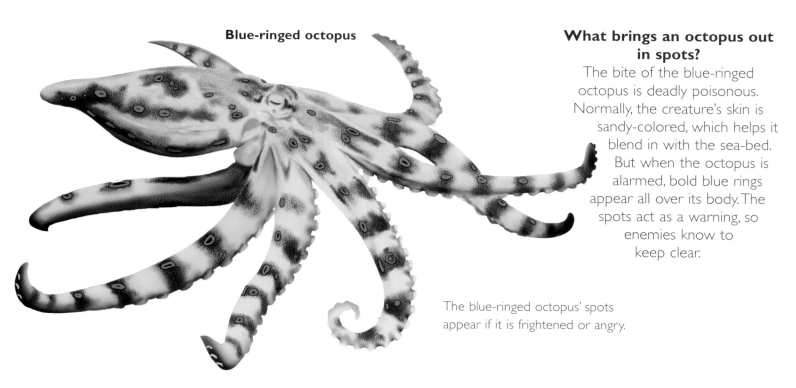

What brings an octopus out in spots?
The bite of the blue-ringed octopus is deadly poisonous. Normally, the creature's skin is sandy-colored, which helps it blend in with the sea-bed. But when the octopus is alarmed, bold blue rings appear all over its body. The spots act as a warning, so enemies know to keep clear.

The blue-ringed octopus' spots appear if it is frightened or angry.

How does a jellyfish sting?
The long, trailing tentacles of jellyfish are armed with thousands of tiny stinging cells. Some cells contain tightly-coiled barbs. When a careless fish brushes against a tentacle, the barbs fire, to pierce the victim's skin and release a paralyzing poison.

Which is the world's most poisonous reptile?
The bite of the yellow-bellied sea snake is 50 times more powerful than that of the dreaded king cobra. Its bold yellow-and-black colors warn of danger.

Lionfish

Why are lionfish brightly striped?

THE LIONFISH IS A BEAUTIFUL BUT deadly fish of tropical waters. Its long, graceful spines contain a lethal poison. The lionfish drifts lazily though the water with its orange-striped coloring, yet few enemies dare approach it. The fish's bright colors warn that it is poisonous. They are a signal known, and recognized, throughout the animal world.

What "stone" can kill you if you tread on it?

OVER 50 DIFFERENT KINDS OF POISONOUS FISH LURK IN THE WORLD'S OCEANS. Some are armed with venomous spines, others have poisonous flesh. The stonefish, of Australian waters, is one of the deadliest of all sea creatures. If a person treads on the fish, its spines release a toxin (poison) that causes agonizing pain. Numbness spreads through the victim's body, and they may die of shock, heart failure, or breathing problems.

In Australian waters, the scary sea wasp jellyfish is responsible for more deaths than sharks.

The lionfish's striped colors warn enemies to keep well away.

What sea creature can sting a person to death in four minutes?

Jellyfish look fragile, but many species are armed with painful stings. The box jellyfish, of South-east Asia, is so venomous that its sting can kill a person in just four minutes. The small sea wasp jellyfish of Australia is said to have the world's most painful sting.

Which deadly fish looks like a toad?

The toadfish is a poisonous fish that dwells on the sea-bed in warm oceans. The spines on its back fins, and gill covers, contain a strong venom that can cause great pain. With its bulging eyes, large mouth, and blotchy skin, the fish is well-named, for it looks just like a toad.

Which poisonous fish do people eat?

The entrails of the pufferfish contain a powerful poison. Yet other parts of the fish are said to taste delicious! In Japan, the fish is served as a delicacy called fugu. Japanese chefs are trained to remove all traces of the poisonous organs, yet each year people die from eating fugu, that has not been properly prepared.

What is the stingray's secret weapon?

Stingrays live and hunt on the ocean bottom. Their long, thin tails are armed with barbs that can inject a painful poison.

Which marine reptile is the biggest?

The saltwater crocodile is the world's largest sea-going reptile. This fierce giant grows up to 26 feet (8 m) long, and its jaws and teeth are jumbo-sized to match!

Saltwater or estuarine crocodiles are found on eastern sea coasts from India to Australia.

What sea creature is as big as four dinosaurs?

Speedy orcas grow up to 30 feet (9 m) long and weigh over 6 tons.

The blue whale is the giant of the oceans. Indeed, it is the largest animal ever to have lived on earth – four times the size of the biggest dinosaur! An adult blue whale measures up to 100 feet (32 m) long, and may weigh over 200 tons – as much as 60 elephants. Female blue whales are the biggest – the males are smaller.

What is the smallest fish?

The dwarf goby holds the record for the world's smallest fish. Adult dwarf gobies measure only 0.4 in (1 cm) long – about the width of your little finger. These tiny fish are found in the Indian Ocean.

What is the world's biggest crab?

The Japanese spider crab is the giant of the crab world. Its body measures more than 1 ft (30 cm) across, and a rowing boat would easily fit between its outstretched claws, which grow up to an astonishing span of 11 feet (3.5 m). At the other end of the scale, the tiniest crab is smaller than a pea.

What record-breaking fish came back to life?

Coelacanths are giant primitive fish that scientists knew from fossils, but believed had died out millions of years ago. Then in 1938, a living specimen of the "extinct" species was caught off South Africa. Now scientists in submersibles have studied coelacanths living on the sea-bed, off the island of Madagascar. Coelacanths are giant, blue-scaled fish with muscly fins which they may use to perch on the ocean bottom.

Killer whale

What is the world's largest mollusc?

Molluscs are a family of shelled creatures that include slugs, snails, clams, and also squid, and octopus. The largest mollusc is the giant squid. These creatures commonly grow 12 feet (3.6 m) long, but specimens as large as 69 feet (21 m) have been found washed up on beaches. Scientists know little about these mysterious deep-sea creatures, which have never been seen swimming in the ocean depths.

What is the biggest fish?

Fish vary more in size than any other group of animals with backbones (vertebrates). The largest fish is the whale shark, which grows up to 49 feet (15 m) long and weighs 20 tons. Though giant in size, whale sharks are not fierce hunters. They feed mainly on tiny shrimp-like creatures called krill.

What are the tiniest sea creatures?

Thousands of kinds of tiny creatures live in the world's oceans. The smallest are made up of just one cell, and must be magnified a thousand times or more before we can see them. Plankton is the name given to the billions of tiny plants and animals that float near the surface of the oceans. They are the main food of many fish, and other sea creatures.

Which is the fastest marine mammal?

The orca, or killer whale, is the speed champion among sea mammals. It can race along at up to 34 mph (56 kph) to catch its prey.

What is a chimera?

ACCORDING TO GREEK LEGEND, THE CHIMERA WAS A TERRIBLE monster with a lion's head, a goat's body, and a dragon's tail. Strange deep-sea fish, called chimeras, also look as if their bodies have been assembled from the parts of other creatures. They have large heads with staring eyes like bushbabies, and buck teeth like rabbits. Their bodies end in long, thin tails like rats' tails.

What is a kraken?
In olden days, myths and legends about dangerous sea creatures reflected the perils of ocean travel. Norwegian legends told of the kraken, a giant, many-armed monster that rose from the depths, wrapped its tentacles around unlucky ships, and dragged them down to the bottom. This legend is thought to be based on sightings of the mysterious deep-sea squid.

What is a mermaid's purse?
Dogfish are small sharks. The tough case, in which a baby dogfish develops, is called a mermaid's purse. Sometimes the empty cases are found washed up on beaches, but it is unlikely that mermaids keep their treasures there!

Which fish has devil's horns?
The manta ray or devilfish has two fins that curve forward from its head like devil's horns. The ray uses its "horns" to scoop food into its mouth as it swims along the sea-bed.

Are there sea monsters in Massachusetts?
Early American settlers lived in fear of a huge sea serpent that was said to live off the coast of Gloucester, Massachusetts. The monster was supposed to have been scaly with a long tongue, but nobody really knows what it looked like – or if it even existed!

Manta ray

Which white whale ate Captain Ahab's leg?
Herman Melville's classic novel, *Moby Dick*, tell the story of Captain Ahab and his hunt for the great white sperm whale that tore off his leg. In his ship, the *Pequod,* Ahab and his sailors sail all around the world in search of the whale. When they finally catch up with Moby Dick, they struggle for three days to catch him. Ahab finally harpoons the great monster just as the whale sinks the ship, and the unfortunate captain is dragged down to a watery grave.

Which nymph ate sailors?
An ancient Greek legend tells of a beautiful nymph, called Scylla, who argued with the Gods and was turned into a terrifying monster by them. This horrific creature was said to have six heads, each with three rows of teeth. It lived in a sea cave, but would venture out of the deep to prey on creatures like dolphins, sharks, and even sailors!

Who survived being eaten by a whale?
According to the Bible's Old Testament, a man called Jonah was traveling by sea when a storm blew up. Superstitious sailors cast the unlucky traveler overboard. A whale swallowed Jonah, but spat him out unharmed three days later. It would be truly miraculous if someone survived in a whale's stomach for three days, because there would be no air to breathe.

The giant manta ray looks scary, but is generally harmless to humans.

What fish carries the "sword of the sea"?
The killer whale has a tall, thin back fin 6.5 feet (2 m) long, that sticks straight out of the water, like a sword. Another sea creature, the swordfish, has a long snout shaped like a sword, but edged with tiny teeth. This large, powerful hunter catches its prey by swimming among a shoal of fish and slashing about wildly with its "sword." There have also been reports of swordfish piercing and sinking boats.

Do unicorns live in the sea?
Narwhals are small whales that swim in icy Arctic waters. Male narwhals have a strange left tooth that grows outward from the gum to form a long, spiralling tusk. In times past, narwhals' tusks found on beaches were sold as precious unicorn horns.

Are mermaids real?

IN BYGONE TIMES, SAILORS WHO HAD SPENT LONG MONTHS at sea sometimes reported seeing mermaids – creatures with the head and body of a woman, and a fish's tail. Experts now believe these stories may have been inspired by dugongs – rare sea mammals with rounded faces, which hold their bodies upright in the water.

Female dugongs sometimes cuddle their babies in their front flippers while they suckle, another human-like trait.

Dugong

Hammerhead shark

The flattened shape of the hammerhead's "hammer" may also help it float and manoeuvre.

What has up to 3,000 teeth?

Hunting sharks have triangular teeth with serrated (jagged) edges like a saw. A shark may have as many as 3,000 teeth in its mouth, arranged in up to 20 rows, but only the teeth on the outer edge of the jaw are actually used for biting. The inner teeth move outward to replace worn or broken teeth, so the shark's working set remain razor-sharp.

Which shark has a head like a hammer?

THE HAMMERHEAD SHARK IS NAMED FOR ITS CURIOUS HEAD, SHAPED like a giant letter "T." The shark's eyes and nostrils are set on the ends of its "hammer." As it moves along the sea-bed, it swings its head from side to side. Some scientists believe that the widely spaced eyes and nostrils help the hammerhead to home in on its prey.

Are all sharks deadly?

No. Scientists have identified about 380 different kinds of shark. Relatively few species are fierce predators, that hunt large prey, such as seals, squid, and penguins. Most sharks, such as whale sharks and basking sharks, feed on tiny creatures which they filter from the water, using their sieve-like mouths. No harm will come to you if you meet one – unless you die of fright!

The great white shark is nicknamed "white death." Its scientific name means "jagged teeth."

How do sharks track down their prey?

Sharks have many senses that help with hunting. An excellent sense of smell allows the shark to detect tiny amounts of blood dissolved in the water, and track down distant wounded animals. A special sense called "distant touch" helps it to pick up vibrations, caused by swimming creatures. At closer range, sensory pores, on the shark's snout, detect tiny electrical signals given off by prey animals' muscles. Sight and hearing also help the shark, as it moves in for the kill.

What would sink if it didn't swim?

Most fish have a special organ, called a swim bladder, that helps them to float. Sharks have no swim bladder, so they must keep swimming to avoid sinking. Moving forward also keeps a supply of oxygen-rich sea-water flowing over the shark's gills, which helps it breathe.

What makes one shark bite another?

The smell of blood sometimes excites sharks so much they go into a "feeding frenzy." A group of feeding sharks will start to snap wildly and bite one another, and may even tear one of their number to pieces in the excitement.

Great white shark

What is the world's most deadly shark?

The great white shark is the world's most feared sea creature. It is responsible for more attacks on humans than any other shark. Great whites grow to 23 feet (7 m) long. Their jaws are so powerful they can sever a human arm or leg in a single bite. Tiger and mako sharks are also known as killers.

What creature holds the record for long-distance ocean travel?
Gray whales are the champion travelers of the oceans. Each year, they journey from their breeding grounds in the tropics, to feeding grounds in the Arctic, and back again – a round trip of up to 12,500 miles (20,000 km).

Gray whale

Gray whales swim such huge distances on migration that scientists use satellites to track them.

Can dolphins talk?
Dolphins make all sorts of noises, from clicks and squeals, to groans and whistles. A school of hunting dolphins keep in constant touch with one another through these noises, and "talk" together to co-ordinate their hunt.

Each dolphin has its own special whistle, which helps the other members of its school to pinpoint its position during a hunt.

Why do whales and dolphins come to the surface?

WHALES AND DOLPHINS LOOK A LOT LIKE FISH, BUT THEY ARE REALLY sea-going mammals. Like all mammals, they breathe oxygen from the air, and so must surface to breathe. One or two nostrils, called blowholes, on top of the animal's head allow it to breathe, without lifting its head from the water. But dolphins and some whales sometimes rear right out of the water to look around, a technique called spy-hopping.

Dolphins

What hunts by sonar?

Dolphins hunt with the aid of their own built-in sonar system, called echolocation. As they swim along, they produce a stream of clicking sounds. Sound waves from the clicks spread out through the water. When they hit an object, such as a shoal of fish, they bounce back. The dolphin can sense the size, and movements, of its prey, by listening to the echoes.

What sleeps in a duvet of seaweed?

The sea otter makes its home among the kelp weed beds, of the eastern Pacific. While resting, the otter wraps seaweed fronds around its body, so it does not drift away with the ocean currents.

What eats its lunch in a bubble?

Humpback whales feed on small fish and krill floating near the sea surface. Sometimes they use a technique called bubble-netting, to catch their prey. The whale lurks below a shoal of fish, then swims slowly upward, blowing a stream of bubbles. The fish are trapped inside the net of bubbles and cannot escape from the whale's open jaws.

Which is the friendliest sea creature?

Dolphins are naturally playful and friendly to humans. They often swim alongside boats, riding on the bow-wave. Dolphins called "friendlies" regularly visit tourist beaches to swim with people. There are many reports of dolphins rescuing drowning people, and even saving swimmers from sharks.

The sea otter is a skillful tool-user

Which is the cleverest sea creature?

DOLPHINS ARE AMONG THE WORLD'S MOST intelligent creatures. Tests in aquariums show they learn to perform new tasks quickly, and can even pass on their skills by "talking" to dolphins in other tanks. Sea otters are clever too, for they are one of the few animals able to use tools. The otter feeds on sea urchins, crabs, and other shelled creatures. It breaks open the shells by smashing them against a flat rock, balanced on its chest.

Sea otter

Which sea creature feeds on its mate's blood?

DEEP-SEA ANGLERFISH HAVE UNUSUAL SEX LIVES. THE FEMALES ARE UP TO 20 times bigger than the males! When a tiny male meets a female, he clamps on to her side with his powerful jaws and won't let go. Eventually he becomes fused to her body and feeds on her blood. The female has a handy supply of sperm to fertilize her eggs – but has to carry the "hanger-on" wherever she goes.

Which creature has a midwife at the birth?

Pregnant dolphins give birth to a single baby up to a year after mating. Experienced female dolphins known as "midwives" help at the birth. They may support the mother's body or help lift the baby to the surface so it can breathe.

What makes a fiddler crab sexy?

Male fiddler crabs have a built-in "sex symbol" – one claw that is much bigger than the other. On the sea-shore, the males attract attention by scuttling up and down waving their giant claws. The females choose the most energetic males, with the biggest claws to mate with.

How do humpback whales go courting?

Humpback whales make many different sounds, including clicks, squeaks, moans, and roars. To attract a partner, the male humpback sings a "song" made up of different noises. Each male sings a different tune, lasting for hours, or even days. Humans enjoy the whale-song too – recordings of humpbacks have been made into hit CDs.

How do deep-sea creatures light up each others' lives?

In the darkness of the deep sea, many fish use light to attract a mate. Deep-sea viperfish, and dragonfish, have lines of tiny lights running along their bellies. Males and females have different patterns of lights, and can recognize the opposite sex when they see the right pattern.

The fiddler crab's giant claw gives him sex appeal, but is little help when feeding.

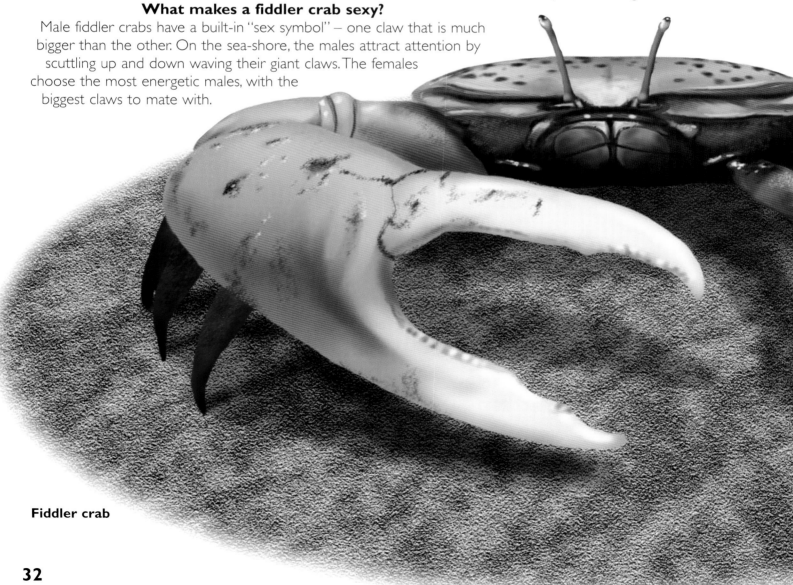

Fiddler crab

How do octopuses show their feelings?

Octopus and squid can change their skin color from brown to green, or blue. They use this skill to camouflage themselves when hunting, but also change color to express emotions, such as anger, and to attract a mate.

How does the damsel fish look after its eggs?

Most fish take little care of their eggs – they just spawn (lay and fertilize their eggs) and swim away without a backward glance. Some kinds of damsel fish are different. The females glue their eggs carefully to rocks. The males are caring fathers. They guard and check the eggs until they hatch, and shoo off any other fish that approach to eat them.

Which male fish gets pregnant?

Sea-horses have extraordinary breeding habits. The female lays her eggs in a little pouch on the male sea-horse's belly. The eggs develop in the safety of the pouch. About a month later, an amazing sight occurs, as the male "gives birth" to hundreds of tiny sea-horses.

Green turtles

Green turtles swim hundreds of miles to lay their eggs on the beach where they hatched out.

What sea creature comes ashore to breed?

GREEN TURTLES SPEND THEIR WHOLE LIVES AT SEA, but come on land to breed. The female swims ashore and clambers up the beach. Then she digs a deep hole and lays her eggs. When the baby turtles hatch they dig themselves out of the sand, then dash down to the waves, and swim away quickly.

Blue whales

A blue whale calf drinks 175 pints (100 litres) of its mother's milk a day.

Which creature has the world's largest baby?

FEMALE BLUE WHALES, THE LARGEST WHALES, ALSO BEAR THE biggest babies. A newborn blue whale calf measures 23 feet (7 m) long, and may weigh 2.5 tons — as much as a full-grown elephant! The thirsty baby drinks huge quantities of its mother's milk and puts on weight fast. At six months old, it may be as much as 54 feet (16 m) long.

What glues its eggs to the roof of its cave?

Female octopuses breed only once in their lifetime. After mating, the female lays long strings of eggs, and glues them to the roof of her cave. She tends her eggs for up to six weeks, and never leaves her lair to go hunting. Many females die of hunger or exhaustion, before their eggs hatch out.

What fish swims a long way to breed?

Young salmon hatch out and grow in shallow streams inland. After several years, they swim downriver, to the sea, and spend their adult lives in the ocean. To breed, they swim back and fight their way upriver, to spawn in the same stream where they hatched out.

What creature's birth was a mystery for centuries?

Eels were once a common sight in European streams and rivers. But their breeding habits were a mystery, for the eggs and baby eels were never seen. Then in the 1920s, experts at last discovered that the eels swim downriver, and make their way across the Atlantic to breed. They spawn in the warm waters of the Sargasso Sea off the coast of Florida. When the eggs hatch out, the young eels drift slowly back to Europe, and swim upriver.

How do young sea otters learn their skills?

Otters are naturally playful creatures. Young sea otters chase each other through the waving seaweeds, and turn somersaults in the water. Mother otters sometimes bring their young an injured fish to play with. As the pups take turns to catch their weakened prey, they learn hunting skills that will be vital when they are older.

Sea catfish

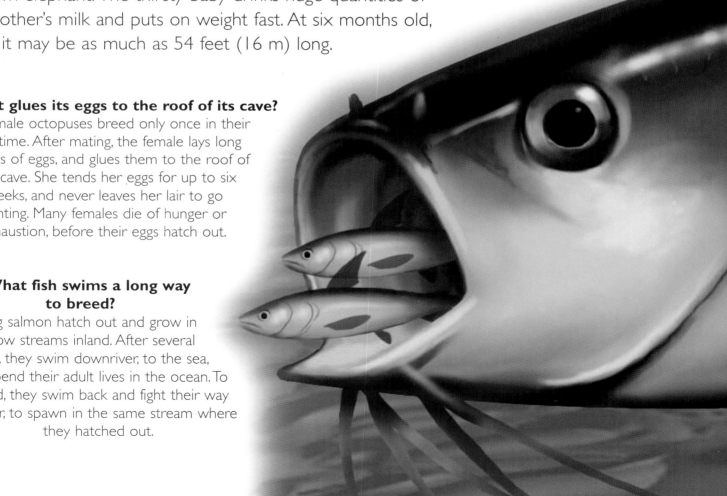

Which young fish eats its brothers and sisters?

Sand tiger shark eggs hatch out inside their mother's body. The tiny embryo sharks feed on one another, until only one big, strong baby is left, ready to be born.

How does the dugong protect its baby?

Female dugongs give birth to a single calf, a year after mating. A close bond forms between mother and baby. As the female and her calf swim through the murky sea-grass, she calls out constantly, to make sure her baby is safe.

Which sea father has a mouthful of babies?

FEW FISH LOOK AFTER THEIR BABIES, BUT FISH known as mouthbrooders are the exception. Mouthbrooders, such as sea catfish, protect their young by hiding them in their mouths! In sea catfish, the male is the caring parent. The babies swim in a cloud near their dad's head. When danger threatens they scoot back inside his mouth.

Young catfish swim close to their father's mouth so they can dash inside if danger approaches.

Birds

Do birds have fingers?

YES, THREE OF THEM. THE FIRST, THE THUMB, SUPPORTS A SMALL BUT important part of the wing called the alula, or bastard wing; the second and third support the main flight feathers.

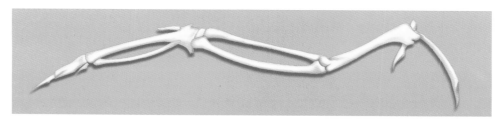

The skeleton of a bird's wing

Why do birds' knees bend backwards?

They don't. What looks like the bird's knee is in fact its ankle, and below it is an extended foot bone, leading to the toes. Its real knee is usually hidden by feathers.

Which bird has the longest wings?

The wandering albatross has a wingspan – the distance from one wingtip to the other, when the wings are stretched out – of more than 9 feet. The longest ever measured was a male with a wingspan of 5 feet (3.45 m); females are usually smaller.

Which birds trot on lillies?

Jacanas are sometimes called "lily-trotters": they live on ponds and lakes, walking on lily pads, to catch the insects that live on them. Their long toes spread their weight out, so that the leaves don't bend and sink.

How many toes do birds have?

Two, three or four. A typical perching bird has three pointing forward, and one back; birds that run on hard ground have only three, all pointing forward. Ostriches have only two toes, shaped rather like the hoof of an antelope. Woodpeckers have two toes pointing forward and two back; owls can turn their fourth toe either forward or backward, for perching on a branch, or to get a better grip on prey. Swifts have all four toes pointing forwards.

Why don't birds fall off a branch when they go to sleep?

Tendons, from the tips of the toes, pass behind the ankle joint. This joint is bent when the bird sits down, so the toes are automatically clenched round the twig it is standing on. No muscle power is involved in this grip, so the bird can sleep, without danger of falling.

What is a wishbone?

Sometimes called the "merrythought," the wishbone is created by the bird's collarbones being joined together at their inner ends. This forms a curved strut holding the wings apart while the bird is flying. The strongest fliers have the widest angles in their wishbones.

A jacana walking on lily pads.

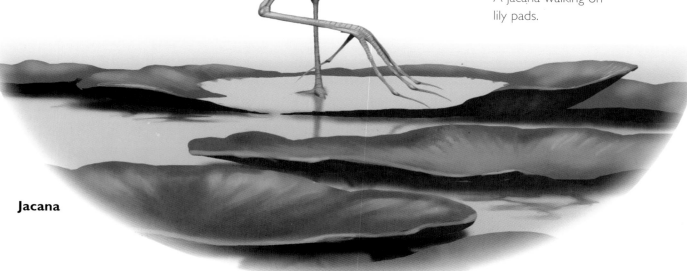

Jacana

Bald eagle

The sharp, hooked beak of an American bald eagle helps it tear apart its prey.

Why do some birds have hooked beaks?

FOR CATCHING AND TEARING THEIR PREY. HAWKS, EAGLES, AND VULTURES, but also owls and shrikes, need to be able to take a firm grip on struggling prey animals, and then pull them apart to eat them. The edges of an eagle's beak act like a pair of scissors, to cut through skin and flesh. Gulls have a sharp hook at the tip of their bill to hold on to slippery fish or squid.

Can a bird change the shape of its beak?

Yes! An oystercatcher's beak changes in a few weeks, from short and blunt while it is eating cockles and mussels, to long and narrow when its diet changes to worms and other soft prey.

Why are bird bones filled with air?

The long bones of birds are like tubes, often with criss-crossing inside, to make them stronger for their weight. Not all birds have equally hollow bones: those that dive into water, like gannets, terns, and kingfishers, and those that fly very fast, like swifts and some waders, have less air in their long bones.

What keeps a bird up in the air?

The shape of its wings. The upper surface is raised in a curve, so that air travelling above it has to move faster, than air moving under the wing. Air moving faster is at a lower pressure than slower air, so the higher pressure under the wing pushes it upwards, as it moves through the air. The first humans to discover how this "aerofoil section" works were Australian Aborigines, when they invented the boomerang.

What is the world's fastest bird?

People will always argue about this. Most think that the peregrine falcon is the fastest bird by far, but when its speed was accurately measured, the maximum in level flight was 58 mph (96 kph). Measurements by radar show that eider ducks fly for long periods at 45 mph (75 kph), but the world record is held by the Asian spine-tailed swift, which has been timed at 102 mph (170 kph) in level flight.

Why do geese fly in a V?

When a bird is flying, the air just behind its wingtips swirls upwards. If another bird flies in this turbulent, rising air, it can save about 15% of the energy it would have to use, if it were flying alone. In a V-formation, the leader is the only bird not saving energy: other birds take its place from time to time, to share the burden of leadership. Swans and cranes are among other birds that use this technique.

What has wing shape to do with flight?

Birds' wings are shaped differently depending on how they need to fly. Fast flight demands narrow wings, like those of swallows, while quick flight in woodland needs short, rounded wings, like those of a bluetit. Falcons change the shape of their wings from long and narrow for fast flight, to swept-back for diving at top speed. Gannets have long wings for long-distance flight and gliding: when they dive to catch fish they fold their stretched wings backwards, like the flights of a dart.

What bird can fly for six hours without moving its wings?

With its long, narrow wings, an albatross is perfectly adapted for gliding, even in still air. But when it glides close to the sea surface, it can make use of wind currents from the waves, giving it an almost continuous source of lift, meaning that in this type of flight, it only has to hold its wings still.

Black browed albatross

The albatross can soar for as long as six hours without moving its wings.

Which chick flies on its birthday?

The chicks of the mallee fowl in Australia, which emerge from the heap of warm sand where they hatched, immediately fly up to a branch to roost in safety. They have to look after themselves from the first day: their parents do not look after them at all.

What is the heaviest bird in the air?

The Kori bustard, from East and South Africa, weighs about 31 lb (14 kg): the largest specimen known weighed just over 40 lb (18 kg). Because it finds flying such hard work, the Kori bustard flies only in emergencies, and only for short distances.

How do birds land?

Ideally, by stalling (ceasing to move forward) just as they touch down. Large water birds, like swans, can water-ski to a halt on outstretched feet. Boobies and albatrosses, which spend most of the year at sea, often crash and tumble over when they finally return to land to breed.

Bee hummingbird

The bee hummingbird hovers as it feeds from a flower.

How does a hummingbird hover?

BY KEEPING ITS BODY NEARLY VERTICAL WHILE ITS WINGS BEAT FORWARD AND backward. It is actually flying upward just fast enough to balance its body weight, so that it stays still. A ruby-throated hummingbird, which weighs less than 0.2 oz, has to beat its wings more than 52 times a second to hover in front of a flower.

What is the slowest bird in the world?

Surprisingly, swifts are also among the slowest-flying birds, moving at less than 12 mph (20 kph) while they are feeding. Their insect prey moves only slowly, so they must move slowly to gather it. They fly faster than this at other times, as they wheel and swoop close to buildings and people. Another answer to this question could be hummingbirds, because when they hover they move at 0 mph! Even better, they are the only birds that can fly backward under power, registering a negative speed!

Which is the smallest migrant bird?
The rufous hummingbird, less than 4 in (9 cm) long, flies every year from Alaska to its winter quarters in Mexico, a round trip of 3,800 miles (6,400 km).

Why are lighthouses dangerous?
The beams from lighthouses attract migrating birds, especially during misty conditions. Many birds are killed when they fly into the glass.

Why do migrating birds fly so far?

To MOVE OUT OF AREAS, WHICH ARE SUITABLE FOR BREEDING , back to places where they can survive the winter. The reason for moving back to the breeding area is usually because it contains plenty of food in the summer to feed the chicks.

Why do some birds stay behind?

In Sweden, female and young chaffinches migrate south in winter, but some males stay behind in their breeding territories. European blackbirds do the same: it seems that the males, that stay behind through the winter, can hold on to the best breeding territories, for when the females return in spring.

How do birds sense cold weather coming?

Some ducks and geese migrate when the weather finally turns cold enough, but most birds leave long before the winter comes: marsh warblers start to migrate in July. Their bodies tell them when to go, as changes in hormones cause them to put on fat ready for the journey. The final trigger to move is the length of the day, which gets shorter in the fall and longer in spring.

When do birds behave like sailors?

When birds migrate, they use a mixture of signs, including the position of the Sun and stars for navigating on long-distance flights. They also use local landmarks when they are near their destination. They have a "compass" in their heads with which they can sense the earth's magnetic field, and choose their direction accordingly.

How did a bored nobleman discover migration?

The best evidence that birds migrate comes from banding – attaching light, numbered metal bands to birds' legs and releasing the birds in the hope that they will be found again. The first banding experiment was during the French Revolution of 1789, when a nobleman fixed a copper ring to the leg of a swallow, and noticed that it came back to the same nest for three years in a row.

Where did people think swallows went in winter?

They thought that they hibernated, perhaps in hollow trees, or even in the mud at the bottom of ponds. This is not as crazy as it sounds: in cold weather swallows often roost in groups in hollow trees or chimneys, and in spring they can be seen collecting mud at the edge of pools to make their nests.

Which bird spends its whole life in the summer?

The Arctic tern breeds in the Arctic, to within 430 miles (720 km) of the North Pole, and migrates every year to the Antarctic, a total distance of 23,000 miles (38,400 km) between breeding seasons. It spends its whole life in the summer.

Pigeons

Pigeons are strong-flying birds and good navigators.

How fast do migrating birds fly?

STUDIES USING RADAR SHOW THAT SMALL BIRDS LIKE WARBLERS MOVE AT ABOUT 21 mph (35 kph) when they are migrating, and ducks at about 42 mph (70 kph). They usually fly for only about six or eight hours a day, but one knot ringed in England was found in Liberia, 3,400 miles (5,600 km) away, only eight days later. It had covered an average distance of 420 miles (700 km) per day; since knots fly at about the same speed as ducks, it must have been travelling for 10 hours every day.

Quetzal

Which birds dig holes to nest in?

MANY BIRDS DIG HOLES FOR their nests, including kingfishers and sand martins, in sandy banks, and woodpeckers in trees. Puffins clean out disused rabbit burrows, the quetzal, in Central America, scoops out a large hole in a rotting tree trunk.

Which birds make the biggest nests?

Eagles. A bald eagle nest in Ohio, USA, which was used for 35 years, was more than 8 feet (2.5 m) across and 12 feet (3.6 m) deep, weighing 1.8 tons. Another in Florida was even bigger: nearly 10 feet (3 m) wide and more than 20 feet (6 m) deep.

Which birds can tie knots?

Many of the African weaver finches start their spherical hanging nests by tying blades of grass to a twig with neat, strong knots.

How do birds learn to build nests?

They know instinctively what to do and what materials to use, but older birds build better nests than beginners. This suggests that they get better with practice, and also that they know where to find the best materials.

Which birds treat their nests with pesticide?

European starlings do. Before the female begins nesting in a hole in a tree, the male bird gathers pieces of green vegetation and puts them into the hole. Scientists have discovered that the male chooses plants that give off certain chemicals which kill parasites, such as bird lice. This helps to keep the nest – and the baby birds that are born in it – free from lice.

The ancient Aztecs and Mayas worshipped the quetzal bird as the god of the air.

Which bird lays the world's smallest egg?

THE SMALLEST IS THAT OF THE BEE HUMMINGBIRD, WHICH IS just under 0.5 in by 0.25 in (11 by 8 mm), and weighs 0.02 oz (barely anything at all). The egg of the emperor penguin weighs just over one per cent of the weight of the female.

What birds lay their eggs in a compost heap?

Mound birds, in Australia and New Guinea dig large holes in the sandy ground, and lay their eggs on a pile of rotting vegetation they have collected in the bottom. The compost warms the eggs from below, and the sun warms them from above. The parents remove or add sand to keep the temperature constant. After all this work, when the chicks hatch the parents aren't at all interested!

What is bird's nest soup?

A Far Eastern delicacy, a soup or jelly made from the sticky cement that cave swiftlets use to stick twigs and feathers together to make their nests. Some species use only their saliva for this, produced from glands in their mouth: their cement is said to be the best for making soup.

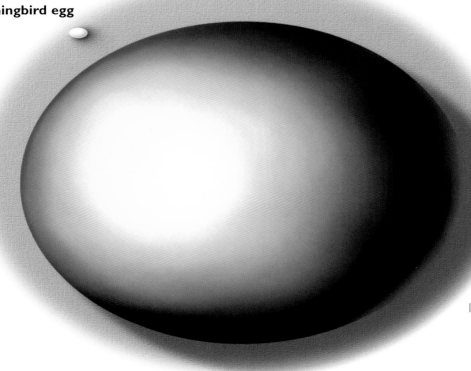

Hummingbird egg

Ostrich egg

From the smallest to the largest – compare the size of an ostrich egg with a hummingbird egg!

Which bird lays a wopper?

The biggest egg is laid by the ostrich: it measures 7 by 5 inches (170 by 135 mm) and weighs 3 lb (1400 g). The biggest egg for the size of the mother is laid by the kiwi, whose eggs, 5 inches (12.5 cm) long, can weigh as much as 1 lb (500 g), a third of the weight of the bird.

Which birds live in communities?

Some, like the sociable weavers of Africa, build huge nests occupied by as many as 100 pairs, but more interesting are those that share the nests of different species. The hamerkop in East Africa builds an enormous nest, more than 3 feet across (1 metre), part of which is shared by gray kestrels and barn owls, sometimes without driving out the original builder.

When does a nest have a roof?

Many small birds, especially in the tropics, build domed nests, with a roof to protect them from rain and sun. The roof might be made of almost anything, from strands of grass, in weaver nests, to bits of plant tied together with spider's webs, in the nests of sunbirds. In Europe, swallows and long-tailed or penduline tits are the best-known domed nest builders.

What's so good about being sat upon?

Most birds keep their eggs warm by sitting on them – so that the embryo can develop – until they hatch. After hatching, the chicks need to be protected from heat as well as cold: many birds shade their chicks in sunny weather.

This lesser whitethroat is feeding a cuckoo chick that hatched in its nest.

Why is it a good idea to hatch first?

A partridge might take three weeks to lay 15 eggs, only incubating them when the last is laid, so that they all hatch together. Owls, eagles, herons and gulls on the other hand, incubate their eggs as soon as the first one is laid, so that the chicks hatch at different times. If food is short, the last chicks to hatch will die.

When are baby birds bigger than their parents?

Shearwater chicks have to be able to survive while their parents fly far out to sea to find food, sometimes for as long as 10 days. They can store fat after a meal to keep them going until the next meal. At the peak of their growth, after about 80 days, they can weigh 12 oz (500 g), twice as much as their parents. They are not fed for their last 10 days on the nest, so that they lose enough weight to be able to fly.

Do chicks eat the same as their parents?

SOME DO, LIKE CHICKS OF SEABIRDS, WHICH EAT FISH. BUT CHICKS of seed-eating birds usually start life eating insects, because they need the special fats and protein that seeds can't provide. Cuckoo chicks eat whatever their foster-brothers and sisters eat, only much more of it.

Cuckoo

Which chicks can't wait to leave home?

LAPWINGS ARE A GOOD EXAMPLE OF

nidifugous (nest-leaving) chicks: they leave the nest as soon as they can all walk, within hours of hatching. Nidicolous (nest-living) chicks stay much longer, in the case of macaws (large parrots) for as long as three months.

Scarlet macaw

Scarlet macaws live in areas like Mexico and Bolivia.

How does a hungry chick get fed first?

A parent feeds the chick that is asking loudest for food. This usually turns out fairly, because chicks that were fed last time the parent came to the nest are quieter than hungry ones. Black storks just dump a pile of fish in the middle of the nest, and let the chicks take what they want.

What is pigeon milk?

This is a fluid rich in protein produced by cells lining the crop of male and female pigeons, used to feed the chicks. Flamingos feed their chicks in the same way: so do emperor penguins, but only the males produce the milk.

Which birds don't look after their chicks?

Mound-building birds like the mallee fowl. They leave their eggs to hatch in a mound of sand, from which the chicks eventually scramble out. If the parents see the chicks, they do not even recognize them.

When do eggs get noisy?

Chicks of nidifugous birds make clicking sounds in the last few days before they hatch. If you play recordings of these sounds to a clutch of eggs, they will all hatch at the same time.

What is an egg-tooth?

The hardened tip of the chick's beak is called an egg-tooth. It is used to break the first hole in the eggshell just before it hatches.

Why do birds sing?

BIRDS DO NOT SING BECAUSE THEY ARE HAPPY! THE TWO MAIN reasons are to attract a mate and to defend a territory. Birds recognize the song of their own species: females are attracted to a male with a powerful and complex song, and other males are driven away from his territory.

When is preening just for show?
All birds have to preen themselves, but some species of duck go through the motions in a special way as part of their display. The bill never actually touches the feathers, but the bird raises its wing to show off the bright patch of color, that is the badge of its species.

Which bird raises a false alarm?
There can be more to alarm calls than just warning other birds of danger. In the Amazon, when several different species are feeding together, in a flock, the white-winged shrike tanager, gives an alarm call when it sees another bird find a tasty insect. All the birds fly away in fright – except the crafty tanager, which dashes in and grabs the prey.

Why do birds sing other birds' songs?
Indian hill mynas are well known for imitating human voices, though they rarely mimic other birds in the wild. But marsh warblers include quotations from hundreds of other species in their song, from both Europe and Africa. This may be because males with more complex songs win more mates. Male mocking birds in America, copy the song of another species when it approaches their territory, possibly to drive it away.

When does a frigate bird blow up?
Male frigates have a huge red throat-pouch, which they inflate to attract females, making a wavering, fluting call as they do so.

Frigate birds have webbed feet, but are poor swimmers.

Frigate bird

Do birds have singing lessons?
Yes. In a famous experiment with chaffinches, scientists found that young males cannot develop the full song of the species without hearing adult males (or at least recordings of them) singing nearby and copying them.

Why do birds preen each other?
Mutual preening helps to remove parasites, such as ticks from places that a bird cannot reach for itself, round its head and neck. Since the only birds that do this are the two members of a breeding pair, it is usually seen as part of the "bonding" process that keeps them together.

Which birds collect ring-pulls?
Male bower birds in Australia and New Guinea decorate the areas round their courtship shelters (or bowers) with brightly colored flowers, seeds and beetle wings. If the bower is near a road, they often use ring-pulls from drinks cans (thrown from car windows) in their collections.

Count Raggi's red-plumed bird of paradise uses its stunning red tail feathers to attract mates.

Count Raggi's bird of paradise

Why does one adult bird sometimes feed another?
Males often bring food to their mates, while they are incubating the eggs, presumably to save them having to go to find food for themselves. In many species this has become a ritual part of courtship. In the African hornbill it is essential, because the female uses mud to wall herself into the nest-hole until the chicks hatch. If the male didn't feed her, she would starve.

Why do birds show off?

FOR MUCH THE SAME REASONS AS THEY SING, BUT WITH MORE emphasis on finding and keeping a mate. Males may display (the technical term for showing off) and even fight while the females watch. Ruffs and capercaillie perform a mass display called a lek. Afterwards, the females choose the most successful males to breed with. The most elaborate displays are seen among birds of paradise and peacocks.

Gannet

Gannets swim under water using their feet and half-opened wings.

How do birds catch fish?

WITH THEIR BEAKS – WHICH OFTEN HAVE A HOOKED TIP OR JAGGED edges, to help them grip their prey – or with their feet, like fish eagles or ospreys. As well as long, curved talons, the feet often have roughened soles to improve the grip. The African fish eagle strikes its prey with its long hind talon and then clenches the others round it.

African fish eagle

Why do gannets end up in fishing nets?

People used to say that gannets can dive to 16 feet (50 m), because they are sometimes found caught in fishing nets set at that depth. But they stay underwater for 10 seconds or less, so they wouldn't have time to get that deep. In fact, they rarely dive more than 32 feet (10 m): the unfortunate birds in the nets must have been caught and killed as the nets were pulled up.

This African fish eagle is just about to strike its prey.

How do jays and oak trees help each other?

AS WELL AS PREYING ON THE CHICKS OF OTHER BIRDS, JAYS FEED on acorns. In the fall, when acorns are plentiful, jays bury some of them to dig up later. Those that they don't find will grow into new oak trees.

Jay

Jays are very noisy birds. They have harsh, raspy voices.

Why don't woodpeckers get headaches?
When a woodpecker drills the bark of a tree, using its head as a hammer and its beak as a chisel, soft, spongy bone, between the beak and the skull, absorbs most of the impact.

When are geese like cows?
Just like cows, most species of geese feed mainly on grass Their short, sharp-edged bill is specially adapted for cutting the grass off close to the ground.

What is a bird pellet?
The indigestible remains of a bird's food, such as bones and shells, wrapped in softer left-overs like fur or wool. The bird throws up these neat packets, rather than trying to pass them through its gut.

Which bird eats only snails?
The Everglades kite, in Florida, is a genuine bird of prey, with strong talons and a sharply hooked beak, but its only food is apple snails. As the Everglades dry up, the snails are becoming scarce, which is why the kite is also becoming rare.

When is a thrush like a blacksmith?
A song thrush uses a stone, called an anvil, to kill snails, which it beats against the stone until the shell breaks.

Why are hummingbirds good for flowers?
They pollinate them when they collect nectar. Grains of pollen stick to the hummingbird's head, and are transferred to the next flower it visits.

Do birds use tools?
Yes. Woodpecker finches, in the Galapagos, use cactus spines to winkle out larvae from their burrows in dead wood, because they can't reach them with their short beaks. Egyptian vultures pick up stones and drop them on ostrich eggs to break them. Green-backed herons, in the United States, have been seen using bread as bait to bring fish within reach of their bill.

51

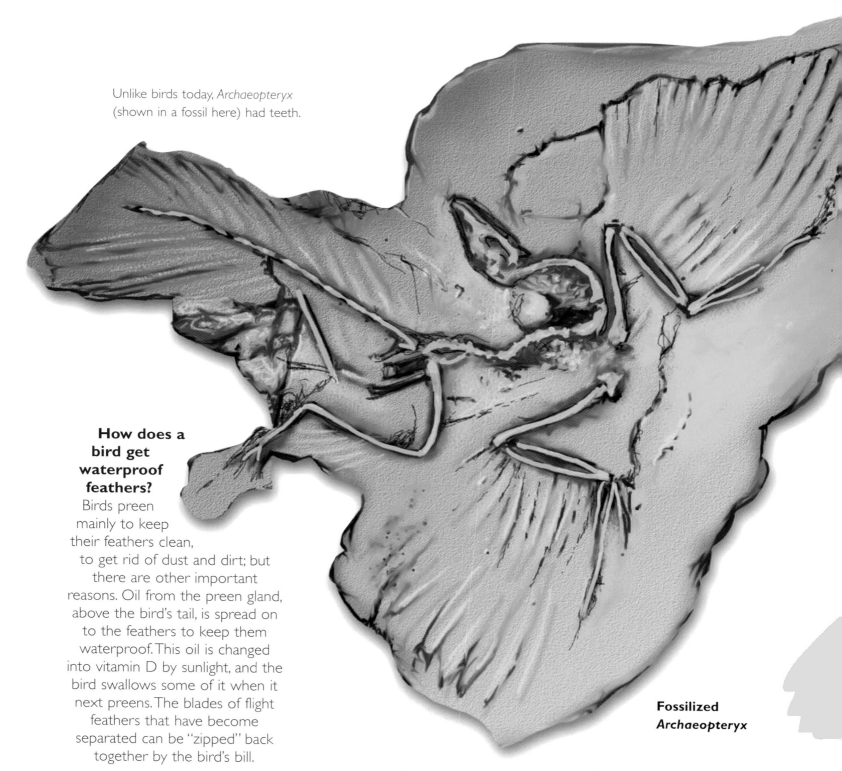

Unlike birds today, *Archaeopteryx* (shown in a fossil here) had teeth.

Fossilized *Archaeopteryx*

How does a bird get waterproof feathers?

Birds preen mainly to keep their feathers clean, to get rid of dust and dirt; but there are other important reasons. Oil from the preen gland, above the bird's tail, is spread on to the feathers to keep them waterproof. This oil is changed into vitamin D by sunlight, and the bird swallows some of it when it next preens. The blades of flight feathers that have become separated can be "zipped" back together by the bird's bill.

What is molting?

Growing new feathers and casting off the old ones. As the new feathers grow, they push the old ones out of their sockets. Most birds do this once a year, though some do it twice, especially when they have different breeding and non-breeding plumages. Many migrant birds start molting before they leave the breeding grounds, stop while they are travelling, and then finish the moult, when they arrive in their wintering area. Geese moult in their breeding grounds, becoming flightless while their young grow their own flight feathers.

What is the link between feathers and dinosaurs?

FEATHERS ARE MODIFIED SCALES, MADE FROM A PROTEIN CALLED beta-keratin, which is otherwise found only in lizard skin. Birds are descended from ancient lizards related to dinosaurs: the earliest known bird, *Archaeopteryx*, has many reptile-like features.

Do birds wear thermal underwear?

Down feathers are the thermal underwear of birds. They are soft and fluffy, covered by a layer of windproof feathers, trapping warm air close to the bird's skin. Chicks, like those of penguins, have very thick down, to keep them warm in the bitter cold of the Antarctic.

Do feathers grow all over a bird's body?

Feathers grow in areas called "tracts," leaving some bare skin between them – though the bare skin is often covered by down, and by feathers fanning out from the tracts. Vultures have bald heads and necks because any feathers growing there would soon be filthy with blood and fat from their food.

Do birds have whiskers?

BRISTLES ARE A SPECIAL KIND OF FEATHER, USUALLY FOUND ON the head and neck (though barn owls have them on their feet). They may protect the eyes and nostrils, or they may act as a net round the mouth of birds that catch insects in flight, like swifts and nightjars.

How many feathers does a bird have?

It varies with the species and size of the bird, with its age, and state of health, and with the season of the year. The smallest number was counted on a hummingbird, which had 940, and the largest on a mute swan, that had 25,216 feathers.

Cormorant

Cormorants are very ancient birds – their ancestors were around 40 million years ago.

Are all feathers waterproof?

No. The body feathers of water birds have curly tips that repel water, but some, like cormorants, can dive better because their wings are not completely waterproof – they don't have to carry so much air underwater. This is why they stand around with their wings hung out to dry between dives.

Why do sand grouse lounge around in pools?

Several bird species, such as the shoebill stork, carry water to their chicks in their bills, and one species, the African sandgrouse, carries it in special feathers on its belly. Sand grouse sit in pools until the feathers are soaked, and then fly back to their chicks.

Which birds make weird music with their feathers?

Snipe have special feathers in their tails that make a "drumming" or "bleating" sound when they dive quickly during their display flights. Mute swans make a high-pitched creaking sound with their wings as they fly.

Do birds enjoy the taste of their food?

Yes. IT IS IMPORTANT THAT THEY TASTE FOOD, NOT ONLY because they can then choose to eat things with a high nutritious value, but so that they can avoid poisons, like those used by many butterflies and caterpillars in self-defence.

How does a penguin find his mate after a year at sea?
By hearing her voice. Even in densely crowded, noisy colonies, mates can recognize each other's calls, and later, those of their chicks.

Why don't cave swiftlets bump into cave walls?
They use "echolocation" to avoid obstacles in the dark. They make a buzzing sound and listen for the echoes it produces from the walls. Outside, they have a normal twittering call, but they start buzzing as soon as they enter the cave.

Is an eagle really "eagle-eyed"?
While it is true that birds of prey can see very well, of those that have been tested, only the wedge-tailed eagle can see better than humans – two and a half times better in fact. Kestrels and falcons have about the same power of sight as we do.

Do birds have an internal barometer?
Yes, they can sense small changes in air pressure. This may be important in predicting coming changes in the weather, which might tell them that it is time to migrate.

Swall

Swallows leave cooler countries, such as northern Europe, at the end of summer, in search of warmer weather.

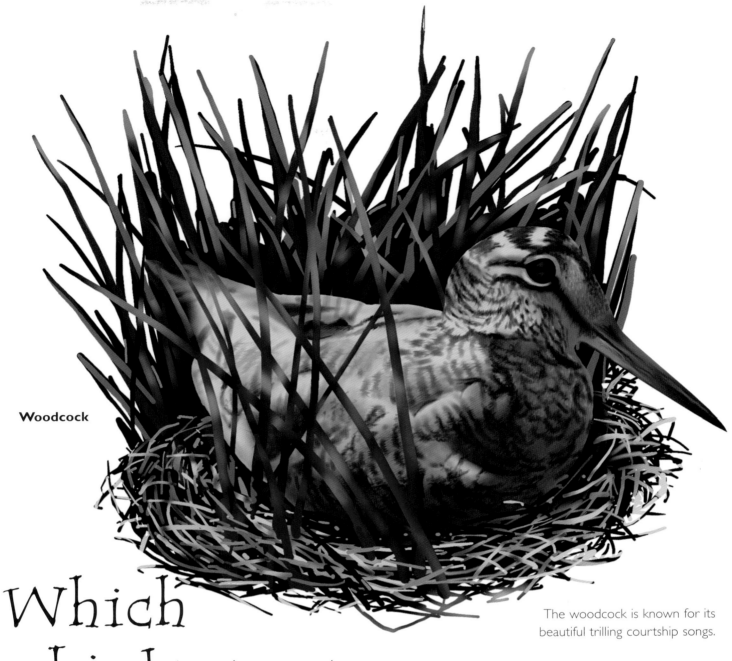

Woodcock

The woodcock is known for its beautiful trilling courtship songs.

Which birds can see backwards?

Woodcock, and many ducks, have their eyes placed

at the sides of their heads, so that they have a 360° field of vision. This enables them to watch out for approaching enemies even while they are feeding.

How does the owl turn its head back to front?

Owls have very large eyes to enable them to gather as much light as possible, and see in the dark; but this means that they cannot move their eyes in their sockets. To compensate for this, they can turn their heads through an arc of 180°

Do ducks get cold feet?

Yes, but it doesn't harm them. A special arrangement of blood vessels cools the blood going out to the feet and warms the blood coming back, so that even when standing on ice, the duck doesn't lose too much heat.

Does a homing pigeon use a compass?

Yes. Experiments with homing pigeons, using magnets, show that they are sensitive to the earth's magnetic field, and use it to help them navigate on long journeys. Other birds probably use the same method.

Why does a kiwi have nostrils at the end of its beak?

Kiwis feed at night, in the forests of New Zealand, snuffling through the leaf litter in search of invertebrates. They find their food by scent, using the nostrils at the tip of their beak: they are the only birds to have their nostrils in this position.

How many kinds of bird are flightless?

THE OSTRICH FAMILY CONTAINS THE BIGGEST FLIGHTLESS BIRDS, including emus, rheas, cassowaries, and the extinct moas and elephant birds. Penguins, in the southern hemisphere, are the most numerous flightless birds, while there are only three species of kiwi, all living in New Zealand. New Zealand also has two flightless parrots, the kakapo and the kea. Other families of birds contain flightless species, such as the cormorant in the Galapagos, the steamer duck in the Falkland Islands, and rails on islands in the Indian Ocean. Also in the Indian Ocean, the dodo, and two species of solitaire, were wiped out in historical times.

Why is a kiwi like a bandicoot?

A bandicoot is a small insect-eating marsupial living in the forests of Australia and New Guinea. New Zealand has no native mammals, and the job of forest-floor insect-eater has been taken over by the kiwi.

A kiwi snuffles for insects on the forest floor.

Kiwi

How fast can an ostrich run?

A biologist once drove alongside a running ostrich on the Mara Plains in Kenya with his speedometer reading 36 mph (60 kph).

Ostrich

Ostriches can run faster than any other birds.

Why are some birds part-time fliers?

Because they give up flying when they molt. Geese that breed in the high Arctic can escape from the few predators that live there by swimming, so they can change all their wing feathers at once, while their goslings are growing theirs. When the time comes to fly south for the winter, the whole family has new flight feathers. Most members of the auk family also molt all their flight feathers at once.

Which bird flies underwater?

Penguins are brilliant fliers. Their narrow, sharp-edged wings are like those of a swift, and their streamlined bodies allow them to move very fast and manoeuvre with great precision. The only reason we call them "flightless" is that they do it underwater.

Which penguin is extinct?

The first bird to be called a "penguin" was the great auk, in the North Atlantic, which has been extinct for more than a hundred years. Nowadays all the true penguins live south of the Equator.

Why can few island birds fly?

Two different reasons lead to the same result. There are fewer predators on islands, so birds that usually feed on the ground don't need to be able to fly to escape; and flying is dangerous on islands, in case a wind gets up and blows the bird out to sea.

**How long can a loony diver
stay underwater?**
The great northern diver (called
the common loon in North
America) is the deepest-diving
bird: it has been accidentally
caught on fishing lines 195 feet
(60 m) underwater. Even at this
great depth, it stays under for
no longer than a minute: 62
seconds is the longest
recorded dive.

The cassowary's hard
helmet protects
its head.

Cassowary

Why does a cassowary wear a helmet?

IT NEEDS ONE TO PROTECT ITS
HEAD FROM THORNS AND
branches as it dashes through the forest. All that
remains of its flight feathers are bare black spines,
curving round its body: they too protect it, by
brushing aside vines and bushes.

**Why don't polar bears
eat penguins?**
The probably would, if they had
the chance, but the only place
the two might meet would be in
a zoo, where the keepers are
careful to keep them apart.
Nature does this by having polar
bears living in the Arctic, and
penguins in the Antarctic.

Why is it dangerous for birds to live on islands?

Until humans came along, islands were among the

safest places for birds to live, but people soon changed that. The first danger came from passing sailors, who came ashore for water and wood, and without knowing it, brought rats with them. Rats are very good predators on island birds. When people started to live in the islands, cats and dogs, and even pigs, continued the damage started by the rats.

How many of the world's bird species are endangered?

Eleven per cent, most of them because of the harm done by people to the natural environment. Draining wetlands and felling forests are the main causes of damage, but the misuse of pesticides and industrial pollution also play a part.

Where is the endangered barn owl a pest?

In the Seychelles, where someone had the bright idea of introducing barn owls from South Africa to kill rats. They instantly started killing birds instead, especially fairy terns, and taking over the nest-sites of the rare Seychelles kestrel.

Dodos were land birds with thick, heavy feathers.

Dodo

Who ate the dodo and the solitaire?

The dodo was a large, flightless pigeon living on Mauritius. All dodos were wiped out when people first came to their islands. Some were eaten by people, and the rest by introduced pigs and rats. By the middle of the 18th century they were all extinct.

Why does the Californian condor owe its survival to a glove puppet?

When condors, nearly extinct in the wild, were being bred in captivity, scientists wanted to avoid the chicks becoming too familiar with humans. They fed them with meat held in a glove puppet, that looked like a condor's head.

Why is the néné important?

The néné was the first bird species to be bred in captivity – at the Wildfowl and Wetlands Trust in England and in Hawaii – with the intention of releasing it back into its home, when it was safe to do so. The operation was a success.

Néné

The néné, also called the Hawaiin goose, has been saved from extinction by being bred in captivity.

Why was North America's commonest bird made extinct?

Before 1840 there were thousands of millions of passenger pigeons in North America, but they were slaughtered for food until only one was left – a female called Martha – who died at 12 years old in 1914, in a zoo in Ohio.

What is Ducks Unlimited?

An organization of North American duck-hunters. They check the breeding success of wild ducks each year, to work out how many they can shoot for food and for sport without endangering the population.

Who is destroying the world's forests?

The increasing human population. In the tropics, people clear forests to grow food for their families or for large companies. The demand for large timber in Europe, North America, and Japan is all too often met by chopping down irreplaceable ancient forests.

How many kinds of bird have become extinct?

MORE THAN 150 SINCE 1600 – THAT WE KNOW ABOUT – AND probably many more, that no one ever noticed. It wasn't just European explorers who did the damage: archaeology shows that when people first arrived in ancient times on Hawaii, and islands in the South Pacific and the Caribbean, they killed many birds that Europeans never even saw.

Why do birds throw away their eggshells?

B ECAUSE THE WHITE INSIDE OF THE SHELL WOULD attract predators. Most ground-nesting birds carry their eggshells quite a distance from the nest, before dropping them. This was proved in a famous experiment, with gulls, by the great ornithologist Niko Tinbergen.

Peregrine falcon

The peregrine falcon is a fast, strong flier and hunts from several hundred feet in the air.

Which bird escaped to Malta
In the reign of Henri IV, of France (1553–1610), a peregrine falcon with a gold band bearing its master's name escaped. It was found 24 hours later in Malta, 1,300 miles (2,160 km) away. It was common at the time to mark hunting birds, and also some quarry birds, such as herons with rings.

How do amateur enthusiasts study bird migration?

All over the world, groups of amateurs, as well as full-time scientists, trap birds to fit numbered lightweight metal rings to their legs and release them. Some of the birds are found again, dead or alive, often in countries far away. Ringing birds in this way is called "banding."

What is a mist-net?

A fine net, supported on poles, used to trap birds for banding. The strands are too thin for the birds to see in time to avoid being caught.

What is a sonogram?

This is a means of printing out the sounds birds make so that they can be studied. A sonogram shows the frequency of the sound and the time it lasts.

How do you count birds?

THERE ARE MANY WAYS, SOME INVOLVING RINGING AND recapturing birds, and some done just by watching. The most reliable way to study bird populations is during the breeding season, when the adults are busy at their nests.

What are Darwin's finches?

A group of related finch species living in the Galapagos. They differ from island to island. When Charles Darwin visited the islands in 1835, he studied the differences between the finches. His findings led to his discovery of the theory of evolution.

What is a duck decoy?

An old way of catching ducks for food, that is sometimes still used today by bird-ringers. The ducks follow a dog into a tapering tunnel of netting, called a pipe, until the tunnel is too narrow for them to escape. They follow the dog as they would a fox, probably to watch it, in case it is hunting them.

One of the best places to count birds is from a beach. This is called a "sea watch."

Birdwatching

What is a honey guide?

Honeyguide

A SMALL AFRICAN BIRD THAT FEEDS ON BEE larvae, honey, and beeswax from wild bees' nests. It has learned to show humans as well as ratels (or honey-badgers) where bees' nests are, by fluttering around them and calling until they follow it. When the ratel (or the human) breaks open the nest to get the honey, the honey-guide has a free feed.

The honeyguide watches the honey badger, waiting for its honey feast.

Why do cattle egrets follow buffalo?
To help them find their food. Cattle egrets are small white herons. They feed on insects, and other small animals that are disturbed by large animals moving through grass.

What is falconry?
The ancient sport of using trained falcon (birds of prey) to hunt. Particularly in some Arab countries, the catch is still taken for human food, though in other places the main point of falconry is to watch the chase.

Why do gulls follow the plough?
Gulls do this because they have learnt that, as the plough turns over the soil, it exposes lots of good things to eat.

When did bluetits learn to open milk bottles?
This habit was first noticed in 1929, in England, when milk began to be delivered in bottles with foil tops. No one can imagine how the first bluetit discovered how to get at the creamy milk, but before long they were doing it all over the country.

Why do rhinos like ox-peckers to perch on them?
Ox-peckers, or tick-birds, are members of the starling family that feed only on the skin parasites of large mammals. They have very sharp beaks and claws, and stiff tails like a woodpecker's to support them as they perch on the animal's body. All large mammals put up with their scratchy feet – and their habit of pulling out hair to line their nests – because they remove troublesome parasites.

Why might GM foods harm wild birds?
Some genetically modified crops are designed to survive being sprayed with weedkiller. If these plants are widely used, more weedkiller will be used, until there are no weeds round the edges of fields. Many small birds, such as goldfinches, feed on weed seeds like thistles.

Which bird acts as a crocodile's toothbrush?

This alarming task is undertaken by spur-winged plovers, which perch on the crocodile's open jaws as it lies with its mouth open to cool off on the bank of a stream. They remove scraps of meat and probably also parasites from the crocodile's gums.

Caption

Why would a dabchick follow a flamingo?

Because the foot-movements that flamingos use to stir up the mud, before they filter it for food, also disturb small animals for the dabchick to eat.

How can a bird bring down a jet plane?

THE GREATEST DANGER IS THAT A LARGE BIRD, OR A FLOCK OF small ones, like starlings, might be sucked into the air intake of the engine, causing it to stop. But sometimes a bird crashes through the cockpit windscreen and injures the pilot.

Which is the wisest bird?

THE EGYPTIAN GOD OF WISDOM WAS OFTEN drawn with the head of a sacred ibis, while in ancient Greece the little owl was dedicated to Athene, the goddess of wisdom. To this day, the scientific name for the little owl is Athene.

Thoth

The Egyptian god of wisdom, Thoth, had the head of a bird and the body of a man.

Can birds predict thunder?
Farmers say that if the dawn chorus is late there will be a storm. This makes sense. The dawn chorus starts at first light, and if heavy clouds make the morning dark, birds will start to sing late, or not at all.

Can we forecast the weather from feeding swifts?
Swifts catch insects on the wing, so when the insects are flying high, so do the swifts. Insects fly higher in windier weather, when rain is more likely: so high-feeding swifts may be a sign of rain. On the other hand, insects fly low in humid or thundery weather. Take your pick!

Why is a bald eagle called "bald"?
Because it is piebald, or black and white – not because it doesn't have any hair (or feathers)!

What is a thunderbird?
It depends where you are in the world. In ancient Zimbabwe, lightning birds were said to look rather like eagles – they were put up to keep storms away. In North America the Indians call the tiny ruby-throated hummingbird a thunderbird, because it makes miniature thunder noises with its wings as it flies. The Romans thought a woodpecker drumming on the sacred oak (the "thunder tree") would bring rain, and this belief survived in Britain after the Romans had left.

Lightning bird

This lightning bird is carved from soapstone.

Why do people say that a tumbling rook brings rain?
It doesn't, but the weather in Britain is so hard to predict that people will try anything! Rooks perform their tumbling display flights in the fall, and it often rains in the fall, so the flights are often followed by rain.

When is an eel really a bird?

WHEN IT'S AN AVOCET. ONE OLD COUNTRY NAME FOR THE avocet was "awl," like a cobbler's tool, because of its sharp, curved bill. The old English word for this, was pronounced more like "eel." Some birds have more than one name, depending on what people notice most about them. The lapwing, named for the way it flies, is also called "peewit" after its call, and "green plover" because that is what it looks like. In Portugal, where they migrate in winter, lapwings are called "birds of winter."

Why do seagulls give up sunbathing?
"Seagull, seagull, sit on the sand; it's never good weather when you're on the land." Or so they say, and there is some truth in it. When the wind blows hard towards the land, gulls often come ashore to feed: and that is the worst weather for fishermen.

Why doesn't one swallow make a summer in the UK?
Because although the first swallows usually arrive at the end of March and in early April, they come only in ones and twos: the main migration arrives at the end of April, when summer is really on its way. This saying is not really about birds at all: it means "one piece of good luck doesn't mean that everything will be OK from now on."

Avocet

The avocet sweeps its curved bill backwards and forwards in the water in search of food.

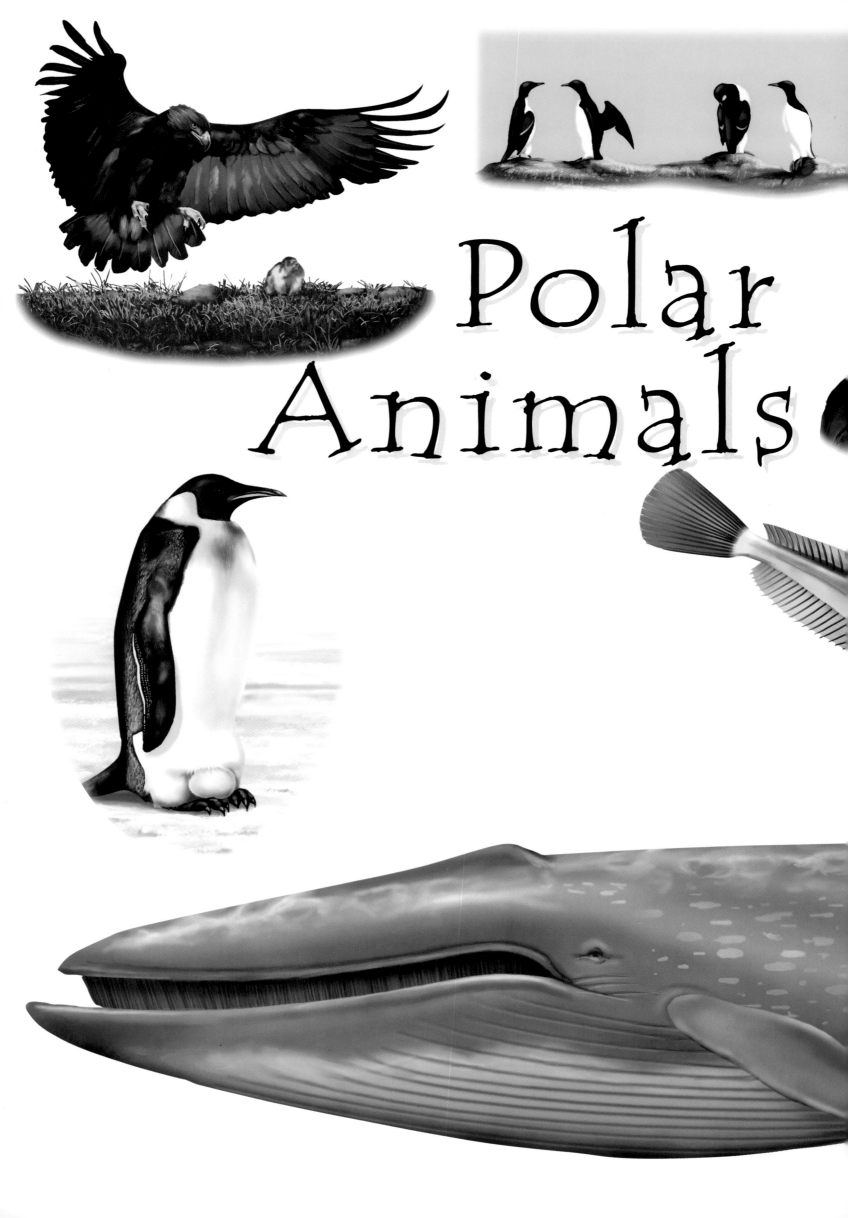

Polar Animals

Arctic fox

The Arctic fox keeps warm with the help of its thick fur coat and a layer of body fat.

How can animals survive the harsh polar weather?

THE POLAR REGIONS ARE THE COLDEST PLACES ON EARTH, YET SOME creatures live there all year round. Snow and ice cover the land and sea for most, or all of the year. Summers are brief and cool, with long hours of daylight. Winters are long, dark, and bitterly cold. In the Arctic, mammals such as the wolf and Arctic fox have a layer of body fat, and a thick coat of fur, to keep them warm. The fur traps air next to the animal's skin, which helps to prevent body heat from escaping.

How do Arctic foxes keep their noses warm at night?
The Arctic fox has a bushy tail up to 16 in (40 cm) long – over half its body length. When the fox is sleeping, it curls its tail around its body to cover its head and nose. The tail acts as a muff to keep the animal snug in biting winds.

Which polar animal has the longest hair?
Musk ox are large beasts related to sheep and goats. Their thick coats contain two different kinds of hair. The shaggy outer layer includes hairs up to 3 feet (1 m) long. The dense, short, woolly fur beneath gives extra warmth.

Which animal has ears adapted to keep it warm?
In hot places, such as deserts, hares have very long ears, which give off body heat to keep the animal cool. In the far north, Arctic hares have much shorter ears, which release less heat, while still giving excellent hearing.

How do birds keep warm in the polar regions?

Birds that live in the Arctic and Antarctic all year round have a dense coat of feathers. Waterproof outer feathers protect the bird against the cold and wet. Underneath, soft, fluffy down feathers help retain body heat.

How do seals keep warm in icy water?

SEALS AND WALRUSES ARE MAMMALS THAT SPEND MOST OF THEIR LIVES in cold water. They have a thick layer of fat, called blubber, below their skin. This fatty layer keeps them warm and well-insulated in the water. Whales and polar bears also have blubber. Whale blubber can be up to 20 in (50 cm) thick.

How do polar animals avoid frozen feet?

An animal's feet can be one of the coldest parts of its body, especially when, as in the polar regions, the feet touch the ice or frozen soil. Mammals, such as polar bears and Arctic foxes, have hair between their toes to prevent their paws from freezing. Some polar birds, such as the ptarmigan, a type of grouse, have feathery feet for the same reason.

Why don't polar animals need snow shoes?

Because their feet act like snow shoes! The feet of Arctic animals, such as polar bears and caribou, are broad compared to those of bears and deer from warmer regions. The broad base of the foot helps to spread the animal's weight over a wider area, so it does not sink into the snow.

Harp seal

The harp seal's blubber keeps it warm in cold water.

How do polar animals perform a disappearing act?

ANIMALS ALL OVER THE WORLD HAVE COLORS AND patterns on their bodies, that blend in with their surroundings. This natural disguise, or camouflage, helps them to hide from enemies and predators. In the Arctic and Antarctic, many creatures have white coats that blend in with the snow in winter. Some creatures have a different-colored coat in summer, so they can also hide when the snow has melted. In winter, the ptarmigan has mainly snow-white feathers. In summer, its mottled brown plumage helps it hide among the bare earth and rocks.

What color is a polar bear's skin?

Believe it or not, the polar bear's skin is black! The hollow hairs of its thick fur, reflect the light and make its skin look white.

How do baby seals make themselves invisible?

Baby harp seals spend the first weeks of their lives out of water, on the ice. Their parents have dark, mottled skins that blend in well with the water, but the young have pure white fur, which helps to hide them from predators, such as polar bears.

How do lemmings avoid catching cold?

Lemmings are furry rodents that make their homes in burrows. They pass the winter months out of the biting winds, in a network of tunnels, dug in the snow.

What Arctic animal has two fur coats?

The stoat is a type of weasel whose camouflage varies with the seasons. In summer its brown fur blends in with the rocky landscape. In the fall it sheds its summer fur, and grows a new, thick coat of pure-white hairs. In its winter coat, the stoat is called an ermine.

Long lines of migrating caribou stretch for 185 miles (300 km) or more, as the animals make their way through the barren wastes, and cross mighty rivers.

Why do caribou follow in each other's footsteps?

Caribou travel as much as 1,240 miles (2,000 km) each year, on migration. To save energy, each deer treads in the footsteps of the animal in front, so it does not have to break a trail through deep snow.

Caribou herd

How do caribou escape the winter cold?

Some hardy animals can survive in the high Arctic all year round. Others, including caribou, visit only for the mild summer season. Caribou herds spend the summer months feeding on small plants in the tundra – the treeless lands on the edge of the Arctic Ocean. In the fall, they make their way south, to shelter for the winter in forests, called the taiga. The caribou make the same round trip each year, following the same routes. Such regular animal journeys, are called migrations.

Snowy owls

Snowy owls feed their chicks on lemmings and other small mammals.

Where does the grey whale take a winter vacation?

Many sea creatures, such as seals and whales, travel great distances when they migrate. Gray whales pass the winter months in the warm seas off Mexico. In the spring, they swim up to 12,000 miles (20,000 km) to Alaskan waters, to feed on the plentiful food there.

How does the snowy owl protect its babies?

Snowy owl chicks hatch out in a nest on the ground in springtime. The young and adult owls have different camouflage. The mother owl has white feathers with dark speckles, so she blends into the snowy landscape. Her chicks have mottled, gray feathers that merge with the rocks and plants near the nest.

What is the most famous Arctic animal?

R UDOLF, THE RED-NOSED REINDEER (OR CARIBOU) WHO PULLED
Santa's sleigh, is certainly the best-loved Arctic animal! In Siberia and Scandinavia, tame caribou are often used to pull sleighs, and heavy loads, and people also ride on them. Throughout the Arctic, humans depend on caribou for meat, and use their skins for clothing. The name caribou probably comes from a Micmac Indian word, meaning "animal that paws through snow for food."

Which Arctic animal makes the scariest noise?
Wolves are found throughout the Arctic, living in packs. Most wolf packs contain between eight and 20 animals. They howl to communicate with other members of their group, and to warn rival wolves away from their territory.

When do grizzlies go north?
The polar bear is the only bear to spend all year on the Arctic pack ice. However, grizzly bears live in the forests that edge the tundra. In summer, they visit the Arctic to feed on berries, fish and mammals. They pass the winter hibernating in dens.

How big do polar bears grow?
Male polar bears can grow up to 10 feet (3 m) long, and weigh as much as 10 adult humans. The females are much smaller.

What do caribou like to eat?
Caribou is a type of deer that feeds mainly on lichen growing on rocks. This is a food that can be found all year round. In summer, the deer feed on a wide variety of plants that grow, and flourish in the long hours of daylight.

Do polar bears really live at the North Pole?
Polar bears live throughout the high Arctic, but are seldom seen near the North Pole itself. These bears catch all their food from the sea. At the North Pole, the Arctic Ocean is covered by a thick crust of ice that never melts, so the bears cannot get to the water, to swim and fish.

Are there cats in the Arctic?
The lynx is a large wild cat that spends most of the year in the taiga forests. It sometimes ventures into the Arctic tundra to hunt hares, voles, and lemmings.

The polar bear's scientific name, *Ursus maritimus*, means "sea bear." These mammals are often classed as sea creatures.

Wolf

Polar bear

Which animal is a champion swimmer?
Polar bears are expert swimmers and divers. They move through the water by paddling with their front paws. They have been spotted swimming as far as 200 miles (320 km) from land.

The eerie noise that wolves make has been used in many horror films!

What Arctic animal was thought to commit suicide?

Lemmings were once believed to commit suicide by throwing themselves off cliffs. Now scientists realize that these rodents breed very fast, so their numbers can rise steeply. When the area where they live becomes overcrowded and food gets scarce, large numbers of lemmings set off in search of a new food source. Many of them drown when they fall into rivers, or lakes, that lie in their path.

Lynx

The lynx's camouflaged coat allows it to creep up on victims.

What do polar bears eat?

The polar bear's favourite food is ringed seals. It hunts its victims at holes in the ice, where the seals come up for air. The bear creeps silently up to the hole, then lies in wait – for hours, if necessary. When a seal pops up to breathe, the bear kills it with a single slash of its powerful paw, and a bite to the neck.

Why should a lemming never panic?

Arctic foxes eat a varied diet, including berries, birds, eggs, and small mammals, such as lemmings. When hunting lemmings, the fox leaps high in the air, then crashes down on top of the lemmings' burrow. The panicked lemmings run from the shelter of their home, straight into the fox's jaws.

How does the lynx go hunting?

Like other cats, the lynx has excellent sight and hearing. It hunts by silently stalking a victim such as an Arctic hare. Then it pounces on its prey with one big leap.

Which animal keeps food in a "fridge"?

Arctic foxes sometimes cache (hide) stores of meat beneath the snow, or under rocks in summer. In cold conditions, the food stays as fresh as it would in the icebox of your fridge.

Which animals form a magic circle round their babies?

When musk ox are menaced by wolves, or other predators, they group themselves into a circle with their young calves safe in the middle. The adult ox face outward and fend off their attackers with their long, curved horns, until the wolves give up.

The wolverine sometimes steals prey killed by other Arctic hunters. It is so fierce that the other predator just gives up its kill.

Which animal has paws like sledgehammers?

THE POLAR BEAR'S MAIN WEAPONS ARE ITS

paws, which can act like sledgehammers. It can kill a human with one swipe of its massive paw. The bear's sharp canine teeth are also sometimes used to kill. Its strongest senses are smell and hearing. A hunting bear can sense prey up to 20 miles (32 km) away.

What small creature likes a lemming for lunch?

The stoat's favourite food is lemmings. With its long, slim body, this fierce hunter can scamper down its victim's burrow, and then overcome its prey with its strong, sharp teeth.

What animal is the glutton of the Arctic?

Wolverines are large members of the weasel family, also known as gluttons. These ferocious creatures look like small brown bears. They hunt lemmings and even large mammals, such as caribou. When the wolverine makes a large kill, it gorges itself on meat, then hides the rest for later, earning a reputation for gluttony.

Which animals gang up on their victims?

WOLVES' MAIN PREY ARE CARIBOU, MOOSE, AND SOMETIMES MUSK ox. They hunt in packs and target young, weak, or injured animals. When the wolves spot a likely victim, such as a caribou calf with its mother, they spread out to surround their prey. The panicked calf tries to flee and is separated from its mother. Then the wolves run their victim down and kill it by biting its neck.

Wolverine

75

Plankton consists of tiny plants and animals floating near the surface of the sea. The plants use sunlight to make their food. The tiny animals feed on the plants or on each other.

Plankton

Antarctica is a vast frozen continent where the weather is even colder and windier than in the Arctic. Conditions are so harsh, that no large land animals live there. Yet some tiny insects and spiders live and breed on the shores of Antarctica. They are some of the hardiest living things on earth.

Which is the most dreaded Arctic animal?
The mosquito is probably the most pesky polar creature. This insect feeds on animal blood. In spring, huge swarms of troublesome mosquitoes hatch out and plague the caribou herds by biting them and sucking their blood. They bite any warm-blooded animals they can find, including humans.

What minibeasts are food for all in the polar seas?

A WIDE VARIETY OF MICROSCOPIC PLANTS AND ANIMALS LIVE in seawater. Together, these tiny living things are known as plankton. In polar waters, plankton forms a vital food source for fish and many other sea creatures. Larger animals, such as seals, whales, and penguins, feed on the plankton-eaters, so, either directly or indirectly, all life in the polar seas depends on plankton.

What minibeast can suffocate a caribou?
The warblefly lays its eggs in the caribou's skin. When maggots hatch out, they burrow into the skin and feed on the caribou's flesh. Sometimes so many maggots hatch out in a caribou's throat, that it dies from suffocation.

Why does the sea turn red and glow at night?
Krill are small shrimp-like creatures that feed on plankton. Their bodies contain light-producing organs that can give the sea a greenish glow at night. In summer, they may occur in such large numbers that they turn the water red.

How do minibeasts survive at the Poles?

SURPRISING AS IT SEEMS, MANY KINDS OF INSECTS AND other small creatures, thrive in the Arctic. Minibeasts are cold-blooded, which means that their body temperature is only about the same as their surroundings. In winter, it is too cold for insects to be active, but they survive in the ice, or frozen soil, as eggs or larvae (young). In spring, when the ice melts, they hatch out in huge numbers, to feed on the plants that flourish in the warmer weather.

When does the sea bloom?
The warmth, and long daylight hours of the polar spring, cause plankton to multiply in vast numbers. This phenomenon is known as plankton bloom. In turn, sea creatures, that feed on plankton, also breed and flourish. So summer becomes a time of plenty in polar waters.

Krill are among the most abundant creatures on earth. All the krill in the sea would outweigh all the people on earth.

Krill

The Arctic clouded yellow butterfly's blood contains a special fluid, that prevents it from freezing.

Arctic clouded yellow butterfly

Do butterflies live in the Arctic?
We think of butterflies as delicate creatures. Surprisingly, some species thrive in the Arctic. Some Arctic caterpillars, and adult butterflies, have hairy bodies which keep them warm in freezing temperatures. Others are dark in color, because dark colors absorb the heat from sunlight quickly.

Marble plunderfish

The marble plunderfish uses the fleshy barbel on its chin like a fisherman's bait, to catch smaller fish.

When does a sea snail dry out?
Some Antarctic sea snails survive the cold by dehydrating (drying out) so the water in their body cells cannot freeze.

Why do fish need antifreeze?
Fish that live in polar seas have special features that help them survive in icy water. The Arctic cod has blood that contains chemicals that work like the antifreeze in a car radiator, to prevent the fish from freezing.

Which Antarctic fish goes fishing?
The marble plunder fish has a fleshy whisker on its chin, called a barbel. To small fish, this slender tentacle looks like a wriggling worm. But when the little fish moves in, to eat the "worm," the plunder fish snaps it up.

Why are the polar seas a popular place to live?

IN THE POLAR REGIONS, FAR MORE CREATURES LIVE in the oceans than on land. In winter, the sea surface freezes over, but under the ice, the water temperature is warmer, than the air on the land. Antarctic waters contain an even greater variety of life than Arctic waters, because the ocean currents there cause nourishing minerals to well up from deep waters, to feed sea creatures.

Icefish

The icefish has pale, nearly see-through skin.

How does the icefish get its name?
Icefish can survive in very cold water, where most other fish would freeze. Unlike all other vertebrates (animals with backbones) the icefish's blood contains no red blood cells; instead, it holds a natural antifreeze. Red blood cells are normally vital because they carry oxygen round an animal's body, but the icefish can absorb oxygen direct from seawater.

Why do polar sea creatures prefer the deep?

Most aquatic animals in polar seas live in

deep water. In shallow waters, creatures that live on the sea bed risk damage from floating sea-ice that scrapes along the bottom. So starfish, sponges, corals, and sea-urchins carpet the rocky bottom of the deep water. When the ice melts in summer, some of these creatures migrate inshore.

Was the Antarctic once a warm sea?

Fossil remains of ancient warm-water dwellers, such as ammonites (shelled creatures) show that the Antarctic was much warmer in prehistoric times. Ammonites were related to squid. They have long since become extinct.

When does a cucumber make a good mother?

In southern oceans, some sea creatures produce larger eggs, and take more care of their young, than similar species in warmer seas. Female sea cucumbers and sea urchins have a special pouch, in which their young develop. This makes these young creatures much more likely to survive.

Can woodlice live underwater?

Glyptonotus antarcticus is a shelled sea creature related to woodlice. In Antarctic waters, this slow-growing crustacean can eventually become giant size, reaching 8 in (20 cm) long.

Which sharks like to chill out in the Arctic?

Most sharks live in warm or temperate waters. Greenland sharks visit Arctic seas, although they usually live in warmer, deeper waters further south. These sharks hunt squid, seals, and small whales.

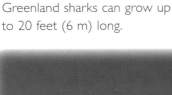

Greenland sharks can grow up to 20 feet (6 m) long.

Greenland shark

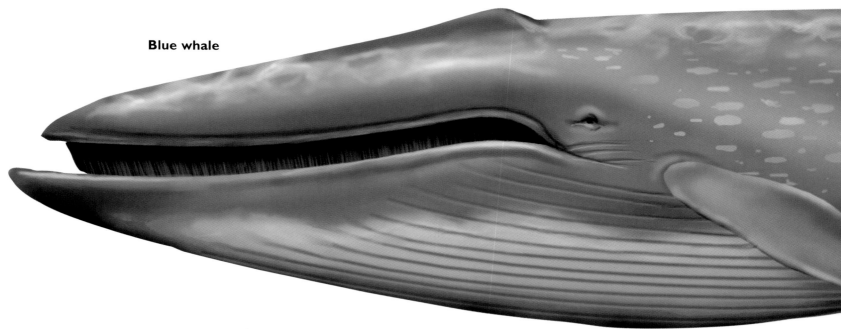

Blue whale

Do killer whales deserve their name?

KILLER WHALES ARE NOT KNOWN TO KILL PEOPLE, BUT
they are deadly hunters of seals and fish. Like narwhals, they
are members of the family of toothed whales. Their sharp,
cone-shaped teeth are powerful weapons.

Which is the biggest polar animal?
Blue whales are the largest animals to visit the Arctic. They are the biggest
whales – in fact, the largest creatures on earth. Mighty blue whales can
grow up to 100 feet (32 m) long, and weigh 150 tonnes. They visit Arctic
and Antarctic waters, during spring and summer, to feed. In the fall, they
migrate to tropical seas, where their young are born.

Which whale uses a battering ram?
Bowhead whales have domed heads and jaws that arch upwards like a
bow. The whale uses its domed head like a battering ram, to smash holes in
thick pack ice, so that it can breathe. It is the only whale to swim in Arctic
waters all year round.

When does a whale not mind being beached?
In southern seas, killer whales sometimes swim right up on to the beach, to
snatch young seal pups. The whale cannot survive on land, so it quickly
wriggles back into the water before eating its catch.

What whale sings like a bird?
Belugas are small white whales
that live in the Arctic. In olden
times, sailors called them "sea
canaries" because of the many
different sounds they make,
including clicks, squeaks, bell-like
clangs, and whistles.

Why was the right whale an unlucky whale?
In the days of whaling, the men of
the whaling ships gave right whales
their name because they were the
"right" whales to hunt down and
kill. Thousands of these whales
were slaughtered during the 18th
and 19th centuries. The whales'
blubber was melted down to
make oil to light lamps, and their
bones were used to make
umbrellas, brushes, and
women's corsets.

Do killer whales have friends?
Yes – other killer whales! Killer
whales live and hunt in groups
called pods. Members of the pod
work as a team when hunting.
They spread out to surround small
ice floes on which seals are resting.
Then the killers charge and tip the
floe from different sides. The
helpless seals slide off into the
water, and the hunters snap
them up.

Blue whales have small eyes in proportion to their giant size, but each eye is still as large as a basketball.

Do giant whales eat mighty meals?

BLUE WHALES DO NOT REACH THEIR GIANT SIZE BY eating large sea creatures. Instead, their meals are made up of thousands of tiny creatures, mainly krill. In place of teeth, these whales have long, thin plates of bone (baleen) hanging down from their upper jaws. These plates work like a giant sieve to strain krill, and small fish, from mouthfuls of seawater.

Which male whale likes to impress the females?
Narwhals are small Arctic whales. Males have a long, spiralling tusk growing out from their heads. Scientists are not sure what the tusks are for, but many believe their main purpose is to impress female narwhals!

The narwhal's tusk is a very long tooth, growing out from the upper jaw.

Narwhal

Are seals vegetarian?
No! All seals are meat-eaters. They feed on squid, fish, shellfish, seabirds, and sometimes even other seals.

Which seal has a beard?
The bearded seal has a magnificent set of long, whiskery hairs on its nose. It uses its sensitive "beard" to feel for shellfish lurking on the seabed, and fish hiding in cloudy water.

What spotted seal snacks on penguins?
The leopard seal has a spotted skin like the leopard. Like its namesake, the seal is a speedy and deadly hunter, with large, powerful jaws. Its favourite prey are penguins and young seal pups.

Do elephant seals have trunks?
Male elephant seals have a wrinkled bag of skin on top of their nose. The bag can be blown up balloon-style, to form a kind of trunk. When inflated, the seal's trunk acts as a loudspeaker, amplifying his roars as he calls to frighten off rival males.

Which seal needs a new name?
Crabeater seals of the Antarctic do not eat crabs. They would be better renamed krill-eaters, as these small, shrimp-like animals are their main food. To catch krill, the seal speeds along with its mouth open, sieving krill from the water with the help of its jagged teeth.

Leopard seal

Leopard seals are fast movers, like the big cats after which they are named.

How do leopard seals hunt penguins?

THE LEOPARD SEAL LURKS BENEATH AN ICE FLOE ON WHICH THE BIRDS are standing. When the penguins dive into the sea, the seal darts forward and seizes a bird in its teeth. Having caught its prey, the leopard is in no hurry to feed. It beats its kill against the water, to turn the penguin inside-out, and remove its skin. It may take over an hour to finish its meal.

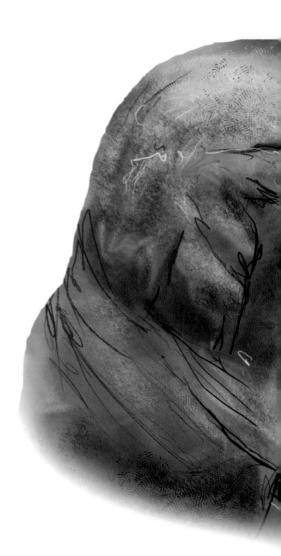

When is a seal an elephant?

The elephant seal is the heavyweight champion of the seal world. Large males may grow up to 21 feet (6 m) long and weigh up to 8,800 lb (4 tonnes). Females are much smaller. Southern elephant seals live in Antarctic waters.

Do walruses like to party?

Yes! Walruses are very sociable animals. They often gather in large, noisy groups on land, basking in the sun, or huddling together, to conserve body heat in cold weather. The walrus pack provides safety in numbers because it is more difficult for enemies to pick out weak, or young animals, from a big group.

Why do walruses have tusks?

BOTH MALE AND FEMALE WALRUSES HAVE SHARP, CURVING TUSKS up to 3 feet (1 m) long. These strong, elongated upper teeth have many uses. Walruses eat clams and other shellfish, and use their tusks to rake along the seabed to find food. The tusks are also used as levers when walruses haul their massive bodies up on to the ice. Long, curving tusks may add sex appeal when walruses are courting. The males also use theirs to gore their rivals when fighting contests to win female partners.

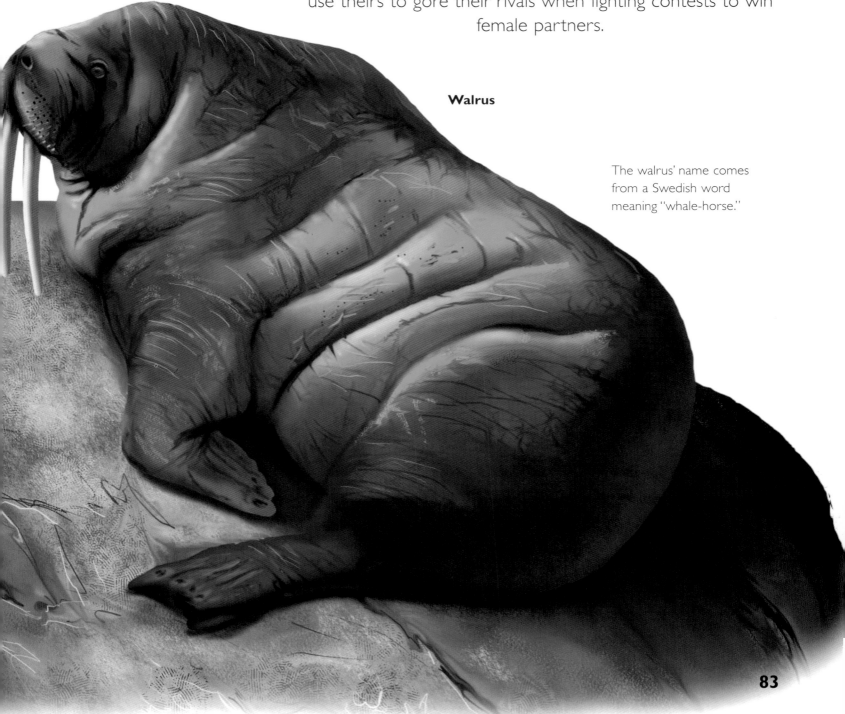

Walrus

The walrus' name comes from a Swedish word meaning "whale-horse."

Loons are expert swimmers and divers.

Loon

Ptarmigan are ground-nesting birds, whose chicks are raised by both parents. If the young are threatened by a predator, such as an Arctic fox, the parent bird flattens itself against the ground, then suddenly flies up, heading straight for its enemy's head. The chicks scatter to safety in the confusion.

What Arctic bird stores its food in a pouch?
Little auks are small, hardy seabirds that live in the Arctic all year round. They feed on plankton floating in seawater, and store their catch in a throat pouch.

What bird is known for its clumsiness?
Loons are diving birds that spend most of their lives in water. Their legs are set far back on their bodies, which makes them graceful in the water, but awkward on land. In fact, the name loon probably comes from the Icelandic word "lomr," which means clumsy.

What is the favourite food of snowy owls?
Snowy owls feed mainly on lemmings. These birds time their breeding cycle, so their chicks are born when there are plenty of lemmings to feed them. In years when lemmings are particularly abundant, the owls breed quickly and raise more chicks. When lemmings are scarce, they may not breed at all.

What Arctic bird makes friends with the polar bear?
The ivory gull is a pure-white bird that spends all year in the Arctic. Through the long polar winter, it survives by following the polar bear, as it wanders the pack ice. The gull feeds on scraps of food left by the bear and on its droppings.

What do Arctic birds like to eat?

ARCTIC BIRDS EAT MANY DIFFERENT FOODS. SEABIRDS, SUCH AS loons and puffins, dive into the seas for fish and shellfish. Wading birds and land birds, such as snowbuntings, feed on insects. Dabbling ducks eat water plants in marshy pools, and birds of prey hunt rodents. In summer, all these living things are plentiful in the Arctic, so there is enough food for these birds to rear their chicks.

How does the eider duck keep its chicks warm?
Eider ducks nest in clumps of grass on Arctic islands. The female bird plucks down feathers from her breast to line her nest and warm her chicks. Her soft, fluffy feathers are used to fill pillows.

What Arctic bird stands out in the snow?

MOST HUNTING BIRDS, AND MANY OF THEIR VICTIMS, HAVE PALE OR camouflaged feathers, so they can hide in the snowy landscape. Ravens are black, so they stand out against the snow, but they are so fierce that few enemies challenge them. These clever birds live off their wits, feeding on dead meat and scraps in winter. In summer they team up in pairs to steal other birds' eggs and young. One raven distracts the parent bird, while the other steals from the nest.

Which bird is a deadly Arctic predator?
The golden eagle visits the Arctic in summer. This fierce predator hunts on the wing, soaring silently over the tundra in search of lemmings and ground squirrels. When it spots a victim moving in the grass below, it swoops down and seizes its unlucky prey in its powerful claws.

Golden eagle

The golden eagle uses its sharp claws, called talons, to catch its prey – a lemming.

Why do birds fly to the ends of the Earth?

FEW BIRDS LIVE IN THE ARCTIC OR ANTARCTIC ALL YEAR ROUND.

Most visit in spring and summer only, when the long days bring warmth and plenty. As the ice melts, flowers bloom and the air is filled with buzzing insects. Lemmings, and other rodents, emerge from their burrows, so there is plenty of food for birds to eat. Many birds also come to the polar regions, to raise their chicks in safe nesting sites, where there are few enemies to harm them. In the fall when the chicks are grown, they leave for warmer regions that do not freeze over in winter.

Where are the best polar nesting places?

Seacliffs and Arctic marshes are favourite nesting spots for migratory birds. In winter, these sites are bleak and deserted. In summer, cliff ledges and marsh rims are packed with thousands of noisy, squabbling birds.

How do birds know when to migrate?

The secrets of bird migration are still a mystery. But scientists believe that the shorter daylight hours of early fall may signal to the birds that it is time to leave.

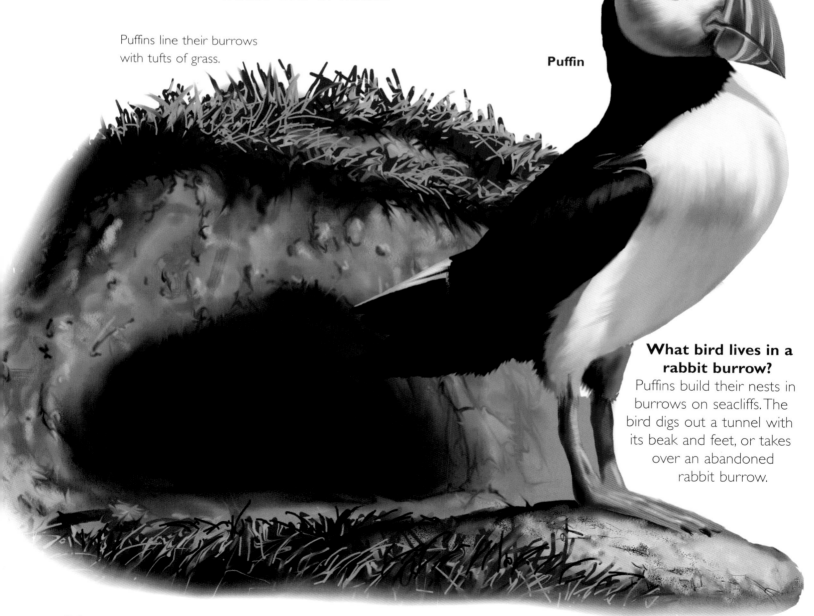

Puffins line their burrows with tufts of grass.

Puffin

What bird lives in a rabbit burrow?

Puffins build their nests in burrows on seacliffs. The bird digs out a tunnel with its beak and feet, or takes over an abandoned rabbit burrow.

How do snow geese save energy?

Snow geese migrate great distances, flying in long lines or V-shaped groups. These formations save energy because each bird flies in the slipstream of the one in front.

Snow geese raise their young in the Arctic, then fly 2,000 miles (3,200 km) to the Gulf of Mexico for the winter.

How do migrating birds find their way?

YEAR AFTER YEAR, BIRDS USE THE SAME ROUTES AS THEY migrate to and from the polar regions. Some young birds learn the way by flying with their parents, and following the experienced birds in front. Other birds find their way alone, purely by instinct. Birds navigate using the sun, moon and stars, and landmarks such as coastlines to establish their position. Some birds can also sense the Earth's magnetic field.

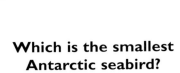

Snow geese

Which is the smallest Antarctic seabird?

Wilson's storm petrel is the smallest Antarctic seabird. Yet this little bird migrates almost as far as the Arctic tern, flying all the way from Antarctica, to northern Canada, and back again each year.

Why do guillemots lay pointed eggs?

Guillemots are seabirds that nest in crowded colonies on cliffs. Their eggs are pointed so if they get knocked, they roll round in a circle, and don't fall off the cliff ledge.

What bird is the long-distance flying champion?

The Arctic tern holds the record for long-distance migration. This bird nests, and rears its young in the Arctic in June, when it is light all day and all night too. Then it flies halfway round the world to take advantage of the Antarctic summer.

This map shows the amazing round trip of 25,000 miles (40,000 km) completed by the Arctic tern each year.

Which giant bird is the wanderer of the air?

THE WANDERING ALBATROSS HAS THE LARGEST wingspan of any bird. Its outstretched wings measure 11.5 feet (3.5 m) across. The albatross uses its strong wings to soar in the winds that blow across the southern oceans. It spends almost all its life in the air, and touches down on land only to breed.

Wandering albatross

What bird brings luck and stormy weather?

In olden days, albatrosses were believed to bring rough weather. Yet sailors also thought these birds were lucky, and believed that killing one brought bad luck. *The Rime of the Ancient Mariner* is a long poem about a sailor who brings disaster on his ship, by killing an albatross. His shipmates hang the dead bird around his neck.

Which seabird lays the heaviest egg?

Albatrosses raise only one chick every two years. Their eggs are the heaviest of any seabird, weighing up to 21 oz (585 gm) and taking up to 80 days to hatch. The parent birds take it in turns to incubate the egg while it develops. The father bird spends weeks sitting on the nest.

Six species of albatross nest in Antarctica. The wandering albatross is the giant of the family.

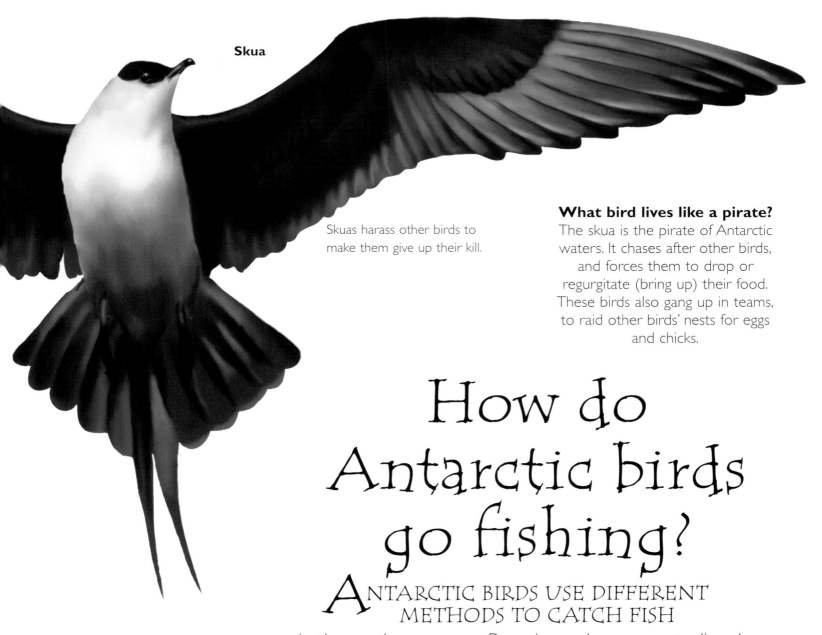

Skua

Skuas harass other birds to make them give up their kill.

What bird lives like a pirate?

The skua is the pirate of Antarctic waters. It chases after other birds, and forces them to drop or regurgitate (bring up) their food. These birds also gang up in teams, to raid other birds' nests for eggs and chicks.

How do Antarctic birds go fishing?

ANTARCTIC BIRDS USE DIFFERENT METHODS TO CATCH FISH in the southern oceans. Penguins and cormorants dive down and swim underwater to overtake their prey. Terns and shearwaters hunt from the air and plunge into the sea to make their kill. Storm petrels flutter along the surface, trailing their legs as if they were walking on water. Albatrosses swim in the waves, watching out for fish in the sea below.

What bird is nicknamed "stinker"?

Giant petrels are large seabirds related to albatrosses. They are nicknamed "stinkers" because they smell so awful. These birds live as scavengers, feeding on dead seals and other sea creatures, and hunting fish and other birds.

What bird will eat absolutely anything?

The sheathbill is a white bird, with a horny sheath on its beak to protect its nostrils. It survives the freezing Antarctic winter by grabbing whatever food it can. It feeds on krill and dead fish, and steals other birds' eggs and chicks in spring. When times are hard, the sheathbill even resorts to eating seal and penguin droppings!

What do polar birds use to build their nests?

Polar birds build their nests with whatever materials they can lay their beaks on! On the barren shores of Antarctica this includes seaweed, feathers, lichen, moss, mud, straw, and even stones.

What do shags use to glue their nests together?

Blue-eyed shags nest in colonies on the coasts of Antarctica. The weather is so harsh there that these birds may use their nests all year round, not just to raise their chicks. Shags build large nests of seaweed, moss, and lichen, stuck together with the only glue available, their own droppings!

How do emperors keep their eggs warm?

EMPEROR PENGUINS DON'T BUILD nests, and an egg left on the ice would freeze in seconds. When the female lays her egg, the male scoops it up onto his feet, and covers it with a warm flap of skin. He incubates the egg for two months during the worst winter weather, until the female returns to help feed the newly-hatched chick.

Emperor penguin

Out on the windy pack ice, male emperor penguins incubate their eggs.

Where do penguins live?
Penguins live only in the Southern Hemisphere. There are 16 different species. Most live in the far south, in Antarctica, or on islands in the south Pacific or Atlantic Oceans. A few species occur further north, and one even lives on the remote Galapagos Islands, near the Equator.

Which penguin is the deepest diver?
The emperor penguin can dive to depths of 870 feet (260 m), and stay below the surface for 18 minutes. The emperor is the largest penguin, growing up to 4 feet (1.2 m) tall.

Why is a penguin like a cork?
To leave the water, penguins swim up to the shore at speed, and then pop out of the water like a cork from a bottle, to land on the ice feet-first. They sometimes use this technique to escape from predators, such as leopard seals.

When is a penguin like a toboggan?
On land, penguins walk with an ungainly waddle. When descending snowy slopes, they toboggan along on their stomachs, pushing with their feet for extra speed.

How did chinstrap and Adelie penguins get their names?
The chinstrap penguin has a narrow line of black feathers running under its white throat, like a chinstrap. Adelie penguins were named by the French explorer Dumont d'Urville, who discovered Antarctica in 1840, after his wife Adelie.

Why do penguins steal pebbles?

Penguins breed in large, noisy colonies called rookeries. Some make no nests, but chinstrap and Adelie penguins build nests of pebbles. Aggressive chinstraps sometimes steal one another's pebbles, or take over Adelie nests.

Which penguin lays its eggs on ice?

Most Antarctic penguins breed on land in summer. But emperor penguins breed in winter, out on the freezing ice. In April, they trek 60 miles (100 km) to traditional nesting sites, where they mate. Then the females head back to the sea, and the males are left to incubate the eggs.

Can penguins fly?

Penguins are flightless birds, but they are strong swimmers and divers. Underwater, they "fly" along, using their wings as flippers to push against the water. When swimming at speed, they often leap out of the water and dive back in again, an action known as porpoising.

How do penguins keep warm?

In the harsh Antarctic climate, penguins keep warm with the help of a layer of fatty blubber, and two layers of feathers. Their outer coat of tiny oily feathers overlap to keep the down feathers below, dry. Penguins also have partly feathered beaks and small feet, so only a small part of their body is exposed to the freezing air and ice.

Adelie penguins

Seven species of penguin live in Antarctica. These are emperors.

One guillemot threatens another by spreading its wings and pointing skywards with its beak. Its opponent backs down by preening its feathers or bowing with outstretched wings.

How do guillemots keep the peace?

GUILLEMOTS REAR THEIR CHICKS ON CROWDED CLIFF LEDGES. EACH breeding pair has only a tiny space to feed its chick. In these overcrowded conditions, fights between rival birds would quickly lead to chicks or eggs falling to their deaths. Squabbling guillemots resolve their differences by using ritual movements that show threat and submission, so physical fights are rare.

What bird dances to attract a mate?

Sandhill cranes migrate to the Arctic to breed. The male and female birds court one another by performing "dances" with many different steps. The birds dip down and bow low, make skipping movements and leap up to 20 feet (6 m) in the air.

Which penguin flirts with its eyebrows?

Rockhopper penguins have tufts of feathers above their eyes that form spectacular "eyebrows." Males and females court by squawking at one another and waggling their heads to show off their impressive tufts.

How does a male caribou prove its strength?

Fall is the mating season for caribou. The males strut and roar, then charge at one another and lock antlers. The deer that wins this test of strength also wins the herd of females.

When is wrinkled skin a turn-on?

Like elephant seals, male hooded seals have a bag of loose, wrinkled skin on top of their heads. During the breeding season, the male attracts the females, and warns rivals away, by roaring and inflating his "hood" into a big black balloon.

What makes polar bears fight?

Polar bears live mostly solitary lives, roaming the lonely pack ice. Females breed only once every three years. If two male bears come across a female who is ready to mate, a fight breaks out. The males wrestle fiercely in the snow, for only the victor will get the chance to mate.

Guillemots

What is a beachmaster?

Southern elephant seals breed on islands off Antarctica. Rival males fight fiercely, rearing up and tearing at each other's necks with their teeth. The seals' necks are padded with thick skin and fat, but the animals are soon bloody. The victor becomes "beachmaster," winning a stretch of beach and his own group, or "harem," of females.

Elephant seals

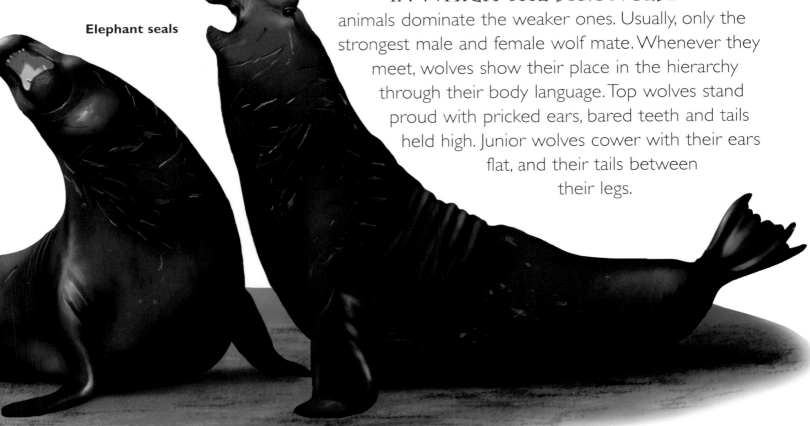

What makes a wolf leader of the pack?

WOLF PACKS HAVE A STRICT SYSTEM, IN WHICH THE STRONGEST animals dominate the weaker ones. Usually, only the strongest male and female wolf mate. Whenever they meet, wolves show their place in the hierarchy through their body language. Top wolves stand proud with pricked ears, bared teeth and tails held high. Junior wolves cower with their ears flat, and their tails between their legs.

Which animal can walk a great distance at only two days old?
Caribou calves are born in June in the Arctic. In minutes, they are able to stand on their long legs and wobble around. In a day or two, they are ready to keep up with the herd as it moves on in search of fresh grazing. In the fall, the calves travel south with the herd to the sheltered forests.

Where do narwhals go to raise their young?
Narwhals spend most of their lives swimming near the edge of the Arctic pack ice. But they migrate to the fiords of Greenland and Scandinavia to give birth. The young spend their first weeks in the warmer waters of these sheltered inlets, where they are fairly safe from enemies such as killer whales.

Which animal drinks milk underwater?
Like other mammals, young whales feed on their mother's milk. The female's nipples are located on the underside of her body, so the calf must take a deep breath, and dive down below its mother to drink.

What animal has several dens?
Ringed seal pups are born in an ice den, scraped out by their mother with her flippers. The female makes several dens, so she can move her pup to safety if it is threatened.

What seabird takes a long time to raise its chick?
On the windswept shores of Antarctica, wandering albatrosses take ten and a half months to rear their young. The parent birds take turns to feed their chick on an oily, foul-smelling mixture made of regurgitated fish.

Why do Brant geese raise their young in a hurry?

Brant geese arrive to breed in Arctic marshes as soon as the ice melts. The young must be raised before the brief summer ends, so the birds lay their eggs at once. The eggs hatch out quickly, and the chicks grow fast. In less than two months the young birds are ready to take off with their parents as they head back to warmer climes.

Young Brant geese learn to swim soon after they hatch out.

Polar bear cubs spend two years suckling their mother's milk and learning hunting skills. Then they are on their own.

Polar bear cubs

What games do polar bear cubs play?
Young polar bears are curious and very playful. They chase one another, slide down snowy slopes, and tussle in the snow. Through play, they learn the skills they will need to survive, once they are weaned.

Which chicks are looked after in a creche?
Emperor penguin chicks hatch out in July – midwinter in Antarctica. They spend about eight weeks riding round on their parents' feet, clear of the ice. Then, they are left in "creches" with other young penguins, while their parents go off to hunt for food.

Where are polar bear cubs born?

POLAR BEARS GIVE BIRTH IN MIDWINTER TO UP TO three cubs. The young are born in a snug snow den, hollowed out by their mother. They live in the den for three months, feeding on her rich milk. Then, the female breaks through the snow plugging the entrance to the den, and the cubs scamper out into the icy world for the first time.

Brant geese

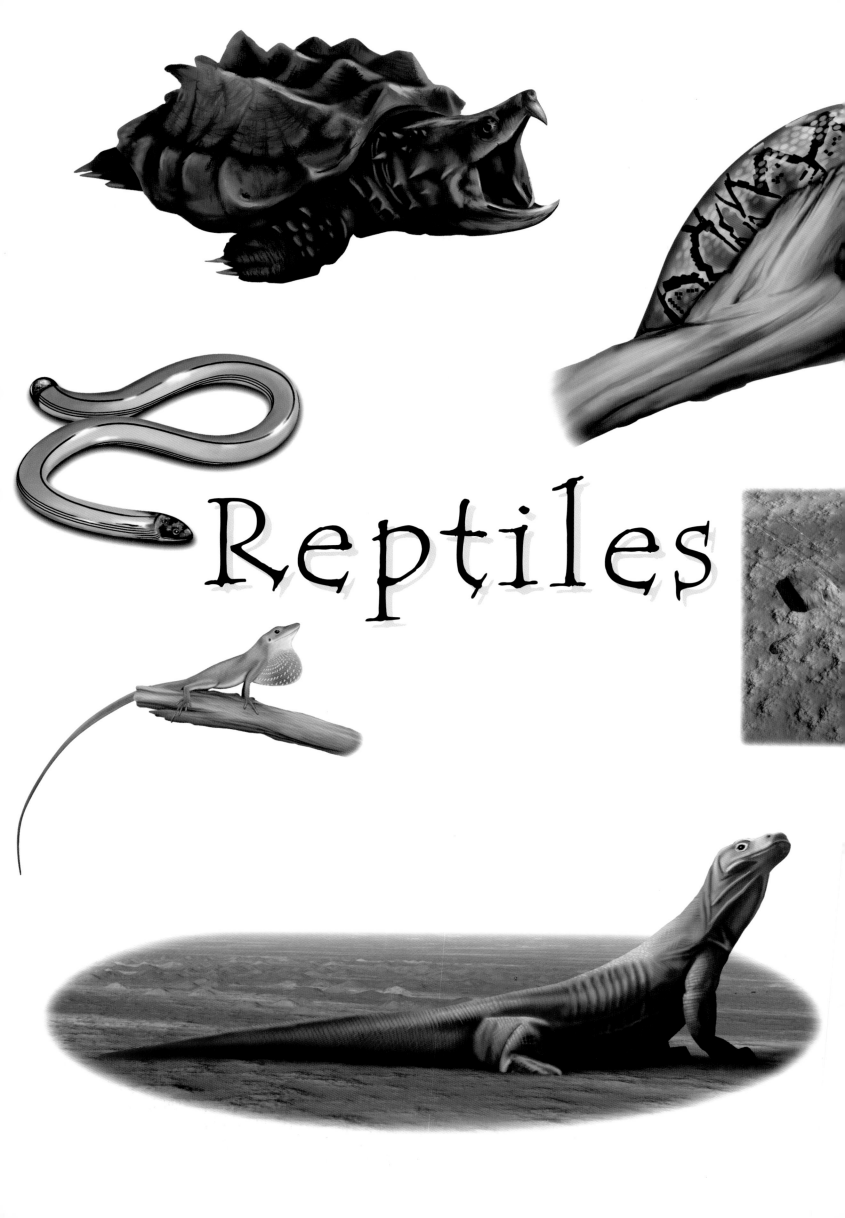

Reptiles

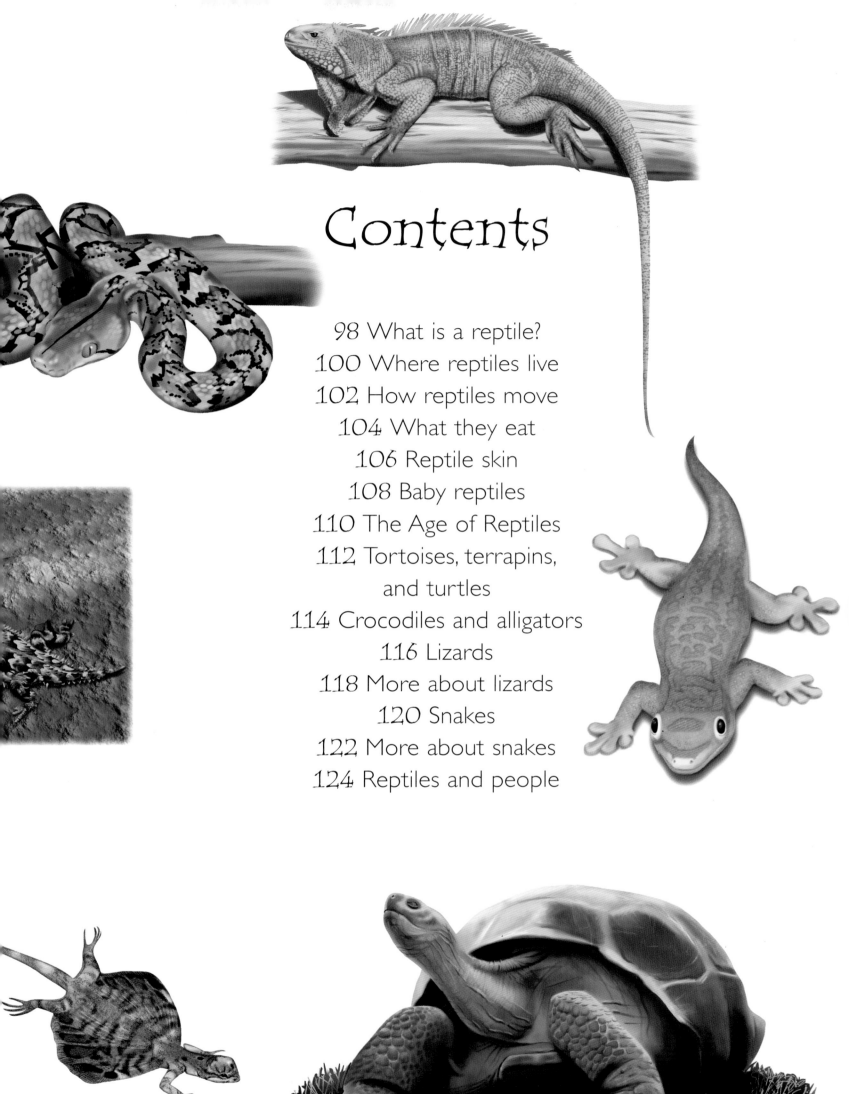

Contents

This Nile crocodile has a typically pointed snout.

Nile crocodile

Do all reptiles look alike?

N̲O! THE SLOW-MOVING TORTOISES, AND THEIR RELATIVES, ARE SHAPED like half an orange, and covered in armor made of bone and horn. Crocodiles have sprawly legs and long tails, flattened at the sides. They are armored with little plates of bone. Lizards also have sprawly legs but they have a scaly skin, which is often brightly colored. And, of course, snakes have no legs at all.

Are reptiles terrifically noisy animals?

Most reptiles are very quiet. But some hiss with anger or fear. Some make grunts or barking calls when they are up and about at night, to keep in touch with each other. Crocodiles are the noisiest reptiles – they can roar like a lion.

When are reptiles invisible?

Some reptiles are brightly colored and easy to see. But most are camouflaged with shades of brown, green, and gray, so that they disappear into their background. Often they sit very still, and are almost impossible to spot.

Have some reptiles got three eyes?

Not three eyes that can focus, and actually see things, but many reptiles have a light-sensitive area in the top of their head, and this is some-times called a third eye. The "third eye" may act as a short-cut to the brain, and some actions, that depend on light, are probably controlled by it.

So, what is a reptile?

A reptile is an animal that you are most likely to see in the warmer parts of the world. It may be smaller than one of your fingers, or many times as big as you are. But like you, it will always have a skeleton and it will always breathe air. It may be colored brightly, or have dull shades of brown or gray, but its skin will be hard and dry to the touch.

What does cold-blooded mean?

Cold-blooded means that an animal does not have a thermostat inside its brain, like we do, to keep its body at the same temperature all the time. Cold-blooded animals, like reptiles, rely on the sun to heat them up.

How many kinds of reptiles are there?

There are about 6,000 different kinds of reptiles. These can be divided into groups that include: around 20 crocodiles and alligators; 600 tortoises, terrapins, and turtles; 2,500 lizards, and a similar number of snakes. One group contains only one animal – a living fossil called the tuatara.

Iguanas belong to the lizard family. This one is sunning itself on a tree branch.

Green iguana

What is the world's smallest reptile?

The smallest of all reptiles are dwarf geckos, which live in the West Indies. They are less than 2 in (6 cm) long when fully grown – and over half of this length is tail! Very little is known about these tiny lizards, but like all geckos they feed on insects.

What is the world's biggest reptile?

The longest reptile is a snake, called the reticulated python. It often measures over 18 feet (6.1 m). The heaviest reptile is the saltwater crocodile. An old male may weigh as much as 2,200 lb (1,000 kg).

Are reptiles very brainy beasts?

COMPARED TO MAMMALS, AND MOST OF ALL TO OURSELVES, REPTILES ARE not that smart. They use their instincts for most of the things they do. It's difficult to study the intelligence and behavior of wild reptiles, but pet lizards can recognize their owners, by voice and appearance.

Do reptiles eat a lot?

No. Cold-blooded animals live on a low-energy system. Compared to mammals they eat very little. They also breathe infrequently, except when they are very warm and active.

Reticulated python

How old do reptiles get?

As a rule, reptiles live longer than mammals, or birds of a similar size. Very big reptiles live for much longer than warm-blooded animals, and it's likely that a really large crocodile may have passed its 200th birthday. Big tortoises live to a similar age.

The reticulated python is happy both on land and in water.

Where do the biggest reptiles live?

THE LEATHERY TURTLE LIVES IN THE SEA. THE BIGGEST REPTILES OF ALL – crocodiles, and the largest snakes – always live near water. Strangely, the biggest land reptiles all live on tiny islands. These include the Komodo dragon, which is the biggest lizard, which lives on the island of Komodo, and the giant tortoises of the Galapagos Islands.

How do reptiles while away the winter?

Without the sun, they slow down, and some of them stop altogether! As the weather gets colder, reptiles move more slowly, eat less, and rest more. In places where winter weather is really harsh, they find safe places to hibernate. Often hundreds of them sleep together through the cold season.

How do reptiles get to be on remote islands?

Scientist think that reptiles first got to small islands like Komodo by accident, probably floating on trees, that were washed into the sea by big storms. Once they had reached the islands, the reptiles found that they had no enemies. They had no need to hide and, in time, they became very big

Komodo dragon

When people first saw the Komodo dragon they thought it was a real dragon.

Where do reptiles live?

Reptiles make their homes in all sorts of places – in deserts and forests, on plains, and in the water. Sea snakes and sea turtles live in the oceans. Crocodiles are always found near water, but usually in fresh water rivers and lakes. Many lizards, and some snakes, are good climbers and hunt for their prey in the branches of trees. Others burrow underground, often to escape from harsh weather. A few geckos and lizards make their homes in human houses. People often welcome them, because they eat insect pests.

Why do most reptiles live in hot places?

Because they are cold-blooded, and need heating up by the sun! Reptiles use the sun's energy to keep warm, rather than making warmth for themselves, as we and other mammals do. Where the weather is hottest, life is easy for reptiles.

Which reptile lives at the North Pole?

No reptile lives right at the North Pole, but several kinds are found north of the Arctic Circle, where the weather is extremely cold, for much of the year. In Europe the adder lives further north than any other reptile. You could find it in the Arctic Circle, in northern Sweden and Finland.

Which reptiles like to get in the swim?

Water is the home for crocodiles and alligators, sea snakes, and turtles. Terrapins live in fresh water and some snakes spend much of their lives near rivers or lakes, though they often come on to dry land. Very few lizards are water-living creatures.

Why aren't there any snakes in Ireland?

Legend says that St. Patrick cast all the snakes out of Ireland. In fact, snakes are very bad sea travelers and rarely manage to reach island homes, unlike many tortoises and lizards. At the end of the last Ice Age snakes slithered into England when it was still joined to Europe. But by the time they reached the west coast, the sea had melted, and Ireland was cut off, so the snakes were stuck in England, Wales, and Scotland.

Are reptiles good at DIY?

No. Reptiles are not home-makers like many mammals. Some may dig burrows to live in, but more often they find a crack in the rocks, or a hole in the ground, where they can shelter. A few take advantage of the den-making skills of other creatures. The tuatara lives in a burrow made by a bird, and some snakes lodge in prairie dog townships.

Sea krait

The sea krait uses its curving body to push through the water.

Which reptiles live in trees?

Forests are the home for many kinds of reptile. With their long claws, lizards are good climbers, and even snakes squirm their way up trees to hunt birds and insects. Tortoises find shelter on the forest floor and terrapins often live in forest rivers.

How hot do reptiles like it?

Although they are cold-blooded, the body temperature of reptiles can soar, to a level that would kill any mammal, so they can be happily active in heat that would be uncomfortable for us. In the hottest places it is too warm even for reptiles, so they hide underground, during the daytime, and come out to hunt in the cool of the night.

How do reptiles help us study evolution?

Scientists compare reptiles that are found on remote islands, with their relations on the nearest mainland. They can often discover which sort of reptile reached the island first, because it has had most time to develop, and so is least like its mainland cousins.

What are sidewinders?

Sidewinders are snakes that live in sandy deserts. They move across the loose surface by looping their bodies up in the air, and pushing hard against the ground where they land. The track that a sidewinder leaves in the sand is just a series of straight lines, at an angle to the direction in which it is traveling. They show where its body touched down for a moment.

How speedy are reptiles?
They may look as if they are running fast, but because their bodies are generally curving from side to side, most reptiles actually move quite slowly. The fastest speed recorded for a snake is about 10 mph (6 kph) and for a lizard 27 mph (16 mph).

Geckos are expert fly catchers.

Can reptiles climb trees?
Many kinds of lizards live in trees, using their sharp claws to cling on as they climb. Some snakes also live in trees. They wriggle up the tree trunks, holding on with the big scales on their undersides.

Gecko

Where do reptiles move faster than humans?
It's a close thing! Water reptiles, such as turtles or crocodiles, can outswim a human easily. On land, a really hungry crocodile could move fast enough to catch a person. Otherwise, humans can outrun most reptiles – except where the ground is very rough. Beware!

How does a snake manage without legs?
Snakes generally move by throwing their bodies into big curves, and holding against the ground with the scales of their undersides. They must have a rough surface to move over. Put a snake on a piece of glass and it would wriggle about helplessly.

What runs upside-down?
Geckos are lizards that sometimes come into houses and run about on the ceiling. They do this without falling, because their toes have little flaps of skin that make their feet into suction pads, which hold them safely.

Are reptiles long-distance runners?

No. Reptiles run out of gas very quickly, so they can't run far. If a reptile has a long distance to travel it will do so slowly, in its own time.

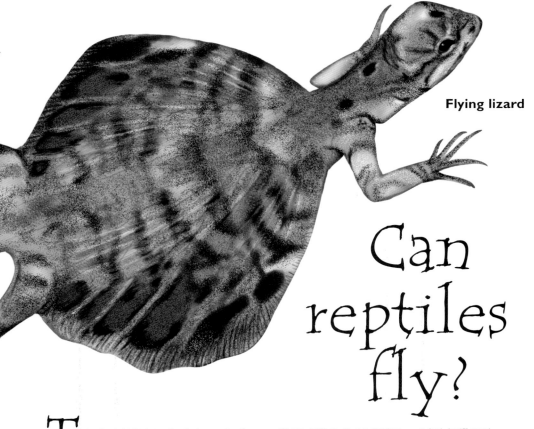

Flying lizard

Flying lizards glide through the air, rather than fly.

How fast does a snake strike its prey?

A striking prairie rattlesnake moves its head at an average speed of 8 feet (2.44 m) per second. But a human's fist, punching towards an opponent, moves faster.

How do snakes swim?

Snakes swim by curving their bodies and pushing hard against the water. Snakes, that swim well, are usually long and slender. Some have flattened sides, so their whole bodies are like a long paddle that moves them through the water.

Why do reptiles have a curvy walk?

Most reptiles have legs that stick out from the sides of their bodies. They always use diagonal limbs (left front foot, right hind foot) together. Because of this, they swing their bodies into a big curve, which makes it easy for them to take a long stride. Even reptiles, like snakes and some lizards, that have no legs at all, move in a series of curves. Small crocodiles may gallop, but other reptiles never do, even when they are going as fast as they can. However, some lizards can run on their hind legs.

Can reptiles fly?

THE PTEROSAURS, WHICH LIVED AT THE SAME TIME AS THE DINOSAURS, had huge bat-like wings and flew well. Today, the best that a few forest-dwelling reptiles can do is to glide from one tree to another. The champion gliders are little lizards that have long ribs, some of which they fold back against their sides. Leaping from a branch, they spread their ribs, opening umbrella-like fans of skin. Then they glide, like brightly colored paper darts, for up to 60 feet (20 m). Some other lizards, and a few snakes, flatten their bodies as they leap, but they cannot glide far.

Loggerhead turtles are very good swimmers.

Loggerhead turtle

How do turtles swim?

Turtles have webbed feet, which they use like frogman flippers to swim. Sea turtles use their two front feet together and steer with their hind flippers. Although they look ungainly on land, in the water turtles are graceful animals.

Which reptiles catch their food with their tongues?

Best-known of the tongue-catchers are the chameleons, which stalk insects in bushes and trees. When the chameleon is close enough, it opens its mouth – slowly, slowly – then suddenly shoots out its tongue, sometimes as much as 10 in (25 cm), and grabs the insect on its sticky tip in as little as 1/25 second!

Which reptiles are toothless?

Turtles, terrapins, and tortoises never have any teeth. Instead, they have hard, horny jaws, that can cut and tear at all sorts of food. The snapping turtle has jaws powerful enough to cut off the toes of a swimmer unlucky enough to step on it!

The chameleon is an expert climber.

Chameleon

What do reptiles eat?

ANTELOPES, FISH, WORMS, INSECTS, JELLYFISH, CACTI, AND MANY other kinds of plants! But most reptiles are very picky and most will eat only one kind of food. A meat-eater would not try chomping on a plant, no matter how hungry it was, though plant-eaters sometimes nibble at insects or worms. Crocodiles, which are the biggest reptiles, catch the biggest meals.

How often do reptiles eat?

Reptiles that eat large meals don't need to eat very often. One that has just gorged itself, on a huge meal, may not eat again for several months. Very big snakes and crocodiles have been known to go for over two years between meals!

Do most reptiles eat big meals?

Big reptiles eat big meals for their size. A crocodile may scoff a buffalo, or a young giraffe, but a little lizard is content with a few insects.

How do reptiles find their food?

Some use their eyes, first noticing the movements made by their prey, before starting to stalk it. Others use their sense of smell, which in many cases is better than that of any bloodhound.

How does reptile poison work?

The venom that some reptiles produce works in two ways. Part of it paralyzes the nervous system of their prey. The other part acts as a digestive juice, to break down the prey's body, so venomous reptiles can digest their meals more quickly.

Why are some reptiles poisonous?

POISONOUS REPTILES USUALLY FEED ON ANIMALS THAT MOVE FASTER THAN they can, so they would probably get away if they were just bitten, but the venom (poison) stops them from escaping. Not all reptiles are poisonous. But two kinds of lizard, and about a third of all known snakes, have venomous bites.

Do reptiles pick up their food to eat it?

Most reptiles use their heads and teeth to catch their prey, but they don't hold it in their claws. Tortoises, and some terrapins, put their front feet on their food while they tear at it with their jaws, but they can't pick it up to make eating a meal easier.

Do reptiles need to drink?

All animals need water and reptiles are no exception. Some drink large quantities when water is available and are able to store it in a dry season. Giant snakes that may not eat for a long time still need to drink between meals.

Gila monster

Do reptiles chew their food?

No, they don't. Reptiles that feed on flesh generally swallow their meals whole, or in very large chunks. Plant-eating reptiles have teeth or jaws that cut their food up, but they don't grind it into small pieces, like horses or rabbits do.

Which reptiles like eating jellyfish?

Almost all marine turtles eat some jellyfish, but the leathery turtle feeds on little else. It seems strange that this armored reptile, which may weigh up to 1,500 lb (680 kg) and be as long as a tall man, should eat only soft, jellylike creatures.

What reptiles are vegetarian?

The chief plant-eaters among the reptiles are the land tortoises and some lizards. Pet tortoises often eat favorite plants in your garden! The giant tortoises from the Galapagos Islands feed mainly on hard, prickly cacti. Some plant-eating lizards always go for yellow flowers. The strangest plant-eater of all is the marine iguana, which feeds on seaweed.

Galapagos tortoise

Why do reptiles change color?

Reptiles, particularly lizards, can change their colors for many reasons. They tend to be more intensely colored In bright light, and paler in dull light. Often this helps to camouflage the animal. The lizard may also change color when angry, or frightened, as changes in color can make it look bigger or fiercer. The most striking color changes are in courtship displays, when male lizards confront mates or rivals.

How quickly can a reptile change color?

Flash changes of color take a fraction of a second. Pigment changes take longer – but not that long, as a chameleon can make a complete color change in only two minutes! However, becoming paler in dim light may take hours or even weeks.

Can reptiles see in color like we can?

Reptiles that are active in daylight can probably see much the same colors as we can. Lizards can distinguish red, orange, yellow, yellowish green, blue, and violet. Giant tortoises can see orange, blue, and green and some terrapins are very sensitive to reds. They may even be able to see infra-red, which is invisible to us.

Do reptiles change color as they grow?

Brightly colored reptiles, such as lizards and snakes, may change color as they grow. This is usually because, as they become bigger, they begin to live in slightly different places and need to match different backgrounds. The dull browns and grays of turtles and crocodiles remain the same all their life.

The coral snake's bright colors warn off predators.

coral snake

Are reptiles slimy?

No, REPTILES ARE NEVER SLIMY. IN SOME CASES THE SKIN IS ROUGH TO TOUCH, but many people are surprized at how beautifully silky the skin of a snake or a lizard can feel. The scales that cover most reptiles have very few glands, like our sweat glands, which is why the skin is dry. The scales help to protect the animal, and the thin skin between them is often folded. When a reptile, like a snake, eats a huge meal, its skin can bulge as the folds are stretched out.

How can you tell male and female reptiles apart?
Some male lizards are brightly colored in the breeding season, which makes them attractive to females. (It also makes it easier for us to tell their sex.) The other differences between the sexes lie in shape, size, and smell.

This anole lizard uses his brightly colored throat fan to attract a mate.

Which reptiles wear armor?

THE BODIES OF TORTOISES, TERRAPINS, AND TURTLES ARE ENCASED in bone that forms their protective shell. The shell is made even stronger by a cover of plates of horn. Crocodiles also wear armor, made of little bones called osteoderms, which are set in the skin. This armor protects them against most enemies.

Why are some reptiles bright red and black?
The venomous lizards and some small poisonous snakes, called coral snakes, are black and orange or red. This is called warning coloration, for it tells predators that animals with this color are dangerous. Really large poisonous snakes are not brilliantly colored, perhaps because they are not attacked by small predators.

Why do some snakes borrow dangerous colors?
A predator that has had a bad experience with a poisonous snake, will probably avoid other snakes with a red and black warning coloration. So a few non-poisonous snakes are also red and black. They have evolved by tricking predators into thinking they are dangerous when they're not.

Which reptile has an invisible shadow?
Lichen bark geckos are little lizards that live in Madagascar. They are hard to see as they rest on the trunk of a tree, because they completely match the color of their background. They also have a narrow flap of skin that runs round their body and drapes on to the tree. This hides the animal's shadow, which might be a give-away to hunters.

How do reptiles regulate their temperature?
They manage to keep at the best temperature, for their needs, by moving in and out of the sun and shade. As they bask in the sunshine they absorb the heat that they need for being active. Once they are active they create a little more heat. The leathery turtle, which is very active, is thought by some people to be partly warm-blooded, like a mammal.

How fast does a baby reptile grow?

In the early days of life most baby reptiles grow quite quickly.

Some alligators, which are about 8 in (20 cm) long at hatching, grow about 12 in (30 cm) a year for the first three years. After that they slow down, though they carry on growing for many more years.

Are reptiles good, caring parents?

Not usually! Most reptiles don't look after their families at all, so the babies have to fend for themselves. Baby reptiles are like small copies of their parents. Most are born from eggs laid by the mother. They hatch out of the egg, fully formed and ready to go. They may be a different color from the adults, and often feed on different food for a while, but for a young reptile, independence is the name of the game.

When do male reptiles get really angry?

In the breeding season. Male reptiles may fight for territory, and sometimes for mates. The most fearsome fighters are the big monitor lizards, which wrestle and tear at each other with their sharp claws. Some snakes twist round each other and sway in a battle — it looks as if they are dancing. The winner probably earns the right to the biggest female, and the best place for egg-laying.

Which reptile lays most eggs?

Geckos usually lay only one or two eggs, but most reptiles produce more than this. Usually a big, old female lays more eggs than a small, young female. The biggest clutches of eggs are laid by green turtles, which normally produce over 100 — and sometimes as many as 200 — eggs!

How long does a baby reptile take to develop in the egg?

A long time — much longer than birds with eggs of a similar size. The baby tuatara takes the longest time of all reptiles to develop in its egg — up to 14 months! For many reptiles, the length of time in the egg may depend on the the temperature — the cooler it is, the more slowly they develop.

How does a baby reptile get out of its egg?

Before it hatches, a baby reptile grows a small, sharp bump on the end of its snout. This is called the "egg caruncle." When the little creature needs to break out of the egg, it twists its head from side to side and the caruncle breaks through the shell. Soon after this, the caruncle disappears.

Adders

These adders are "dancing," or fighting for a mate.

What is a reptile's egg like?

REPTILES' EGGS ARE WHITE OR DULL COLORED, WITHOUT A POINTED end, like birds' eggs. Some have a hard shell, but many have a papery outer layer. They all have a yellow yolk, which is food for the embryo (developing young), plus a watery white. Some, but not all, have an air sac, which helps the young to breathe as they hatch out.

Crocodile young hatch from their eggs fully formed.

Do any reptiles make good mothers?
Most reptile mothers don't look after their young. Crocodiles and alligators are the main exception. These scaly mothers guide their young, or sometimes carry them in their mouths, to the water. There they stay with them, to protect them from predators, often for several months.

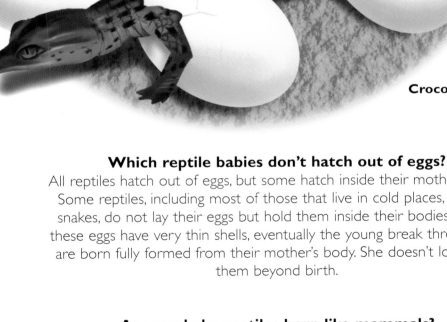

Crocodile young

Do reptile fathers ever help to bring up their families?
The male mugger, an Indian crocodile, sometimes crushes the eggs that are about to hatch, very gently in his mouth, to help his babies into the world. With the female, he then escorts them down to the water. After this he may help to guard them, but does not teach them to care for themselves.

Which reptile babies don't hatch out of eggs?
All reptiles hatch out of eggs, but some hatch inside their mother's body. Some reptiles, including most of those that live in cold places, and sea snakes, do not lay their eggs but hold them inside their bodies. Mostly these eggs have very thin shells, eventually the young break through and are born fully formed from their mother's body. She doesn't look after them beyond birth.

Are any baby reptiles born like mammals?
In some geckos and skinks the eggs that the mother holds inside her body, are very small. She overcomes this by giving some nourishment to the growing young before they are born. This is almost like the way that baby mammals develop in the womb.

Plesiosaurs swimming

Plesiosaurs were very common sea creatures during the Age of Reptiles.

When did the first reptiles roam the Earth?

T HE OLDEST KNOWN FOSSILS OF REPTILES DATE BACK ABOUT 280 MILLION years. They were small lizard-like creatures that lived in damp forests. Palaeontologists, who study fossils, tell us that they probably laid shelled eggs, and hid from danger in tree stumps.

What was the Age of Reptiles?
The Age of Reptiles lasted from about 200 million years ago, until about 65 million years ago. During this time all the main kinds of land animals, and many of those that lived in the sea, were reptiles. Most of them are now extinct.

Why are modern reptiles sometimes called 'living fossils' ?
All the reptiles alive today are very similar to those that lived in the distant past. If we could go back to the days of the dinosaurs, we would see crocodiles and turtles, and some snakes and lizards. These "living fossils" can tell us a lot about prehistoric life.

What did the dinosaurs eat?
The dinosaurs are the best known prehistoric animals. *Tyrannosaurus*, which stood as tall as a house, was a flesh-eater that tore at its food with up to 60 teeth, each like a double edged saw. Not all dinosaurs were flesh eaters – many ate plants. Some chewed them thoroughly; others gulped them down, and swallowed stones to help break them up in their stomachs.

Brachiosaurus was the tallest known dinosaur. With its long neck it would have been as tall as a three-storey house.

Brachiosaurus

How do dinosaurs get their names?

Names like *Tyrannosaurus*, which we use today, were given by the scientists who first studied the remains of the creature. Usually the name tells us something about the animal, or where it came from. *Tyrannosaurus* means terrifying lizard!

What color were dinosaurs?

NO ONE KNOWS. IN A FEW CASES PIECES OF FOSSILIZED SKIN have been found. Most look hard and warty. Very occasionally, there are marks that show where the living animal had stripes or color changes. Like most modern reptiles, the dinosaurs were probably rather dull colors.

How can we tell what dinosaurs ate?

Teeth are always the clue to what an animal eats. Slicing daggers, like the teeth of *Tyrannosaurus*, could only belong to a flesh-eater, while a set of flat-topped grinding teeth like those of the duck-billed dinosaurs shows clearly that these animals fed on tough plant food.

Which was the first dinosaur to be discovered?

It is likely that ancient people sometimes found the bones of dinosaurs, but didn't know what they were. The first dinosaur to be discovered and recognized as a huge reptile was a flesh-eater called *Megalosaurus*.

Which was the first dinosaur to be given a name?

The first dinosaur to be given a name was not, strangely, the first one to be discovered. Some big teeth were found by a doctor's wife in Sussex, UK, in 1823. They turned out to belong to a big plant-eater that was called *Iguanodon* by the scientists who studied it.

Where is the best place to find dinosaur fossils?

In a museum! Lots have wonderful collections of fossil bones. But the best place to find them yourself – if you are very lucky – is in stream beds or by the seashore, where rocks of the right age may contain ancient remains.

Alligator snapping turtle

The alligator snapping turtle can live to over 100 years old.

How does the snapping turtle fool its prey?

THE ALLIGATOR SNAPPING TURTLE SITS IN THE WATER WITH ITS MOUTH open. It doesn't need to be very active, for on its tongue is a pink, worm-like growth which it waves gently in the current. Any fish stupid enough to nibble the "worm" is caught in the snapper's sharp jaws.

What's the difference between a tortoise and a terrapin?

Difficult to tell at first, because tortoises and terrapins are both slow-moving armored reptiles. Tortoises live on dry land in many warm parts of the world. They usually have high-domed shells, and feed mainly on plants. Terrapins live in fresh water. They have flattened shells, which make them more streamlined as they swim. They often have partly webbed feet and they feed on fish and other animals. Some terrapins are quite large, fierce predators.

So what is a turtle?

Some people use the word "turtle" to include tortoises and terrapins. But true turtles are big animals that live in the sea. Their shells are streamlined and they can't pull their heads inside for protection. Their feet are paddles covered in a mitten of skin, and they eat a mixture of sea plants and animals.

How many tortoises and terrapins are there?

There are 240 different kinds of tortoises, terrapins, and turtles to be found in the world today. The scientific name for the whole group is the *Chelonia*. The biggest is the leatherback turtle, which may reach 13 feet (1.8 m) in length and weigh an astonishing 1,500 lb (680 kg). The smallest is the speckled tortoise, which is only about 4 in (10 cm) long when fully grown.

How is the shell joined to the tortoise?

A tortoise's armor is made of bone overlaid with horn. The bones are part of the skeleton, which have grown together to make a complete box. The backbones, ribs, hips, and shoulders are all attached to this.

How do tortoises breathe?

Because their bodies are enclosed in a bony box, tortoises can't stretch their rib cage, and so they can't breathe like other animals. Instead they have special muscles that pull at the lungs, so that air is forced in, and pushed out.

What drove many tortoises to extinction?

Human beings, unfortunately. The big members of the tortoise family are all very rare because they live on small islands. When sailors visited the islands in the past, before the days of refrigeration, they killed tortoises to get fresh meat. Many kinds of tortoise became extinct because of this.

Which Greek poet was killed by a tortoise?

The poet Aeschylus is supposed to have been killed by a tortoise in 455 BC. An eagle, that had caught a tortoise, thought the poet's bald head was a stone. It dropped its prey to crack it, but instead broke the poet's skull. Or so they say!

Why did the hawksbill turtle need protecting?

Tortoiseshell is the horny outer layer of the hawksbill turtle's shell. For many years hawskbills were hunted for their shells, which were made into all sorts of trinkets, boxes, fans, and combs and sometimes used to decorate furniture. Now the hawksbill is endangered it's strictly protected, though in some parts of the world young hawksbills are reared specially to be killed for their shells.

How did a tortoise outrun a hare?

The ancient story of the hare and the tortoise tells how these two animals decided to have a race. The hare was so confident that he would win, that he didn't bother to start until it was too late. The tortoise, plodding along, reached the finishing line first.

Why are some cats and butterflies called tortoiseshells?

They get their name because of their colors. The underside of the wings of the butterfly, and the coat of the cat are blotched with black, brown, and gold. These are the colors of tortoiseshell taken from the hawksbill turtles' shell.

Which creature lives in a box?

The box turtle is a small tortoise, with a hinged shell. When it is alarmed it pulls in its head and feet and shuts the lid, so it is totally enclosed in its shell. A hunter like a fox is fooled by the bony box.

Can tortoises climb trees?

THE CHINESE BIG-HEADED TURTLE HAS LONG claws and a long tail. This cumbersome creature is more agile than it looks. When it's out of water, it sometimes scrambles up trees for safety. All its relatives stay firmly on the ground!

Chinese big-headed turtle

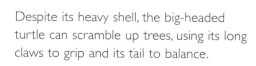

Despite its heavy shell, the big-headed turtle can scramble up trees, using its long claws to grip and its tail to balance.

Crocodiles have pointy snouts.

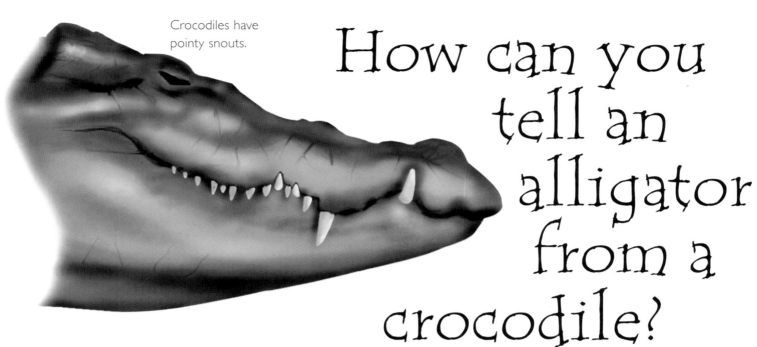

How can you tell an alligator from a crocodile?

BY ITS SMILE! ALLIGATORS AND THEIR RELATIVES THE CAIMANS ARE VERY similar to crocodiles, and their cousin the gharial. They are all water-living hunters with long jaws crammed with sharp pointed teeth. The easiest way to tell one from the other is that when an alligator has its mouth closed, you can't see any of its lower teeth. A crocodile shows a big tooth, sticking up, at either side of its mouth.

Alligators have wide, flat heads and rounded noses.

Like alligators, caimans have wide, flat heads and rounded noses.

Which mother carries its babies in its fearsome mouth?
Mother crocodiles help their young by breaking away the hard cap of soil over the nest, and digging down to the eggs. They sometimes break the eggs gently in their mouths, to free the babies, which are only about 8 in (20 cm) long. When the family is complete, the mother either leads them down to the water, or carries them – carefully! – in her mouth. For the first months of their life, she protects them by driving away enemies, such as storks or other crocodiles.

What does a baby crocodile eat?
After it has finished eating the yolk from its egg, the baby crocodile starts to catch insects. These are its most important prey until it is about two.

Gharials have long, thin snouts that they use for fishing.

Why is the crocodile in danger?
Some types of crocodile have become very rare, because people have destroyed their habitat. Many other types have been hunted to the brink of extinction. Only now that crocodiles are disappearing, have people discovered their importance to the environment.

What are crocodile tears?

Crocodile tears are not real tears of sadness. So someone crying crocodile tears is insincere. This idea came from a sea captain, called John Hawkins. He said that a crocodile would cry, then eat any creature stupid enough to be sorry for it.

Do crocodiles use birds as toothbrushes?

In a way, yes! The Nile crocodile often rests with its mouth open. Birds venture into its open jaws, to pick at bits of meat stuck between the teeth, and perhaps feed on parasites lurking there as well. The birds have to leap out of the way if the crocodile suddenly snaps shut its jaws. By taking flight, they can also warn the crocodile of approaching danger.

Why don't crocodiles need sunshades?

The heavy skin of a crocodile is protected by scales. In some place these are like thick toenails, in others they have become bone. The bony scales are called osteoderms. Osteoderms act as armor against attack, and also against overheating when the crocodile is basking in the sun.

Do crocodiles like getting water up their noses?

No. They prefer calm water to swim in. To swim, a crocodile holds its front feet close to its body and forges forward, using its powerful tail like a paddle. If the water is choppy, the crocodile has to raise its head, to stop the water getting up its nose.

Where are crocodiles farmed?

In many parts of the world where crocodiles have become very rare, people are now breeding them in crocodile farms. Some are released into the wild but most are killed, and used for leather and for meat.

Which animal has 45 sets of teeth before it is fully grown?

Even if it could, a crocodile never has any need to wear false teeth. As the animal grows and its teeth wear down, they are replaced by sharp new ones growing in its jaws. By the time it is a young adult, a Nile crocodile will probably have used up 45 sets of teeth!

How do baby crocodiles call their mum?

When they are ready to hatch, baby crocodiles croak to their mother, from inside the egg. Then she knows it's time to help them hatch. In the water she warns them of danger by twitching her body. The babies feel the water swirling and cluster round her for safety.

When do kids walk like crocodiles?

When they walk two by two. A line of schoolchildren walking in pairs is called a crocodile. This is probably because they don't walk in a straight line, but curve a little from side to side, like a crocodile's long body as it swims.

The spur-winged plover picks pieces of meat from between the crocodile's teeth.

Basking crocodile

Which is the biggest living crocodile?

THE SALTWATER CROCODILE. THE LARGEST ONE RECORDED SO FAR IS OVER 23 FEET (7 m) long. Others are said to have grown even bigger – in some cases to over 29 feet (9 m) long – though no accurate records of these have been kept.

Why should you avoid being bitten by a beaded lizard?

You can tell a beaded lizard because its scales make it look as though it has been sprinkled all over with beads. But the great difference, between beaded lizards and other lizards, is that they have a poisonous bite. They eat mainly small helpless creatures, and use the bite for self-defence.

Which lizard has eaten people?

The biggest of all lizards is called the Komodo dragon. This fearsome creature measures up to 10 feet (3 m) long and weighs over 330 lb (150 kg). It normally feeds on carrion (animals it finds already dead), but it has been known to kill and eat humans!

What lizard flies?

Lizards cannot fly like birds, but some forest dwellers can glide for about 65 feet (20 m) between trees. As they leap from a branch they spread a flap of skin, supported by ribs.

Which lizards have the biggest stomachs?

American horned lizards and the Australian moloch lizard feed on nothing but ants. A single meal may consist of 2,500 ants! Their stomachs have to be much larger than average, so they can eat such big meals, and may be up to 13% of their total bulk.

What is a sandfish?

A sandfish is not a fish at all, but a smooth, shiny-skinned lizard called a skink, that lives in sand dunes. Its legs are tiny, so to get about in its sandy home it wriggles its way along with side-to-side movements, like a snake.

What creature shoots blood from its eyes?

If a horned lizard is attacked, it can increase the blood pressure in veins, in its eye sockets until they burst. Blood squirts out in a thin stream, traveling up to 48 in (122 cm) and splattering the attacker. Predators, that get the lizard's blood in their eyes, or mouth think it is poisonous and leave the lizard alone.

Where do lizards live?

There are at least 2,500 different kinds of lizards. Except for Antarctica, and some very small islands, they live in almost every country in the world. Most of them are found in warm places, but a few live as far north as the Arctic Circle.

Is it true that some lizards have no legs?

Yes, quite a lot of lizards are legless – they wriggle along like snakes. Scientists think that the ancestors of these lizards were burrowing creatures, which wriggled their way through the soil. Their legs were not used for this activity, so gradually grew smaller, and eventually disappeared altogether.

The Californian legless
lizard looks more like a
snake than a lizard.

**Californian
legless lizard**

How does a frilled lizard scare its enemies?

Frilled lizard

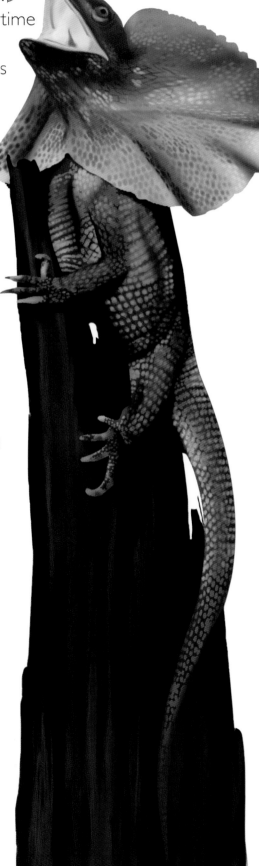

THE FRILLED LIZARD TURNS
ON ITS ENEMIES, OPENS
its mouth wide and at the same time
spreads a big ruff of brightly
colored skin round its neck. This
makes it look much larger, and
fiercer, than it really is. Quite
often the bluff works and
the lizard escapes with
its life.

Is it true that lizards never stop growing?

Like all reptiles, lizards grow fast
when they are young. After they
are big enough to mate, they grow
more slowly, but it is likely that
they don't ever stop growing
completely. Tiny lizards are
probably short-lived, but the big
ones are almost all very old.

What creature can grow two tails?

A lizard's tail may break if bitten by an
attacker. At first the tail wriggles all on
its own, and the predator is distracted
by the twitching tail, while the
lizard escapes.

What creature blows itself up like a balloon?

Chuckwallas live in North American
deserts. If one is attacked it dives
into a crevice in the rocks and
swallows air, so its body is blown
up like a balloon. However hard
the predator tries to dislodge it, it
is unlikely to succeed, for the
chuckwalla is stuck in its crevice
and can't be budged.

If its vivid ruff doesn't scare
off enemies, the frilled lizard
will either run away or run
towards its enemies, hissing.

Horned lizards are
decreasing in number,
though no one is really
sure why.

Horned lizard

marbled gecko

This gecko is shedding its skin in one large piece.

When is a lizard like a hedgehog?
When threatened by a larger enemy, the spiny lizard of South Africa rolls itself up and holds its tail in its mouth. The predator is faced with a prickly ball, which it usually leaves well alone.

Which lizard can move its eyes independently?
The chameleon! Its eyes are partly surrounded by skin, and look as if they are in little turrets. Each eye can be swiveled independently, so a chameleon can always see what is going on around it.

Why do lizards pretend to be beetles?
One little lizard, that lives in the Kalahari Desert, has a tail colored like desert sand. The rest of its body is black and white, so while the tail disappears into the background, the body looks like a desert beetle that tastes horrible. Predators that have learnt that the beetle is nasty avoid the lizard. As it grows too big to be mistaken for a beetle, the lizard loses its black and white coloring and becomes camouflaged against its desert background.

How does a lizard shed its skin?

LIKE US, LIZARDS NEED TO SHED THEIR SKIN. BUT WHILE WE LOSE OUR SKIN ALL THE time in minute flakes, lizards shed theirs from time to time in large pieces. Sometimes a lizard will pull a piece of skin off with its teeth, and eat it. Underneath is a bright new skin.

When does a lizard look like a snake?
Several kinds of lizard are left alone by their enemies, because they look like poisonous snakes. They have similar coloring and move their heads in a snake-like way. One lizard, that lives in Pakistan, has a tail that looks like a viper, which it waves to warn off enemies. Some lizards escape from their enemies because when they stand still they look like plants!

Where can you see lizards in the sky?
Look up into the sky on a summer night in the northern hemisphere, and you can see the constellation of Draco, the dragon or lizard, with its tail curling round the Little Bear. In the southern hemisphere, a constellation called the Chameleon has its long tongue pointing toward a smaller star group called the Fly.

Where does a lizard hold the purse strings?

In the past, the Japanese carried purses fastened by toggles called netsuke. These were often carved in the shape of lizards twined around each other.

Lizards can move much faster on their hind legs than they can on all fours.

Gould's monster

Why do some lizards have very fat tails?

Lizards that live on the edge of deserts, where there is rainfall and food for part of the year only, eat as much as they can in times of plenty. They store food as fat in their bodies, usually round the tail, which grows very big and fat. When there is no food, the tail slims down again as the fat is used up, to give the lizard energy.

Do lizards eat seaweed?

The only seaweed-eating lizard is the marine iguana from the Galapagos Islands. It lives on the seashore and dives into the water, to feed on weeds that grow on rocks. The sea off the Galapagos is cooled by the Humboldt Current, but the iguana can drop its heart rate so it does not slow down in the cold, as other reptiles do. The marine iguana also has special glands that get rid of salt from the water.

Can lizards walk on water?

No! But the basilisk lizards of South America can run over water for a few seconds, at their top speed of about 5 mph (8 kph). The water surface film does not support them for long. But by the time they sink they have usually escaped the enemy that was chasing them into the water.

Why are some lizards black?

You can often find black lizards in high mountains, where the sunlight is bright but the air is cold. Their black skins allow them to warm up better than if they had a pale skin. In just one hour in the sun, the lava lizard of the Peruvian Andes mountains can raise its temperature to 91.5°F (33°C) – when the temperature of the air around it is only 35°F (1.5°C).

Why do lizards stand on tip-toe?

SOME DESERT-LIVING LIZARDS STAND ON TIP-TOE BECAUSE THE GROUND HAS got too hot. Others stand on their hind legs, so they can see further. Still others run on their hind legs so they don't waste energy wriggling from side to side.

How many kinds of snake are there?
There are around 2,500 different kinds of snake known in the world today. Most live in warm countries, though you are not likely to see them, since they are generally shy creatures.

Which is the smallest snake?
The smallest snakes are the blind or thread snakes. They are rarely spotted, as they burrow underground. Some are only 6 in (15 cm) long when fully grown. They normally feed on ants and termites, which they hunt by smell.

Can snakes shut their eyes?
A snake has no eyelids, so it can't shut its eyes, even when it's asleep. As it moves about, its eyes are protected by a transparent scale, called a brille. Many people think that snakes have an evil stare, but this is simply because they can't blink.

Can snakes hear through their jaws?
Snakes have no eardrums, so they can hardly hear any airborne sounds. But they do have an ear bone that connects with the lower jaw, so they can sense vibrations through their jaw, from the ground or the water. Like other animals, they have an inner ear which is used for balance.

The fork in the snake's tongue is very sensitive.

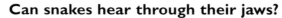

Why do snakes have forked tongues?

So THEY CAN 'TASTE' THEIR WAY about the world. As the tongue flicks out of the snake's mouth, it picks up tiny particles of scent left by other animals. Inside the snake's mouth is a pit lined with cells that are very sensitive to smells. The tongue flicks in the air, or on to the ground, then is pushed into the pit to test for smells that might lead to food. The deep fork means that the snake can sample a wider track than it could with a simple, undivided tongue.

Why do snakes swallow their food whole?
Snakes' teeth are sharply pointed, good for holding food, but no use for cutting it up or chewing it. So when a snake has caught a meal, it has to swallow it in one piece. It may have to unhitch its jaws, so that a really big meal can go down. You can tell when a snake has just eaten well because of the bulge in its body.

Do snakes ever have legs?
No snake has legs, but a few kinds have tiny claws toward their rear end. These, and some small bones inside the body, are the only remains of the legs that their ancestors once had.

Which is the biggest snake?

THE LONGEST OF ALL SNAKES IS THE RETICULATED PYTHON FROM Indonesia. It is often longer than 19 feet (6 m), with some running to over 32 feet (10 m). The heaviest snake is the anaconda, which is usually shorter than the python, but much stouter. An anaconda measuring only 17 feet (5.2 m) weighs as much as a python of 24 feet (7.3 m).

The golden tree snake is one of several flying snakes.

How does a flying snake fly?
No snake can fly like a bird, but the golden tree snake comes nearest to it. As it launches itself from a branch, it pulls in its belly, so it is concave, like a long wing, and shaped like this it can glide for several feet.

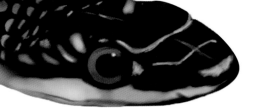

Golden tree snake

Are snakes aggressive?
Most snakes are peaceable animals, and hurry away from trouble if they can. Humans are not the natural prey of snakes, so most are aggressive toward us only if they are cornered. Most are non-poisonous, but even so, it's best to leave them alone.

What is a snakestone?
A snakestone is the name that used to be given to fossils of ammonites, because their curled shells reminded people of snakes. You can sometimes see these fossils in antique shops, with snakes' heads carved on to them.

What is a constrictor?
A constrictor means a squeezer – it's a snake that squeezes its prey to death. It does this by throwing a loop of its body round the prey. It then squeezes so hard that the prey is soon suffocated, and the snake can swallow its meal.

By stretching its mouth, the boa constrictor can swallow its prey whole.

Boa constrictor

121

Can snakes spit their venom?

SPITTING COBRAS HAVE A TINY HOLE IN THEIR POISON FANGS, THROUGH which they can spit their venom. The poison can be spat up to 6 feet (2 m) with a spread of over 19 in (0.5 m). Snakes aim for their enemies' eyes, where the venom causes severe pain and at least temporary blindness.

Why haven't snakes got legs?

The early ancestors of snakes did have legs, and they could walk about like other animals. Most scientists think that some of these snakes took to burrowing in the ground, where legs were not much use, so they lost them. Since then some snakes have returned to the surface, but their legs have gone for good.

What is a front-fanged snake?

It's a snake with a poisonous bite. The poison is made in glands, high up at the back of the jaw, then channeled to the fangs (hollow teeth) in the front of the mouth. When the snake bites, poison flows down the fangs straight into the wound.

How do you milk a snake?

Milking a snake means taking venom from it. This is a job for an expert, who holds the snake so that its mouth is open, and its fangs are in a small jar. The snake is usually fairly cross at this treatment and bites at the jar, so that venom flows into it from its fangs. The venom is used to make medicines for blood-clotting disorders, as well as antidotes (cures) for people who have been bitten by snakes.

Which is the most dangerous snake?

The snake with the deadliest poison is the olive sea snake, but like all sea snakes, it is shy and rarely spotted. Far more dangerous are land-living species, such as cobras and rattlesnakes. The eastern diamondback rattlesnake is said to be the most dangerous snake in North America. In fact, all venomous snakes can be dangerous. People should not try to kill them, as they have their own place in the ecosystem.

Which Greek god has snakes around his staff?

Hermes, messenger to the gods, is often shown carrying a staff with two snakes twined round it. Greek mythology says that these were originally two white ribbons. Then Hades, who ruled over the kingdom of the dead, gave Hermes the job of laying his staff on the eyes of the dying, and turned the ribbons into snakes.

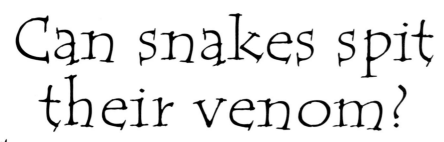

Black spitting cobra

What was a snake doing in the Garden of Eden?

The snake in the Garden of Eden is supposed to have tempted Eve, the first woman in the Old Testament creation story, to take the fruit of the tree of knowledge – and this has led to all our troubles ever since!

How do snake charmers charm snakes?

Snake charmers in India keep cobras or other very poisonous snakes in a sack. To entertain people, they play the flute, and the snake writhes out of the sack and dances to the music. But, since the snake has no ears it can't actually hear the music! In fact it weaves its head about as it watches the movements of the flute, or feels the vibration of the charmer's tapping feet.

Cobras are one of only four types of poisonous snakes.

Rattlesnake

Rattlesnakes are dangerous to humans only if disturbed.

How does a rattlesnake rattle?

A RATTLESNAKE'S RATTLE IS MADE OF INTERLOCKING PIECES OF HARD material like toenails, which tap against each other when the end of the tail is twitched. The rattle grows longer each time the snake sheds its skin, so an old rattlesnake will have a bigger rattle than a young one. The rattle is used to warn off large animals.

What is "a snake in the grass"?

The phrase "a snake in the grass" means a hidden enemy. It was first used in Roman times, when people went barefoot or wore open sandals, and were sometimes in danger of stepping on venomous snakes.

How do some snakes play possum?

When they are caught, or badly frightened, some snakes pretend to be dead. A snake playing possum rolls limply on to its back, dislocates its jaws, and hangs its tongue out of its mouth. But the snake is not dead, and after a few minutes of acting, it will turn over and slip quickly away.

How many people do reptiles kill every year?

Poisonous snakes bite large numbers of people every year, though there are no reliable figures to say how many attacks are fatal. Modern treatment means that far more people survive snakebites than used to be the case. Saltwater crocodiles and Nile crocodiles attack, and probably kill, up to 3,000 people a year.

Which animal in Britain has killed most people?

The adder is the biggest poisonous animal in Britain, but it has not caused the most human deaths. Guess which creature has – the honey bee! Some people are allergic to bee stings and have died from them.

How many reptiles do people kill every year?

It's not possible to say, but we are more dangerous to reptiles than they are to us! Most of the large tortoises, that used to inhabit remote islands, have been hunted to extinction, and countless smaller reptiles have been lost because of habitat destruction. Today most marine turtles, and most crocodiles, are so rare that they are nearly extinct. A large number of lizards and snakes are in the same position.

Which reptiles are valued for their skin?

Many reptiles have been hunted to the brink of extinction for their beautiful skins. The skins of large lizards and snakes are really valuable, as is the skin of the underside of the crocodile. Some hunters sell the skin of marine turtles' flippers, pretending that it's something more valuable.

Do reptiles make good pets?

REPTILES ARE NOT LIKE OTHER PETS; THEY MUST HAVE WARMTH, the right food, and housing if they are to thrive. They may need vitamin supplements and ultra-violet light to keep them healthy. Many people don't realize that reptiles are hard to look after, need a lot of attention and money spent on them, and may soon grow very large and become hard to manage.

What is the worst time of year to meet an adder?

Early in the spring is the most dangerous time to meet poisonous snakes, in cooler parts of the world. In spring snakes aren't very quick to warm up, and you could step on one before it has a chance to get away. Most snakebites occur at this time.

Are reptiles welcome in the garden?

Yes – apart from large poisonous snakes! Few reptiles, that wander into your garden, are likely to eat cherished plants. Their food generally consists of pest species, such as mice and large insects. In Northern Europe, a legless lizard, called a slow worm, feeds largely on small slugs – creatures that most gardeners are pleased to be rid of.

Loggerhead turtles

Loggerhead turtles arrive on a breeding beach.

What help is on hand for sea turtles?

Endangered sea turtles are being helped by people who organize sanctuaries on their breeding beaches, where the young can hatch in safety. Sometimes the young are kept in the sanctuary, until they are large enough to stand a good chance of survival in the ocean.

What are herpetologists?

People who study reptiles. Herpetologist comes from a Greek word meaning creeping, that was used to describe reptiles. There are no commonly used terms for specialists who study, for instance, only lizards or turtles.

What is lucky in China but evil in the West?

Dragons! These mythical beasts are scaly, sharp-toothed and long-tailed. They have leathery wings, and some can breathe fire. In Western folklore they are evil, destroying people and their crops. In China they are a force for good, warding off evil spirits.

In China the dragon is seen as a sign of good.

Which snakes once won a battle for humans?

Hannibal, the Carthaginian general, ordered jars of live snakes to be thrown aboard the ships of his enemy. His terrified foes soon gave in.

Do people ever eat reptiles?

A FEW REPTILES EAT PEOPLE, BUT THIS IS NOTHING TO THE AMOUNT OF alligator meat, snake meat, and turtle meat eaten by humans. In some parts of the world, reptiles are farmed for their meat. Reptile meat is good, for it is tasty and has very little fat.

Creepy Crawlies

Do all spiders have webs?

Not all spiders make a nice round web. Some weave hammock-shaped webs, flat sheets of silk, or simply trip wires radiating from their lair to trap insects. Some hunt without using a web, but all spiders can make silk.

How many kinds of spider are there?

There are over 30,000 species discovered so far, but there could be as many again that haven't yet been found. Spiders can live virtually all over the world on land.

Red-kneed tarantula

The largest spiders, like this red-kneed tarantula, are little danger to humans.

Which are the biggest spiders?

T HE "BIRD-EATING" SPIDERS OF SOUTH AMERICA ARE BOTH THE HEAVIEST and widest species, with weights up to 3 oz (80 g) and leg spans up to 10 in (26 cm). Very few of them actually eat birds, but the bigger species do eat small frogs, lizards, and snakes.

Which spider makes the biggest webs?

The tropical orb web spiders can have webs over 16 ft (5 m) across. Up to 2,300 ft (700 m) length of silk strand can be produced by the silk glands of one of these spiders. The silk is so strong it can actually hold a human.

Crab spider

A crab spider can change color to match the flower it is on.

Are spiders good parents?

Most spiders don't really look after their young. Many lay their eggs in a cocoon, for protection, but often the female will die before they hatch. Mother wolf spiders carry the cocoon attached to their spinnerets (the organ that makes their silk), and *Pisaura* carries her cocoon in her fangs until hatching time, when she builds a silk tent, on a plant, for the babies to live in. The tiny *Theridion sisyphium* lives in a thimble-shaped tent above its hammock web. In the tent it looks after the egg cocoon, then feeds the tiny babies below it with the regurgitated juices from the prey.

How many insects do spiders eat?

We can only guess at the millions of insects eaten by spiders every day. W.S. Bristowe, who studied spiders in England, once calculated that, over a year, spiders ate a weight of insects greater than the weight of all the people living in England.

Why do spiders spit?

Scytodes, a small black and yellow spider, found in Europe and the USA, has an unusual way of catching its prey. As an insect approaches, the spider raises its fangs and ejects two streams of gum from them, swinging its head so that the two lines of gum fall in a zigzag over the prey. Once the prey is pinned down, the spider moves in to bite and eat it.

How many eyes does a spider have?

Most spiders have eight eyes, but there are species with six, four or two. The shape and arrangement of the eyes help to tell which family a spider belongs to. Many spiders use touch more than sight, but the eyes of jumping spiders are well developed.

Can spiders fly?
Spiders do not have wings, but many species can parachute, or sail through the air by letting out a long thread of silk until they are carried away by the wind. Many young spiders leave the nest by this "ballooning" technique. They can be carried thousands of metres above the earth.

Which spiders give presents?
Male spiders are often smaller than their mates. Sometimes the female may attack the male in order to eat him. Many American wolf spiders "sing" to the female to distract her and try and save themselves. The male spider *Pisaura mirabilis* of Europe makes himself safe by catching a fly, wrapping it into a silk parcel, and presenting it to the female, who eats it as they mate. He does this in the hope that she won't be hungry enough to make a meal of him.

Black widow spider

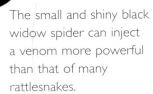

The small and shiny black widow spider can inject a venom more powerful than that of many rattlesnakes.

How common are spiders?
Very common indeed. We do not notice most of them, because they are small and are mainly active at night, but in good conditions there may be about 2,000,000 per acre (5,000,000 to the hactare).

Can spiders change color?
The crab spiders, such as *Misumena*, live in flowers. They lie in wait for insects, sitting on flowers whose colors they match. They are even capable of changing color over a few days to match the flower. Most kinds of spider stay the same color, but their natural coloring or pattern is often perfect camouflage for their habitat.

Which spider likes to go fishing?
The bolas spider hangs underneath a branch on a silky trapeze, then lets down a silk line about 2 in (5 cm) long with a sticky blob on the end. The spider swings this around to catch passing insects.

What is a spider's web made of?
A spider's web is made of silk. Spiders have glands on their abdomen which produce the silk, which can be made sticky, elastic or very strong. Some spider silk is much stronger than steel of the same thickness.

Which spiders are human killers?

ALL SPIDERS ARE POISONOUS, BUT ONLY A FEW HAVE STRONG ENOUGH FANGS, and powerful enough venom, to harm people. The black widow, found in many warm parts of the world, including the USA and Europe, is a small, round spider which likes hiding in quiet places. It is not aggressive, but if it is attacked, it may bite. After a few minutes, the bite is terribly painful. The victim feels dizzy, and can suffer from paralysis. It is rarely fatal, though, and nowadays cures are available. The Australian Sydney funnel-web spider is a larger species with a dangerous bite. A bite from this spider causes heart failure and breathing problems. Again, drugs are now available to reverse the effects. The recluse spiders of the USA, and the Brazilian wandering spider, have bites that can be fatal. However, the chances of being killed by a spider are less than those of being struck by lightning.

When do scorpions dance?

THE MATING RITUAL OF SCORPIONS LOOKS LIKE A DANCE. THE partners grab one another's pincers, to protect themselves from each other. With pincers held, they move back, forward and sideways, sometimes for hours. Finally, the male deposits a packet of sperm and moves the female over on top of it. The sperm goes into her body and fertilizes the eggs.

Where do the biggest scorpions live?

The largest scorpions live in tropical forests. Some, such as the imperial scorpion of Africa, are up to 7 in (18 cm) long. These scorpions aren't very poisonous.

Do all scorpions sting?

All scorpions have poisonous stings at the ends of their tails. They use them mainly to defend themselves. Only a few are truly dangerous to humans. Most scorpion stings are unpleasant, rather than deadly.

Where do baby scorpions hitch a ride?

After hatching, the young of many scorpions climb onto their mother's back. They use her large pincers as a climbing ramp. They ride there until after their first molt (when they lose a layer of skin). After this they leave their mother and start to fend for themselves.

Why do ticks drink blood?

Ticks don't find food very often, and they must be ready to latch on to anything that can provide it, as it passes. An adult tick may have to wait months, or even years, before fastening its jaws into a passing mammal and sucking its blood. It has to have a meal of blood before it can lay its eggs.

Scorpions first appeared on earth 345 million years ago.

Imperial scorpion

How many legs does a millipede really have?

In spite of their name (*mille* is Latin for a thousand), millipedes never have a thousand legs. The most that they have is 200 pairs (400 legs), and some species have only 20 pairs (40 legs). The leg movements are co-ordinated in "waves" running from front to back.

Will you ever be attacked by a centipede?

Centipedes have a pair of poison fangs, that they use to catch their prey. Most centipedes in countries with a mild climate, do not have a powerful enough bite to do serious damage. Anyway, they usually run away rather than attack. But some large tropical centipedes can inflict a nasty bite if threatened.

Millipedes have two pairs of legs for each segment of their bodies, while centipedes have just one pair per segment.

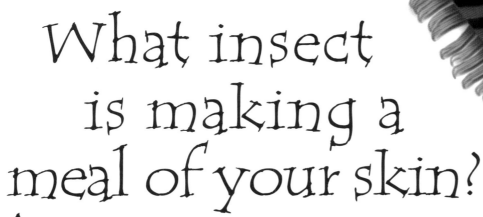

What insect is making a meal of your skin?

A LARGE PART OF HOUSE DUST IS MADE UP OF TINY FLAKES OF HUMAN SKIN, and this is what the house dust mite eats. It likes warm, damp conditions, such as in beds and mattresses, which can also provide plenty of skin. Although most people are not affected by these mites, some people are highly allergic to them.

Giant millipede

How can you tell a millipede from a centipede?

Most millipedes are slow-moving plant-eaters with short legs and chewing mouthparts. Centipedes are fast-moving meat-eaters with fangs that they use to kill prey. They have fewer legs than millipedes.

What do centipedes have for dinner?

Centipedes eat insects, slugs, and other creepy-crawlies; they even eat other centipedes. The largest tropical species can be 13 in (33 cm) long. They can kill animals such as lizards, frogs and mice.

What tick carries a mountainous disease?

A serious illness, called Rocky Mountain fever, is caused by a tiny organism called a rickettsia. It invades the cells of the body and produces severe fever. The disease is carried by woodchucks, but wood ticks, living on these animals, can carry it to humans. The disease was first discovered in Montana, about 100 years ago, when it killed three-quarters of those who got it. Since then, it has been found in other parts of North and South America, but not in such a deadly form.

What animal lives in your eyelashes?

Almost all of us have tiny mites living in the sockets of our eyes. They do no harm and may even help to keep our skin clean. They are so small that we can't see them.

How big are the biggest millipedes?

Some of the millipedes that live in the tropical parts of Africa grow to 11 in (28 cm) or more, with a diameter (thickness) of about 1 in (2 cm).

What weapons does a soldier termite have?

SOLDIER TERMITES ARE TOUGHER THAN THE WORKER TERMITES. MANY termite species have soldiers, with huge armoured heads and biting jaws, to fight off enemies, particularly ants. Other species have soldiers with special "snouts" that can shoot sticky fluid over an enemy. Soldiers are designed only for fighting, so they cannot even feed themselves. They have to rely on the workers to provide food for them.

Why are termites heavier than elephants?

Millions of termites live in the tropics. There may be as many as 3,300 per square yard (4,000 per square metre), sometimes even twice this. The weight of termites in 0.4 square miles (1 square kilometre) under the ground, is more than the weight of all the elephants or zebras feeding on the vegetation above the ground.

Which insect likes a termite bite?

Termites are a tasty food to other insects, particularly ants. Many birds also eat them. There are also many mammals, that are equipped with sharp claws, to break into termite nests, and long tongues to lap the termites up. These include: the South American tamanduas and giant "anteaters," the aardvark of Africa, and pangolins in Africa and Asia.

What's the difference between a termite and an ant?

There isn't a lot of difference between them, ants eat other creatures, but termites like to stick to plants. Although termites are sometimes called "white ants," they are much more like cockroaches than ants. Termites have been around for millions of years, and are great recyclers of plant materials.

What is a termite garden?

Some species of termite, including *Macrotermes,* farm, or grow, a fungus. They make special "fungus combs" out of their own faeces, as a base on which to grow the fungus. These are called "gardens." The fungus breaks down the faeces, and the termites feed on the fungus, and its products. The fungus is a special one, only found growing in termite nests.

Who helps termites digest their food?

Wood-eating termites do not actually digest wood themselves, but rely on protozoa (single-celled animals) that live in their gut to break it down. In the gut of other termites, large colonies of bacteria help to break down food. Termites also contain bacteria that take nitrogen from the air and turn it into body-building protein. Termites owe their success to these tiny creatures in their guts.

Termite

A soldier termite stands on guard with its enormous head and jaws.

Why are some termites magnetic?

Magnetic termites live in Australia. They build a nest in a flat blade shape. The flat sides point east and west, catching the cooler morning and evening sun, but only the narrow edge points north to the midday sun, so that only a little of the nest catches the sun at its hottest. The nest is often used as a compass by people in the bush, and this is how the nest gets its name.

Termite mound

Which insects have air-conditioned nests?

In insect nests, most of the "living accommodation" is below ground. So, in hot climates, they could overheat. Termites such as *Macrotermes* build a hollow nest with a central chimney and side channels to allow the circulation of air. Wind blowing across the top of the tall chimney helps to draw out air and create a breeze.

The cap-shaped roof, of this African forest termite mound, helps keep off the rain.

What is a termite city?

A NUMBER OF TERMITES IN THE TROPICAL DRY SAVANNAS BUILD VERY HIGH mounds. These are where termites live and work. Some of them are very big. The magnetic termite mounds can be 11 ft (3.5 m) tall. In Africa, *Macrotermes* builds nests that can extend up to 24 ft (7.5 m), four times the height of a human. In contrast, some species make their nests entirely within one plant, or underground and they are quite small.

How many eggs does a queen termite lay?

The queen termite's only job is to lay eggs, and she may become much bigger than her surrounding workers, when her huge abdomen is filled with eggs. In some species, the queen lays up to 30,000 eggs a day.

Which termites are suicide bombers?

There are termite species which don't have a soldier caste. The workers defend the nest from attackers. If ants attack the colony, the workers burst their guts open, throwing the slimy contents over the enemy, and killing themselves at the same time.

How do ants defend their nests?

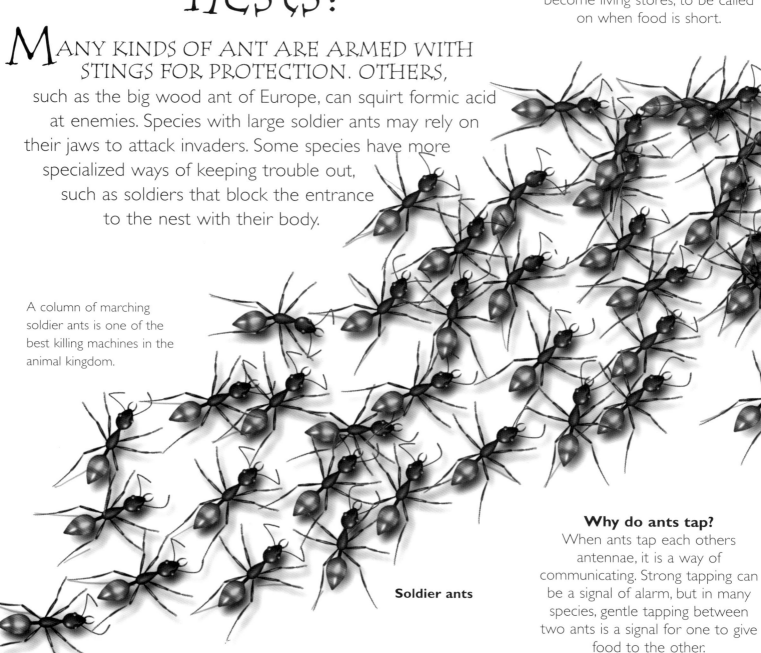

A column of marching soldier ants is one of the best killing machines in the animal kingdom.

Soldier ants

Mᴀɴʏ ᴋɪɴᴅꜱ ᴏꜰ ᴀɴᴛ ᴀʀᴇ ᴀʀᴍᴇᴅ ᴡɪᴛʜ ꜱᴛɪɴɢꜱ ꜰᴏʀ ᴘʀᴏᴛᴇᴄᴛɪᴏɴ. Oᴛʜᴇʀꜱ, such as the big wood ant of Europe, can squirt formic acid at enemies. Species with large soldier ants may rely on their jaws to attack invaders. Some species have more specialized ways of keeping trouble out, such as soldiers that block the entrance to the nest with their body.

When is an ant like a honeypot?
Among *Myrmecocystus* ants, of North America, some of the workers are actually used as storage jars. They never go out of the nest, and are fed the spare nectar gathered by workers. Their abdomens swell massively as they become living stores, to be called on when food is short.

Why do ants tap?
When ants tap each others antennae, it is a way of communicating. Strong tapping can be a signal of alarm, but in many species, gentle tapping between two ants is a signal for one to give food to the other.

Which ants like a thorny home?
The acacia ant makes its small nest just in the spiny tips of twigs of acacia thorn trees, in the Savanna (dry plains with bushes and trees). The ants get some protection from the thorns, and they keep the tree free of other, harmful insects by eating them.

How do ants grow mushrooms?
The leaf-cutter ants, of tropical America, cut out pieces of leaf to take back to their nest and use as a kind of "manure." Back in their nests, underground, they chew the leaves and add them to their "garden." A fungus grows in this garden (each ant species has its own) which makes a nutritious food.

Why do ants need slaves?
Some ants are forced to act as workers for other species. The slave-maker ant, of Europe, raids the nests of other species and carries the young back to their own nest. When they hatch out, these new workers act as slaves collecting food, feeding other ants, and cleaning the nest. Slavery is used by a few ant species.

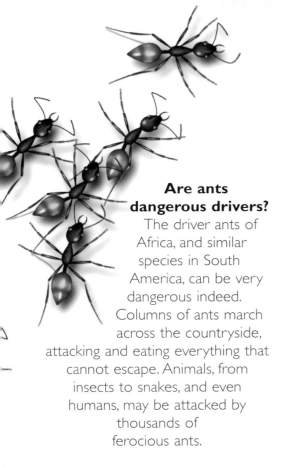

Are ants dangerous drivers?

The driver ants of Africa, and similar species in South America, can be very dangerous indeed. Columns of ants march across the countryside, attacking and eating everything that cannot escape. Animals, from insects to snakes, and even humans, may be attacked by thousands of ferocious ants.

Which ants look after "cows"?

Several kinds of ant feed on a sweet substance, called honeydew, which is produced by aphids (a small bug, such as a greenfly). Some, like the black garden ant, look after herds of aphid "cows" or females, protecting them from predators, and even moving them to new plants on which to feed.

Are all ants sociable?

All ant species are social animals. This means that they live in groups and each of them is given a job to do in the colony. Each colony has at least one egg-laying female, or queen, but she is vastly outnumbered by the ants we usually see, the workers. They are wingless and sterile females – never males.

How many ants are there in an ant nest?

Some estimates put the number of ants in such a nest as high as 7 million. Other species have smaller nests, with numbers ranging from thousands to hundreds. The biggest ant nests are those made by the leaf-cutter ants, some of which travel for 33 ft (10 m) or more underground.

Why do ants have wings?

Ants' wings are only used when they mate. Only fully-grown males and females have wings. Workers do not need them. When they land from their mating flights, females that have been fertilized lose their wings, in some cases chewing them off. They then look for a place to start a new colony and have their young.

Leaf-cutter ants carry huge pieces of leaf back to their gardens.

Leafcutter ant

How do ants know each other?

ANTS PROBABLY DON'T RECOGNIZE EACH OTHER AS INDIVIDUALS. BUT EACH species has its own chemical messengers, and there may be slight differences between nests too. An ant can recognize another as a nest mate, or a stranger, by its smell. Chemicals allow the ants to leave scent trails that can be followed by others to good food sources.

This bee is filling up the "basket" on its back leg with pollen.

Bee collecting pollen

How many bees live in a hive?

In a busy hive there can be up to 80,000 honeybee workers.

There will be just one adult queen bee. She may live for as long as five years, and she is the most important member of the hive. The worker bees have an adult life of only about 6 weeks. The hive may also contain up to 200 male bees (drones) whose only job is to fertilize the queen on a mating flight. Bumblebees have much smaller nests than honeybees. The nest only lasts one season.

Are bees vegetarian?
Yes, bees, unlike their relatives the wasps, are vegetarian. They feed on nectar from flowers. Honeybees have tongues that are made for sucking nectar from shallow flowers. Many bumblebees have longer tongues that can push deep into tube-shaped flowers. Bees also collect pollen from flowers, to take back to the nest to fed their young.

What is bee-bread?
Bee-bread is the mixture of honey and pollen that bees use as food, particularly to feed the larvae that will grow up to be workers.

How do bees become queens?
The job that a bee does in the hive depends on what it eats. A queen bee has a special diet. The workers build some large cells for the young queens, and start special treatment for them. They are fed on rich food, called royal jelly, produced by glands in the workers' heads. This allows them to develop into full queens. Only some bees are queens, because the adult queen in a hive makes a chemical that spreads round all the workers and stops them from becoming queens. If the queen gets weak, or the hive is very large, there is not enough of this chemical to work and it no longer has an effect.

How many flowers a day does a bee visit?
A honeybee makes about 10 trips from the hive, each day, looking for food. It can take up to 1,000 flowers to provide enough nectar for a bee on a trip. So, it could be visiting around 10,000 flowers a day.

A bee's waggle dance

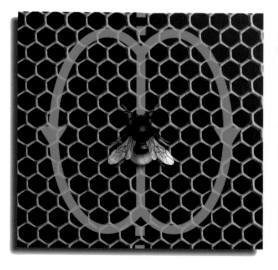

Why are bees good dancers?
When a bee returns from a successful trip to find pollen, it "dances" on the top of the honeycomb, surrounded by other workers. Its movements during the dance tell the other bees how far away the food source is, and the angle to the sun at which they must fly to reach it.

How long have people kept bees?
People have made use of bees for a very long time. Beehives, and their keepers, are shown in ancient Egyptian paintings from 5,000 years ago.

Why are bees hairy?
Some bumblebees are quite good at keeping themselves warm, when the outside temperature is low, and their furry bodies probably help with this. For most bees, though, a hairy body is useful mainly because it gathers up pollen grains, from the flowers as it looks for nectar.

Where is a bee's shopping basket?
Many bees have a special brush of hairs on each back leg, that they use as a shopping basket. When they have collected pollen on their body hairs, they clean it off, and gather it all into the pollen basket on the leg. You can often spot a well-filled, yellow pollen basket on a bee.

This solitary wasp sticks sand grains together to build a flask-shaped nest.

Potter wasp

Where do wasps go in the winter?

Unlike honeybees, wasps do not store up sweet substances in their nests, so the colony has nothing to survive on in the winter. At the end of the summer, after the new queens have mated, the workers all die. Just the queen survives the winter in hibernation, and she starts a new colony in the spring.

Are wasps any use?
Many people think that the yellow and black striped wasps are our enemies. These wasps do have a powerful sting, but it is not often used against humans. In fact, they do an enormous amount of good for people, as they collect a lot of caterpillars and insect grubs, many of which are pests. These are taken back to the nest and chewed up as food for the larvae.

What sort of home does a wasp have?
A wasp's nest is made of tough paper, known as carton. The wasps tear wood fibres from trees, posts, and fences and chew them to make this paper. It is carefully molded into shape, and then inside, it is shaped into six-sided cells that the queen lays her eggs in. The nest may be underground or hanging from a tree.

How many kinds of wasp are there?
There are a surprising number of different kinds of wasp, more than 200,000. Most of them are not the familiar striped social wasps, but are types such as sawflies, wood wasps, sand wasps, and other kinds of hunting wasp.

Which wasp eats its victims alive?
There are lots of parasitic wasps. These wasps paralyze their victim then lay their eggs inside its body. When the eggs hatch, the larvae feed on the victim from inside it, while it is still alive.

137

Does the female mantis eat her mate?

In some species of mantis the male is at risk of being the female's dinner, if he does not avoid her clutches. The first part to be eaten is usually the male's head. Unbelievably, this does not stop it mating.

What is the mantis's main weapon?

The front legs of the mantis are its main weapons. They are very spiny and great for seizing their prey, rather like spiny pincers. They are also good as a defence against attackers. Even humans can get a nasty jab from a mantis if it swivels its front legs and uses its spines to stab.

Praying mantis

The large eyes of the mantis tell it when prey is within range.

Does the mantis prey or pray?

T HE MANTIS OF THE MEDITERRANEAN AREA IS CALLED THE "PRAYING mantis" because of the way that it sits, with its front legs folded up in front of its head, as if it was saying its prayers. It does its share of preying as well. It is a fierce carnivore that will grab and eat insects and even small animals.

How long is the longest stick insect?

The longest stick insect is the saw-footed stick insect of South-east Asia. It grows up to 13 in (33 cm) long – as long as a pet rabbit.

Why are male stick insects rare?

In many, but not all, species of stick insects males are just not needed. Some species, such as the "laboratory" stick insect, manage perfectly well with no males at all. The females can produce eggs without mating, and these develop into more females, just like their parent.

Can a praying mantis fly?

Many mantis females have small, useless wings, or no wings at all. Adult male mantises, though, have fully developed wings and may fly off if attacked.

How does a stick insect disguise its eggs?

A stick insect lays eggs that look like seeds. They are dropped on the ground, and scattered one by one. They have a hard shell with a cap at one end, through which the young will eventually hatch. This may take up to three years, so its very important that they look like a tough seed, rather than a tasty morsel.

What do adult dragonflies eat?

Adult dragonflies catch other insects in mid-air. They hold all their spiny legs out forwards to make a catching basket. Into this fly flies, beetles, and even bees, where they are bitten by the powerful jaws of the dragonfly. Sometimes dragonflies scoop up their prey from plants or from the ground.

Why does a dragonfly need a mask?

A dragonfly larva needs a mask in order to eat. The mask is the lower jaw that can be pushed outward. When the dragonfly is resting, the jaw covers a lot of the face, just like a mask. The larva lives in water and preys on insects, small fish, and tadpoles. The mask is hinged, and can be shot out suddenly. Two hooks on the end stab the prey, so it can be pulled back into the mouth.

All dragonflies start life in water, but adults spend their time in the air.

What is the biggest dragonfly?

THE LARGEST DRAGONFLIES OF THE PRESENT DAY ARE SOUTH American giant damselflies. They have a wingspan of up to 7 in (19 cm), with a body 5 in (12 cm) long. These are dwarfs, though, compared with dragonflies that lived 280 million years ago. Fossils have been found with a wingspan of 29 in (75 cm). That means they would have been about the size of a small dog.

Dragonfly

Why have dragonflies got such good eyes?

An image on a computer screen is made up of a series of dots. The more dots, the more detailed the image. In the same way, insects have compound eyes with many lenses, each producing a "dot" of image. The more lenses, the more detailed the image will be. Dragonflies have as many as 30,000 lenses in each of their eyes, and are very good at seeing movement up to 50 ft (15 m) away while flying.

Why do dragonflies fly in pairs?

Dragonflies seen flying together are usually a mating pair. A male defends a certain territory, and courts females that come into it. Before mating takes place, the male puts sperm from the tip of his abdomen into a special pouch under the front of his abdomen. He then uses claspers, on the end of the abdomen, to grasp the female, and they fly together. The final mating position allows the female to take sperm from the male.

How do cicadas sing?

Anyone who has been in a warm country has heard the loud calls of cicadas. These bugs make their sound using a kind of drumskin on each side of their abdomen. This skin is pulled in by a muscle, then allowed to snap out again, producing one click in the group of clicks that make up the cicada's song. Air sacs help to increase the sound.

Which bugs feed on human blood?

A number of assassin bugs can feed on human blood, but most are not dangerous. One, however is dangerous, not because of the blood it takes, but because it carries a disease. The South American bug *Triatoma infestans* carries the germ that causes Chagas' disease. This illness gives a high fever and a swollen liver, spleen, and lymph nodes.

Cicada

Cicadas are among the strongest singers in the animal kingdom.

Which bug is an assassin?

Assassin bugs are predators (creatures that prey on other creatures) that use their piercing, sucking mouthparts to impale insects, so that they can feed on their body fluids. They inject digestive juices and suck up the resulting "soup." They may carry their prey on their beaks. A few species suck the blood of animals.

What insect makes sweets?

Some kinds of scaled insects produce a syrupy secretion. As the insect produces the secretion, it dries quickly in the hot climate to form sugary, honeydew lumps. It can then be eaten by humans.

Which bug spends years underground?

The periodical cicada, of America, has a life span of 17 years. Almost all of this time is spent as a larva underground. It digs its way through with its big front legs, and feeds on the sap of plant roots. Other cicadas also spend a lot of time underground, but the periodical cicada holds the record. After this long start, adults sometimes live for just a few weeks.

Which insect can color food?

Before the days of artificial food colorings, the red color added to food was cochineal. This is made from the crushed, dried bodies of the female cochineal bug, a kind of scale insect that feeds on cacti in Mexico.

What is cuckoo-spit?
Cuckoo-spit does not come from cuckoos. The frothy "spit" is made by a frog hopper larva. It blows air into a liquid that comes from its anus. The froth that it produces protects the larva from enemies, as well as keeping it moist. Adult frog hopper bugs are very good at hopping, which is why they are called hopper bugs.

How do aphids drink plant juice?
Aphids, such as the greenfly that you find on roses, have special piercing tools on their mouths that point downwards. These are pushed down into the plant vein, and act just like a straw. They inject saliva down one channel of the mouthparts and suck up juices through another.

How do aphids cause havoc?
Sometimes aphids damage crops just because there are so many of them sucking sap, and weakening or killing the plants. In other cases the plants develop deformed leaves that make them useless to sell. Those aphids that fly from plant to plant can also spread serious diseases, injecting them into the plant as they suck sap.

Which insect doesn't like wine?
The vine phylloxera aphid comes from North America. It was accidentally introduced to Europe in the 19th century, where it destroyed thousands of the grape vines.

Looking from above, it is easy to see how shield bugs get their name.

Shield bug

Hawthorn bug

The hawthorn bug is a common species that feeds on hawthorn berries.

Which bugs stink?

T HE SHIELD BUG HAS QUITE A FLAT BODY, THAT LOOKS LIKE A SHIELD WHEN seen from above. It lives on plants, which they eat with their piercing mouthparts. They have glands in their body which produce a smell. In some cases this smells really strong to humans, which is how this bug earned the name stink bug.

Which bug followed us from our ancestors' caves?
The bed-bug is a wingless insect that comes out at night, and feeds on human blood. In the day, it hides in small, dark places. Bed-bugs attack other warm-blooded animals too. They probably first started attacking humans when our ancestors lived in caves close to other animals. Piles of skins and fur would have provided ideal hideaways. Bed-bugs are rarely a problem in hygienic modern houses.

How do some grasshoppers disappear in a flash?

Most grasshoppers are brown or green in color, and patterned for camouflage. But many have hind wings that are a bright contrasting color. This is "flash coloration." If an enemy comes too close, the grasshopper suddenly takes flight, showing the bright hind wings. This can startle and put off a predator. Alternatively, if the predator watches the bright wings, it can be confused when the insect suddenly lands, and disappears behind its camouflage.

Which crickets like to make a noise?

The mole cricket spends much of its time burrowing underground. On summer nights, it makes a burrow that is just the right shape to increase the noises it makes. (This is the same shape that humans have come up with to make their stereo amplifiers!). The cricket sits in the entrance singing continuously. The amplifier is so successful that the cricket can be heard a mile away.

Do grasshoppers have ears?

Yes, but they aren't always where you'd expect them to be. Short-horned grasshoppers do not have ears on their heads, but on their abdomens. In crickets and their relatives, they are on their legs. Each ear has a thin "eardrum" which vibrates when sounds hit it.

Good eyesight and hearing warn a grasshopper of approaching enemies.

Grasshopper

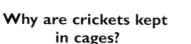

Why do grasshoppers sit on the edge of a leaf?

Grasshoppers have strong chewing mouthparts which bite from side to side. It is easier to use these very well if the grasshopper sits along the edge of a leaf – out of the way of its chomping jaws.

Why are crickets kept in cages?

In China, the song of the house cricket has always been really popular, even in the emperor's court. So, there is a Chinese tradition of keeping crickets in small cages to hear their song. Only the male cricket sings. He may chirp 10,000 times an hour.

How do grasshoppers and crickets sing?

There are two main ways of "singing" if you are a grasshopper or cricket. Short-horned grasshoppers scratch a row of projections (something that sticks up) from the inside of the hind leg against the veins of the front wing. In other grasshoppers and crickets, the bases of the front wings are scratched together to make the sound.

Which creature lets its leg drop off?

If another animal seizes a grasshopper by the leg, the grasshopper will throw its own leg off, rather than let itself be caught. A special lining quickly seals the hole, so that the grasshopper doesn't lose much blood. A grasshopper can work surprisingly well with only one of its long jumping legs to work with.

What is a locust?

LOCUSTS ARE SPECIES OF GRASSHOPPER. THE UNUSUAL THING ABOUT

them is that at times they form huge swarms. Most locusts live alone, just like the average grasshopper, but when conditions are right, and there is plenty of food around, they join together to form massive swarms.

Locust swarm

Each locust has a moderate appetite, but the vast numbers in a swarm can cause devastation to crops.

How does a locust swarm form?

When the rains come, females lay lots of eggs and thousands of new locusts are born. All the locusts join together, and soon thousands of them are moving forward. By the time they get wings, as adults, they may have eaten all the food in the area. After destroying all the crops there, they fly off again and the terrifying swarm of locusts arrives somewhere else to strip the land of vegetation.

How do you stop a locust?

Locust swarms can be sprayed from the air with poisons. But by the time millions of them are flying together, they are difficult to stop. Nowadays, scientists keep an eye on locust numbers, to make sure they aren't building up too much. If they see a dramatic increase in locust numbers, they can often be destroyed before they get out of control.

Where do locusts live?

Locusts live in the Mediterranean region, Asia, Australia, North and South America. The most destructive of all are the migratory locust, and the desert locust, which live in Africa and the Middle East and can destroy crops in just a few minutes.

How many locusts are there in a swarm?

Many millions of locusts move together in the largest swarms. The biggest may cover hundreds of square miles and contain 50,000 million locusts. A swarm like that would weigh as much as 50,000 people.

How high can a flea jump?

HUMAN FLEAS CAN JUMP UP TO 7 IN (20 CM) HIGH, AND CAT FLEAS EVEN higher, up to 13 in (34 cm). This is an amazing jump when you think that fleas are so tiny. Fleas can store energy in a membrane of elastic protein, and it is when this is released that they are clicked into the air.

What do young fleas look like?

Young fleas are tiny, worm-like larvae. The larva lives in the nest on the animal its living on, and feeds on drops of dry blood from the faeces of the adults. After two or three weeks, it turns into a pupa (the stage just before it becomes an adult). It may wait some time before hatching out. The movement of the host animal stirs the adult fleas into moving.

How big do fleas get?

The size of the host makes no difference to the size of the flea that attacks it. The biggest flea in Britain is the mole flea, about ¼ in (6 mm) long (the size of a small fly). The world record is held by an American flea. It was a flea from a mountain beaver, and it was ⅓ in (8 mm) long.

It is elastic under tension, rather than muscle effort, that powers the flea's jump.

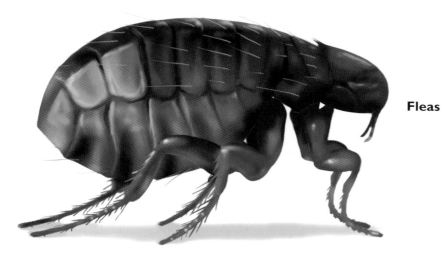

Fleas

Do birds have fleas?

Nine-tenths of the world's fleas feed on mammals, but there are species that attack birds. Because fleas don't have wings they cannot move very far, so they need to live somewhere where they can find lots of hosts to live on. They tend to live in bird nests.

Why do fleas spread the plague?

Plague is a disease that is carried by rats. Fleas that carry the disease live on rats and can then jump onto humans and bite them. The plague spreads very quickly. Outbreaks in the Middle Ages, such as the Black Death, wiped out half the human population in some areas of Europe. Outbreaks of plague still occur.

Do fleas like to live on anyone?

Fleas do tend to live on just one particular type of host. There are cat fleas and dog fleas, for example, that live in the fur of these animals. Rabbits, porcupines, and beavers have their own fleas. "Human" fleas on the other hand, are shared with foxes and pigs. If they are hungry enough, most fleas will take blood from any animal. Human fleas are now rare in houses, and genuine dog fleas are not very common in Britain. Most fleas around now are cat fleas.

What are nits?

Nits are the eggs of the head louse. Female lice lay eggs in the hair of the human host. They stick to the hair of the host because if they fell off they would die. A fine comb is often used to remove nits from hair.

Why do lice have flat bodies?

Lice have low, flat bodies so that they can squeeze between the hairs of the host. They also have short legs that allow them to hold tight if the host tries to scratch them off. Fleas are flat for the same reasons.

What are jiggers?

Jiggers are also called sand fleas. The females burrow into the skin of animals, including the feet of humans. Here they remain for the rest of their lives, laying the eggs that will produce the next generation.

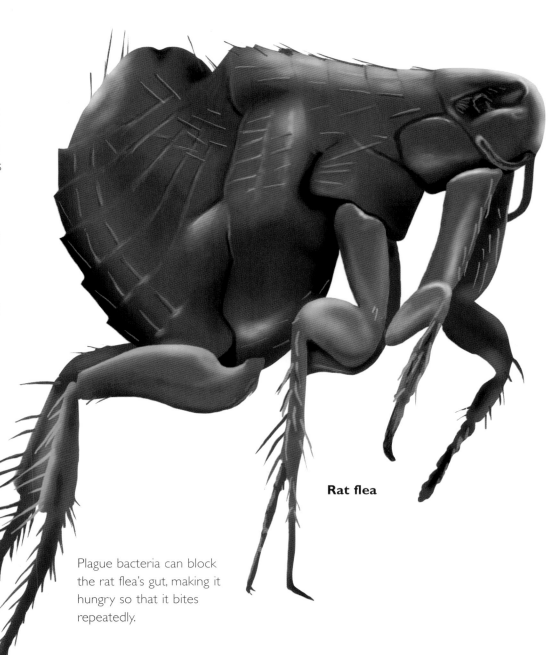

Rat flea

Plague bacteria can block the rat flea's gut, making it hungry so that it bites repeatedly.

What do lice eat?

All lice are parasites. They live on the skin of mammals and birds. One group has chewing mouthparts, and feeds on flakes of skin, feather, sweat, or blood. Another group of lice has piercing and sucking mouthparts and feeds on mammal's blood. Human lice belong to this group.

Are head lice dangerous?

The human head louse lives in human hair and can be an irritating nuisance. But it is not dangerous and doesn't spread disease. It will live on clean hair as happily as dirty. Lice cannot fly, so they like to live in crowded conditions where they can easily step from one human head to another, to get a new feeding ground.

Which louse has killed millions of people?

THE HUMAN BODY LOUSE HAS BEEN RESPONSIBLE FOR KILLING VAST numbers of people. When people are crowded in dirty conditions, in wars or natural disasters, body lice can thrive and multiply. Unfortunately, they can carry typhus. This disease is a killer. It is thought to have caused the deaths of some 3,000,000 people in Eastern Europe in the First World War (1914–18), and to have killed more people in concentration camps in the Second World War (1939–45) than any other cause.

How do flies feed?

THE FLY LANDS ON THE FOOD – A PIECE OF MEAT OR CHEESE – AND SPITS ON IT TO soften it. All flies have sucking mouthparts, with pumping muscles in the head, and it uses these to suck up the softened food. In many flies, the tip of the mouthparts spreads out to form a sponge to absorb the liquid food. Some, such as horse-flies and mosquitoes, have piercing mouthparts, and take blood from whatever they are feeding on.

Why are fruit-flies important to scientists?

Fruit-flies are important because they are small and easily bred in captivity, and have a speedy life history. Scientists have been able to use them to find out an enormous amount about how genes (the units that pass from generation to generation and make us the same as our parents) work.

Why do some flies look like bees?

By trying to look like animals with a dangerous sting, flies may stop many animals from attacking them. The hoverflies, in particular, look like and behave like bees and wasps. The hoverfly *Volucella bombylans* actually has different forms mimicking different bumblebees. It lays eggs in bumblebee nests too, where its larvae steal the food meant for the bumblebee larvae.

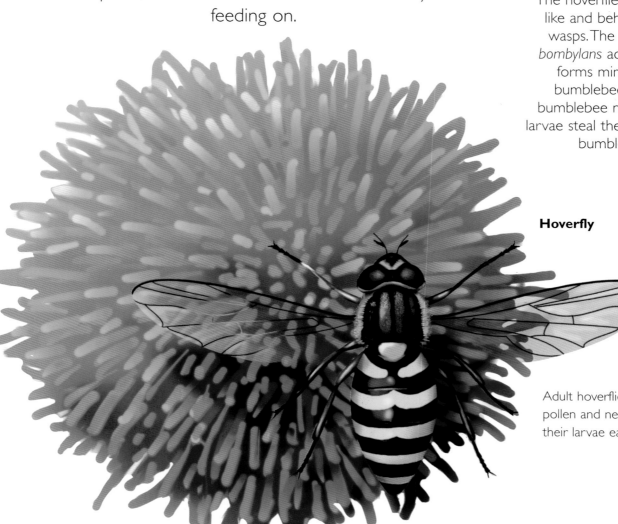

Hoverfly

Adult hoverflies feed on pollen and nectar, but their larvae eat aphids.

Why do flies like animal dung?

Many species of fly lay their eggs on dung, which provides a nourishing food for the larva. The true dung flies have legless larvae which wriggle their way about, sucking in food greedily, until they have grown enough to turn into pupae in the soil below a cow-pat.

Can flies eat your living flesh?

Some flies lay their eggs in the skin of living animals. The larvae hatch and burrow into flesh and feed on it. The warble flies eat the flesh of cattle and deer, causing much irritation. The tumbu fly larva, of Africa, lives under the skin of humans.

How do bluebottles spread disease?

Bluebottles eat the kind of food that is likely to have bacteria on it, such as rotting vegetation or faeces. Often, they will then land on our food, carrying the disease with them to infect an unfortunate human with diarrhoea, or worse.

Can you tell a fly by its wings?

True flies can always be recognised among the insects because they have a single pair of wings rather than four. In fact, the rear wings have been turned into stabilizers. They are club-shaped projections (areas that stick out) from the body that give the fly information about how it is flying.

Why do humans avoid the tsetse fly?

The tsetse fly is the insect that carries sleeping sickness, and can give it to humans. The disease is quite common in wild grazing animals, and doesn't affect them badly, but it can be devastating to humans. Because it is such a serious disease, humans try to live in areas where the tsetse fly is not known to live.

Which flies help the police with their enquiries?

Different species of flies arrive at different stages, during the rotting of flesh, to lay their eggs. The larvae grow, pupate, and then turn into adults to a fast timetable. This allows a forensic scientist (scientists who study how people have died) to make a good estimate of the time of death. They look at what flies, at what stage of growth, are in a dead body.

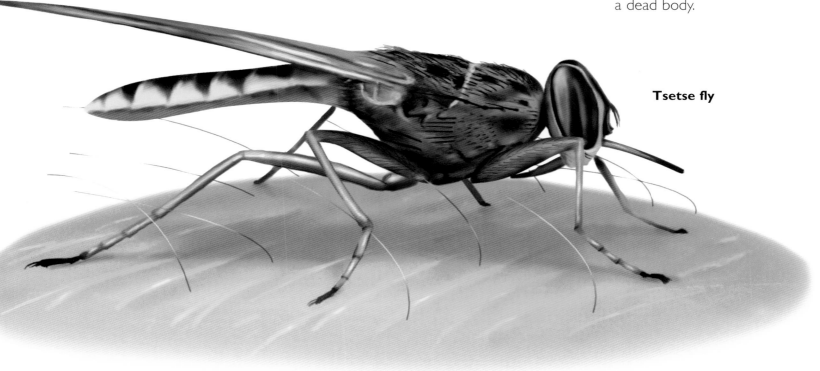

Tsetse fly

The tsetse fly carries the parasite that causes sleeping sickness.

Why are mosquitoes our deadly enemies?

THE FEMALE MOSQUITO IS A BLOODSUCKER, BUT THE DISEASES SHE MAY CARRY IN her saliva are the real danger to humans. In the warmer parts of the world, there is always a danger that a mosquito is carrying the germ that causes malaria. This disease affects a large section of the world population and it makes people very weak and ill.

How does a blowfly taste its food?

It is useful to a fly to know, before it tries to feed, whether what it has landed on is a possible food. The fly has special tasters, in the hairs on its feet, that tell it whether it's on food or not. These hairs may be much more sensitive than the human tongue.

What are "no-see-ums"?

No-see-ums are North American biting midges. They feed on us, using piercing mouthparts to take blood. Biting midges are all very small flies, but those that attack humans have an irritating bite. Being so small, they often manage to bite before being noticed, which is where the name comes from.

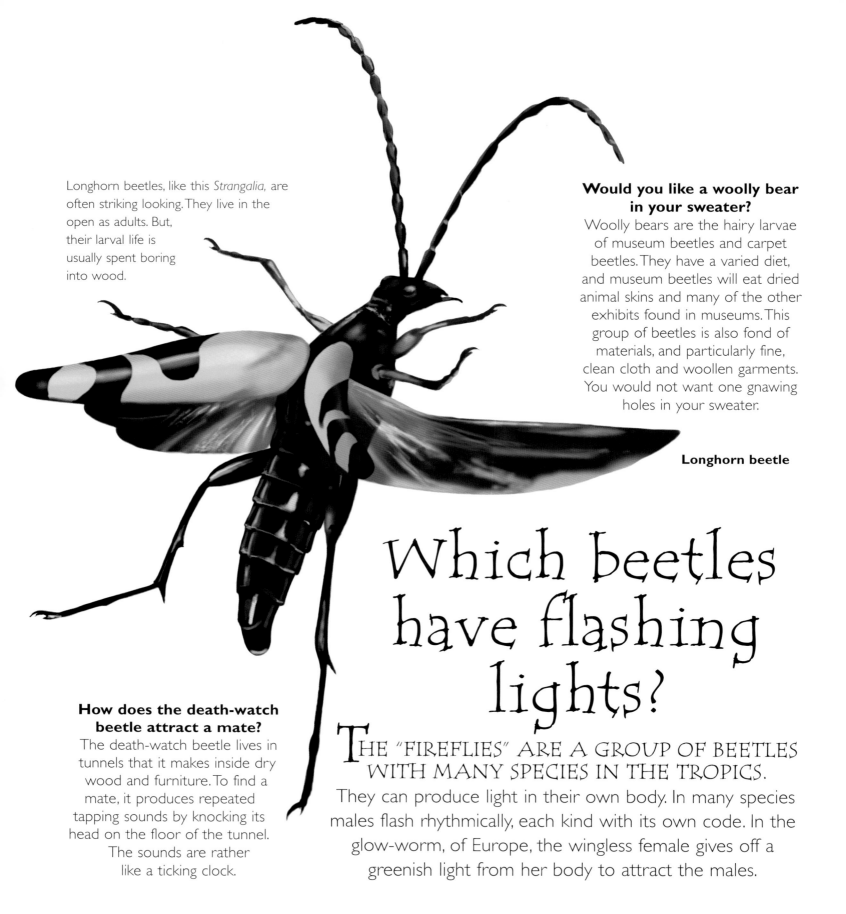

Longhorn beetles, like this *Strangalia,* are often striking looking. They live in the open as adults. But, their larval life is usually spent boring into wood.

Would you like a woolly bear in your sweater?
Woolly bears are the hairy larvae of museum beetles and carpet beetles. They have a varied diet, and museum beetles will eat dried animal skins and many of the other exhibits found in museums. This group of beetles is also fond of materials, and particularly fine, clean cloth and woollen garments. You would not want one gnawing holes in your sweater.

Longhorn beetle

Which beetles have flashing lights?

The "FIREFLIES" ARE A GROUP OF BEETLES WITH MANY SPECIES IN THE TROPICS. They can produce light in their own body. In many species males flash rhythmically, each kind with its own code. In the glow-worm, of Europe, the wingless female gives off a greenish light from her body to attract the males.

How does the death-watch beetle attract a mate?
The death-watch beetle lives in tunnels that it makes inside dry wood and furniture. To find a mate, it produces repeated tapping sounds by knocking its head on the floor of the tunnel. The sounds are rather like a ticking clock.

Which beetle might you find in your cereal?
A number of beetles can get into cereal products such as flour, grain, and biscuits. Apart from weevils there are the large mealworm beetle and the flour beetle. They get into stores in warehouses, and their larvae damage everything that they touch. Flour beetles can infest houses too and eat all the dry food in your cupboards.

Which is the largest beetle?
The biggest beetles in the world are about the size of a mouse. Several tropical beetles are this size, including the rhinoceros beetle of South America. The heaviest beetle measured was a goliath beetle from Africa, weighing in at 3½ oz (100 g).

Why do ladybirds have bright colors?
Many beetles that are brightly colored in red or yellow, like the ladybird, are telling predators that they aren't very nice to eat. Ladybirds will also bleed from their leg joints when attacked, letting out sticky, toxic blood which repels and gums up an attacker.

Why were dung beetles sacred?

THE SCARAB DUNG BEETLES WERE SACRED IN ANCIENT EGYPT BECAUSE THE

Egyptians thought they were linked to the gods they worshipped. These beetles gather a ball of dung that they roll away to a hole, as food for their young. To the ancient Egyptians this ball symbolized the globe of the sun, being pushed across the sky each day by the sun god.

How many beetle species are there?

About 370,000 different species of beetles have been found so far; that's one third of all the known animals in the world. Beetle specialists can only guess how many more await discovery, particularly in the tropics. Estimates suggest that at least as many again will be found, and there could be up to 5,000,000 species. Beetles are easily the biggest group of animals in the world.

Dung beetle

Which beetles shoot their enemies?

Bombardier beetles store chemicals in a special chamber in their body. If they are attacked, the chemicals react to produce a boiling hot mixture that can blister skin. These are shot, like explosives, from a nozzle in the body. They are so hot that they become an irritating gas cloud that repels an attacker.

How are dung beetles useful?

Dung beetles remove and break down vast amounts of dung, and return its goodness to the soil. In Australia there were no insects to deal with the dung produced by cattle, so dung beetles were imported from Africa to help to solve this problem.

Is a weevil evil?

The weevils are a huge group of beetles, that have "elbows" on their antennae. Many weevils are a minor nuisance. Some species are major pests, like the boll weevil that lives inside cotton flowers, and stops cotton fibres from growing. Other species cause serious damage in stored grain.

The dung beetle lays her eggs in a ball of dung that she buries.

Monarch butterflies

In winter, monarch butterflies roost together in vast numbers.

How far can butterflies fly?

MANY BUTTERFLIES FLY VERY WELL. RED ADMIRAL AND PAINTED LADY butterflies do not normally survive the winter in Britain. Some North American monarch butterflies fly to Mexico, to spend the winter in huge communal roosts. They can fly 1,180 miles (1,900 km) in just three weeks.

How do you tell a butterfly from a moth?
Butterflies fly by day, have club-shaped antennae, and are often brightly colored. Moths fly by night, have feathery antennae, and are duller in color.

What do butterflies like to eat?
Adult butterflies do not need to grow, so their food needs are for energy, rather than protein. The typical butterfly food is nectar from flowers. However, some feed on sap oozing from trees, from rotting fruit, and some, including some of the most beautiful, from dung. They will also take in salts from mud.

Where do butterflies go in the winter?
In cooler climates, when butterflies disappear in winter, many people assume they all die. Some do, but some species spend the winter hibernating before breeding the next year. In Britain, these include brimstone, peacock, and small tortoiseshell butterflies. In other parts of the world, butterflies may migrate with the seasons. The North American monarch butterfly spends its winter in sunny Mexico.

How are the colors of butterflies made?
The wings of butterflies and moths are covered in tiny overlapping scales (their scientific name, *Lepidoptera,* means scaled wings). Each individual scale can be filled with color, giving the insect its characteristic pattern. In some butterflies, such as the shiny tropical *Morpho* butterflies, the color is produced by the special structure of the scale as much as the color on it.

Are moths poisonous?

Moths do not have a poisonous bite, but many are poisonous to animals that bite them. Often their colors advertize that they have chemical defences. The cinnabar moth has a caterpillar, with black and yellow warning colors, that feeds on ragwort, a plant with poisonous sap. The caterpillar isn't affected by the poison and stores it in its own body. For the rest of its life it carries the poison which only affects those that attack it, never the moth itself.

How do tiger moths baffle bats?

Bats hunt tiger moths at night. The bats give out high-pitched sounds, and find their prey from the echo that the sounds produce. Tiger moths have "eardrums" on their body. They hear the bats' cries and keep out of the way. They can even produce high-pitched sounds themselves to confuse the bats.

How good is a moth's nose?

The male silk moth can detect the scent of a female ready to mate from 7 miles (11 km) away. His "nose" is actually a pair of feathery antennae. These contain the scent receptors.

The eyespots of the emperor moth make it look like the face of a bigger animal.

Emperor moth

What is a silkworm?

The silkworm is the caterpillar of the mulberry silk moth *Bombyx mori*. Like many other moth larvae, it can make silk threads, but its cocoon is made of incredibly long threads up to ¾ mile (1.2 km) long, ideal for spinning into cloth. Silkworms have been bred in captivity for at least 2,000 years in China.

Which moth encourages its food to grow?

Many moths and butterflies may help their food grow, because they help to pollinate flowers. The yucca moths of Mexico and North America lay their eggs in the ovaries of the yucca flower, then put pollen on the stigma so the flower is fertilized. By doing this it is helping the plant to produce seeds. Of the seeds it produces, some may grow into new plants, but many will be eaten by the moth larvae that are developing within the ovary. Both the moth and the plant benefit.

Which moth smells like a goat?

The goat moth has a larva that produces a strong smell of goat. The larva lives inside a tree for three or four years before it is mature. It can be up to 3 in (7.5 cm) long. It can cause serious damage to the tree because it bores through the wood.

Why do butterflies and moths have eyespots?

The eyespots on the wings of a moth or butterfly can fool a predator into thinking it is a larger animal, and therefore leaves it alone. If it is attacked, the eyespots are more noticeable than the body and head. This can be a lifesaver, if a bird goes for these first, it leaves the butterfly in one piece, apart from a slice out of the wing.

Earthworm

What is the biggest earthworm?

THE BIGGEST EARTHWORM EVER MEASURED WAS 22 FOOT LONG when moving (that's twice the length of a tiger). Most earthworms are under 12 in (30 cm) long, but the South African worm *Microchaetus* grows to over 3 ft 3 in (1 m). Giant earthworms measure 10 ft (3 m). They live in Australia, and in Oregon and Washington, USA.

How long is a tapeworm?
Many kinds of tapeworm infect the gut of animals. In man, the pork tapeworm can grow to 5 ft (1.8 m), but a tapeworm caught from the fish *Diphyllobothrium* can be over 59 ft (18 m) long.

Where do killer worms live?
When humans transport insects to different countries, the effects can be terrible on the species already living in that country. A New Zealand flatworm, called *Artioposthia,* caused havoc, when it arrived in the British Isles. It grows to up to 8 in (20 cm) long, and hunts for earthworms in the top 12 in (30 cm) of soil. It has greatly reduced earthworm numbers in places where it has spread. In Northern Ireland, some pastures have been totally cleared of earthworms by the invader.

How many worms are there in a bucket of soil?
In soil from a fertile meadow, there may be as many as 700 earthworms under each square yard. An average bucket of such soil might contain up to 200. Earthworms play a huge part in turning soil over. This puts air back into it, and returns the goodness to it.

How long does an earthworm live?
So many earthworms are eaten by birds and animals, from moles to foxes, that the average lifespan of an earthworm is probably very short. However, some have been known to live 10 years.

Earthworms are very important for keeping soil fertile.

Do worms eat potatoes?

Roundworms are shapeless worms with two pointed ends. They are very common. Most are tiny, and live in water or damp soil. You can hold up to 1000 in just one handful. One kind of roundworm, the potato-root eelworm, is a serious pest. It weakens the plant by living in its roots. Other roundworms, such as the hookworm of the southern USA, live inside humans as parasites.

Which worms can you catch from a dog?

Dogs often have parasitic worms inside them. These can include a tiny tapeworm called *Echinococcus*. The larva forms a cyst the size of an orange inside the host animal. The worm's eggs are passed out in dog faeces. A dog that has licked itself clean may have eggs on its tongue. If it licks the face or hand of a human, they may be infected. A huge cyst can form in their body, or most deadly of all, in the brain.

Which worm lives inside people?

The human blood fluke is the "flatworm" that causes the disease bilharzia, which attacks millions of people in the Middle East and Africa. The larvae of the worms are released into the water, and burrow into the skin of humans who are wading through the water. Pairs of flukes then live in veins in the gut. Their eggs are passed out through the person's bladder, damaging it as they go.

Why do we cook meat?

Cooking meat can improve the flavour or tenderness, but it is also very useful for killing parasites, and their eggs and larvae, which might otherwise infect us. If there is a tapeworm in the meat, raw or undercooked beef and pork can infect people.

Leech

The leech's body fills with blood as its jaws cut into the human's skin.

Which worm sucks blood?

THE MEDICINAL LEECH SUCKS BLOOD FROM MAMMALS, INCLUDING HUMANS. IN the past, people treated many diseases by "bleeding" the patient. They believed that diseases were caused by too much blood in the body. The leech would use its three teeth to open a wound; its digestive juices anaesthetized wounds and kept blood flowing.

How big is the biggest snail?

The shell of the giant African snail Achatina can be up to 13 in (35 cm) long. That is as long as a rabbit. The extended snail is longer. A captive specimen was once measured at 15 in (39 cm) from head to tail, with a shell 10 in long (27 cm), and a weight of 32 oz (900 g).

Do all snail shells coil the same way?

In most snails, the shells spiral to the right. If you hold the shell so the mouth is facing you, the mouth is on the right. Some species have a left-handed shell. In each species, all the individuals coil in the same direction.

How do snails make shells?

The mantle is a skin that covers the parts of the snail that stay within the shell. The shell substance is produced by the edge of the mantle. The shell has a horny layer, then an inner, strengthening layer of calcium carbonate. This is the same chemical as chalk.

What do snail eggs look like?

Some species produce clutches of up to 100, others fewer. In many cases, they are round and transparent, but other species such as the giant African snail have eggs with a hard chalky shell. The eggs are the size of a small bird's egg.

Giant African snail

Away from its native land, the giant snail has become a giant pest.

Which is the world's fastest snail?

MOST SNAILS ARE SO SLOW-MOVING THAT NOBODY HAS BOTHERED TO MEASURE their speed, but the fastest snail on record was an ordinary garden snail *Helix aspersa*. This could move at 0.03 mph (0.05 kph).

What are the rarest snails in the world?

The *Partula* snails, of some South Pacific islands, may be the rarest in the world, but they are fighting for survival. Giant African snails were introduced to the islands accidentally, but became a farm pest. So, a meat-eating snail was introduced to control them, but preferred to catch the smaller *Partula* snails, which are ¾ in (2 cm) long. The species is now rare, and it is threatened by habitat loss too, but *Partula* snails are being bred in captivity now, to try and save them.

Do all slugs eat plants?

MOST SLUGS ARE PLANT-EATERS. SOME ARE

pests because they attack our crops, but many prefer to feed on dead or decaying plant matter. Shelled slugs, such as *Testacella,* are unusual because they have a tiny bit of shell left on their backs. They are unusual in another way too; they are meat-eaters. They go underground and chase worms. They harpoon them with their tongues, then suck them into their mouths.

What do snails do in a drought?

Although their shells are waterproof, snails' bodies are likely to dry out fast when there is a drought. Most snails are active at night or in wet weather. At other times, they rest in places where water hangs around for a long time. In very dry conditions, many snails make a door for the entrance to their shell. This door, called an epiphragm, is made of a thick layer of dried mucus. A snail can survive for months inside this protection, until damp conditions return.

Which slugs mate in mid-air?

Most slugs and snails are both male and female in the same body. Even so, they usually mate with another slug or snail, and mating rituals may be very complicated. For example, one great grey slug meets another on the ground, and starts a slimy embrace. The pair climb up vegetation, entwining and producing so much slime that it forms a rope up to 39 in (1 m) long. The pair dangles from the end of this as they complete their mating in mid-air.

Great gray slugs

Do slugs and snails have teeth?

Not really. Snails and slugs have no jaws like ours, but they have special ribbon-shaped tongues which are covered in row upon row of horny "teeth." They rasp away at their food and break it into tiny pieces. On a quiet night in the garden, you can hear the noise of snail and slug tongues shredding their food with their file-like tongues.

How do snails move without legs?

Snails move on a single thick pad of muscle known as the "foot." Waves of muscle power move down the underside of the foot, lifting sections and moving them forward, as others are put down. From above the snail appears to glide along. The mucus, or slime, that the snail produces, helps smooth its path, and is sticky enough to help it grip when it climbs.

How do snails breathe?

Slugs and snails have turned the wall of the mantle (the skin of the snail) into a kind of lung. It is well supplied with blood vessels and encloses a cavity that is full of air. This connects to the outside air through a special hole, that can be opened and closed. You can often see this hole on the right of the body if you look at a slug or snail when it's stretched out.

Where do slugs hang out in dry weather?

We always see slugs in wet weather, but where do they go when it dries up? Unlike a snail, a slug cannot hide out in its shell during drought. Many slugs simply burrow deep into the earth and stay there until it is wet again.

Two gray slugs mate in a slimy embrace, hanging above the ground.

155

Desert Animals

Fennec foxes are the world's smallest foxes, but have the largest ears of any fox.

Fennec fox

Do many desert animals have large ears?

Fennec foxes, of the Sahara Desert, have large pointed ears. So do kit foxes of American deserts, and also desert hedgehogs. All these creatures' ears work in the same way as the jack rabbit's do. They radiate heat to keep the animal cool.

How do its ears help a jack rabbit keep cool?

Jack rabbits are desert hares with very long ears. The thin skin inside the ear is criss-crossed with delicate blood vessels. Blood flowing through the ears gives off heat, helping the animal to keep cool in scorching weather.

How do desert animals keep cool?

Deserts are hot, dry places where almost no rain falls. Each day, the sun beats down fiercely from cloudless skies. At first glance, deserts seem lifeless places, but in fact all kinds of creatures live there. Many desert animals spend the scorching midday hours in underground burrows. Burrow-dwellers include snakes, lizards and tortoises, rodents, and other mammals, and even some kinds of birds.

Are deserts always hot?

At night, deserts are often very cold. The temperature drops steeply in the evening because there are no clouds to keep in the day's heat. Some deserts in central Asia are cold even by day. So desert creatures must be able to cope with cold, as well as heat. Dwarf hamsters, of Mongolia, have thick fur, which they fluff out to keep warm at night. Bactrian camels grow thick fur for the winter, and molt again in spring.

Do desert creatures ever sleep for long periods?

Some desert creatures, such as tortoises, enter a deep sleep called aestivation to avoid the hottest summer weather. In harsh Mongolian deserts, furry mammals called susliks sleep out the scorching summer; they also hibernate in winter. Aestivation comes from the Latin word for summer, and hibernation from the Latin word for winter.

How do cold-blooded creatures cope with the heat?

S NAKES, LIZARDS AND MANY OTHER REPTILES LIVE IN DESERTS. REPTILES are cold-blooded creatures – their body temperature is not controlled by a thermostat in their body like ours is, but by their surroundings. Throughout the day, they change their position to regulate their temperature so they can stay active. A desert lizard basks in the sun in the early morning to warm up. When the sun blazes down at midday, it moves into the shade to cool off. It sunbathes again in the evening so its body stays warm at night.

Ground squirrel

When do desert creatures go hunting?

By day, the weather is too hot for most desert animals to hunt. Foxes, and other predators (hunters), rest in their cool burrows. They emerge as night falls, and hunt in the cool of darkness.

Which desert creature has a built-in sunshade?

Ground squirrels, of American and South African deserts, have long, bushy tails. When searching for food in the hot sun, the squirrel fluffs out its tail and holds it over its head, to act as a shady parasol.

Ground squirrels use their tails to shade themselves from the baking sun. In the very hottest weather they retreat to their underground burrows.

What stands on its head to drink fog?

DARKLING BEETLES LIVE IN THE NAMIB DESERT, NEAR THE COAST OF South-west Africa. This desert is often covered in sea fog. When the weather is foggy, the beetle emerges from its burrow and does a headstand, so its rear end points in the air. Moisture from the fog condenses on the beetle's body and trickles down into its mouth.

The darkling beetle stands on its head to drink in the Namib Desert.

Darkling beetle

What is the thirstiest desert creature?
Camels are well-known desert survivors. They can last for days without water – weeks if they have plants to eat. At waterholes and wells, camels "refuel" by drinking huge quantities of water quickly. A thirsty camel can gulp down 22 gallons (100 litres) in just a few minutes!

What stores its food in its tail?
Gila monsters are plump lizards of Californian deserts. The reptile's fat tail acts as an emergency food store in dry weather. Its body converts the fat in its tail into energy and slims down when food is scarce.

Why don't camels get sunburn?
A camel's whole body is suited to desert-dwelling. Long, coarse hair on the animal's head, neck, and back protects its skin from the fierce rays of the sun.

What spends 10 months underground?
Frogs and toads are water-loving creatures. You may be surprised to hear that some kinds live in deserts, too. In American deserts, spadefoot toads spend 10 months of the year hidden in deep burrows. They emerge only during the short rainy season.

What drinks the juice of a poisonous cactus?
In American deserts, pack rats eat the fruit and flesh of the saguaro cactus. They get the moisture they need from the juicy flesh, but must be careful not to munch the sharp spines! Saguaro cactus flesh contains a poison, that stops most animals from eating it, but it doesn't harm the pack rats' strong stomachs.

Why is dew the devil's favourite drink?

The thorny devil is a lizard of American deserts. Its body is covered with sharp spines that protect it from enemies. The spines also act as a water-catchment system. On cold nights dew condenses on the animal's body. Moisture runs down grooves in the spines straight into the lizard's mouth.

The thorny devil drinks dew channelled by its spines.

Which frog is its own water bag?

Water-holding frogs live in pools in Australian deserts. As the dry season approaches and the pool dries up, the frog absorbs water, which it stores under its skin. Its whole body swells until it is completely bloated. Then it burrows into the mud, to survive the drought, and only emerges again when the next rain falls.

What do animals drink in the desert?

Deserts are places where water is always scarce. Sometimes no rain falls for months, or even years. Desert creatures can get by on little or no water. Some types of desert antelopes, such as addax antelopes, almost never drink. They get all the moisture they need from eating grass.

Australian Aborigines sometimes dig up water-holding frogs and drink from them.

Water-holding frog

Kangaroo rats live in North American deserts.

Kangaroo rat

When is a kangaroo really a rat?

Kangaroo rats have strong, springy hind legs shaped like a kangaroo's legs. As they bound along at high speed, their paws make little contact with the burning ground. These rodents also leap high in the air, to reach the young, tasty shoots of desert shrubs. Jerboas, of African and Asian deserts, are rodents with very similar hind legs that live in the same way.

Golden moles leave tell-tale ridges of sand on the surface, as they burrow underground.

Golden mole

Which golden mammal "swims" through sand?

THE GOLDEN MOLE LIVES IN SOUTH Africa. Its forelegs have large, flat claws that help it to shovel sand aside, as it burrows under the surface. Its digging action is like a swimmer's breast-stroke. This little beast can dig a tunnel 2.5 miles (4 km) long in a single night.

Which lizard dances to cool off?

MOST LIZARDS USE ALL FOUR LEGS FOR RUNNING. THE BEARDED LIZARD of Australian deserts is different – it runs on its hind legs to keep its body off the sand. When standing still, it cools its feet by "dancing" – lifting each of its legs in turn.

Which lizard moves like a fish?

Sandfish are African lizards with long, slender bodies, like eels. They move through the sand by thrashing their body from side to side, like a fish swimming in water. The sandfish's feet have scaly fringes that can help it run along the sand.

What wears snow-shoes with hairy soles?

Desert animals, such as camels and addax antelopes, have very broad feet. Their feet act like snow-shoes, spreading the animal's weight over a wide area, to stop it sinking into soft sand. Hot sand can scorch tender animal feet, so the camel's feet have tough soles to protect them. Some other desert beasts, such as sand cats and gerbils, have feet with hairy soles for the same reason.

Which huge desert birds are champion runners?

Ostriches live in deserts and dry grasslands in Africa. These large, heavy birds can't fly, but they have very powerful legs and can race along at speeds of up to 45 mph (72 kph). They are the fastest creatures on two legs!

What young insects like to hop about in bands?

Locusts are desert insects with long hind legs and powerful muscles. Adult locusts can leap up to 10 times their own body length and can also fly. Young locusts are called hoppers. They can't fly, as their wings haven't yet developed, but they are expert jumpers. They gather in groups called bands and hop about the desert. The bigger the group, the faster these young insects hop!

Which desert animal has webbed feet?

Most animals with webbed feet live near water. The web-footed gecko lives in the Namib Desert, in southern Africa. Its webbed feet help it to run on fine sand without sinking in.

What gets there in the end?

Tortoises are slow but steady movers. Their short feet have long claws that grip on to rocks, as these armored creatures haul themselves along. The tortoise's claws also help it to dig burrows.

In North American deserts, skunks defend themselves by spraying foul-smelling liquid at their enemies. The stinking fluid comes from scent glands under the animal's tail, so it does a handstand to aim at victims. Wise intruders back away quickly before the skunk has the chance to strike. Enemies do well to get out of range as quickly as possible.

Skunks aim a jet of foul spray at their victim's heads.

What has poisonous teeth on hinges?

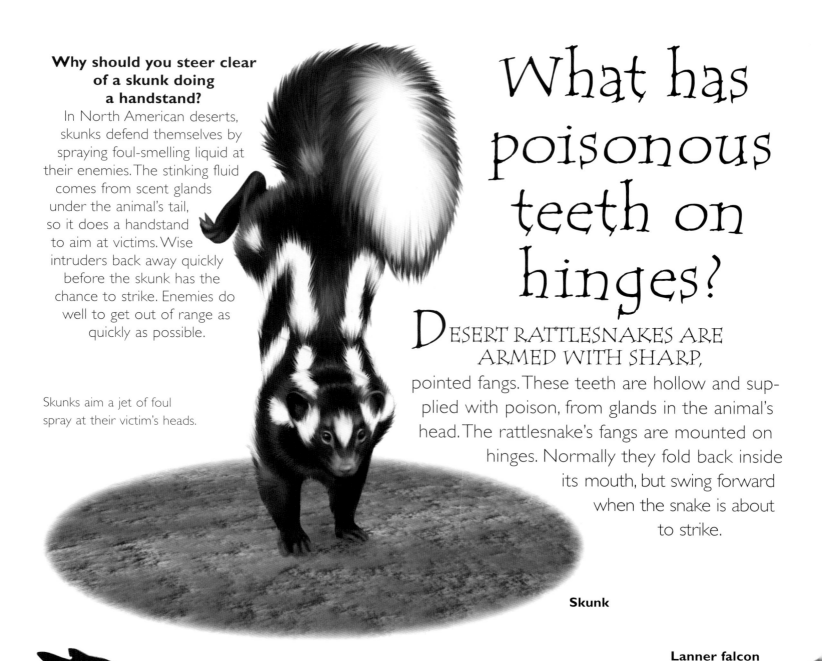

Dᴇsᴇʀᴛ ʀᴀᴛᴛʟᴇsɴᴀᴋᴇs ᴀʀᴇ ᴀʀᴍᴇᴅ ᴡɪᴛʜ sʜᴀʀᴘ, pointed fangs. These teeth are hollow and supplied with poison, from glands in the animal's head. The rattlesnake's fangs are mounted on hinges. Normally they fold back inside its mouth, but swing forward when the snake is about to strike.

Skunk

Lanner falcon

What desert minibeasts are deadly?

Sᴄᴏʀᴘɪᴏɴs ᴀʀᴇ sᴍᴀʟʟ ᴀʀᴍᴏʀᴇᴅ ᴄʀᴇᴀᴛᴜʀᴇs ᴅɪsᴛᴀɴᴛʟʏ ʀᴇʟᴀᴛᴇᴅ ᴛᴏ spiders. They are armed with a venomous sting that curls over their back. The sting is a sharp spine connected to a poison gland at the base of the tail. Most scorpions' stings are no more dangerous than a wasp sting, but some are armed with poison strong enough to kill a person.

Falcons usually have pointed wings and a notch in the top of their beaks.

When does a scorpion use its sting?

Scorpions use their stings mainly in self-defence, against enemies that might attack them. Only rarely do they sting their own prey – insects, mice, and lizards. Scorpions usually kill their prey by crushing them in their powerful pincer-like claws, but if a victim puts up a fierce fight, the scorpion will use its sting to paralyze it.

What desert cat is a deadly hunter?

The caracal is a fast, powerful cat from African and Asian deserts. This strong, agile hunter has large paws that can deliver a mighty blow. The caracal also has sharp claws and fierce canine teeth, to rip its victims' flesh.

What is the gila monster's secret weapon?

The North American gila monster is one of only two lizards in the world with a poisonous bite. It kills its victims by injecting them with poisonous saliva. The creature's bite is not deadly to humans, but it can be very painful.

What is green and covered in poisonous warts?

Green toads of East Africa have poison glands behind their eyes, and also poisonous warts all over their bodies. The warts produce a horrible-tasting fluid, and will put off any predator that has ever tried to eat the toad.

What desert birds are armed and dangerous?

Lanner falcons, of the Sahara Desert, are fierce birds of prey. They have strong feet with razor-sharp claws called talons, and a deadly hooked beak, to tear prey animals apart.

How do rattlesnakes warn off their enemies?

The rattlesnake gets its name from the "rattle" of loose scales on its tail. It shakes its tail to produce a loud, hissing rattle. Enemies recognize the warning and beat a hasty retreat.

Which dog steals a big cat's dinner?

Jackals live in the deserts and grasslands of Africa. They hunt in packs and scavenge whatever food they can find. Small mammals, reptiles, birds, and fruit are all on the jackal's menu. They also steal meat from kills made by other hunters, such as lions, using clever teamwork to fool the lion. One jackal distracts the hunter, while another sneaks up and pulls the meat away.

Caracals leap as high as 6.5 ft (2 metres) in the air to capture flying birds.

Caracal

Why does the jumping rodent fear the snake?

Jerboas are jumping rodents, of African and Asian deserts. They live in underground burrows where they are safe from most predators. But snakes have long, slender bodies – just the right shape to slither down the jerboas' burrows. The snake is the little rodent's most deadly enemy.

What squeezes its prey to death?

King snakes, of the American deserts, do not have a poisonous bite. Instead, they kill their prey by constriction. The snake wraps its body around a victim, such as a rat, and squeezes tighter and tighter. The victim cannot breathe, and soon dies of suffocation.

Which cat can snatch an eagle from the air?

THE CARACAL HUNTS BIRDS, ANTELOPE, MICE, AND LIZARDS. IT CAN PUT ON A burst of speed to overtake a racing antelope, and can also leap high in the air to catch desert birds. This fierce cat can kill even a large bird, like an eagle, with one swipe of its powerful paw.

What hunts with built-in heat sensors?

In American deserts, rattlesnakes can hunt prey, such as kangaroo rats, even in total darkness. Special pits near the snake's eyes are sensitive to heat and can detect the warmth of the rodent's body. The snake homes in on its prey and slithers up for the kill.

How does the rattlesnake kill its prey?

A striking rattlesnake sinks its poison fangs into its victim. Then it lets the animal go. The rat runs off, but is soon overcome by the snake's venom, and drops to the ground. The rattlesnake catches up and swallows its victim whole.

Why are waterholes dangerous?

Hungry lanner falcons hunt by lurking at waterholes. When birds, such as sandgrouse, fly in to drink at the pool, the falcon pounces and seizes a victim in its talons.

The cheetah is the fastest animal in the world.

Why does the ant lion bury itself in a pit?

STRANGE CREATURES CALLED ANT LIONS ARE THE YOUNG OF desert insects that look like dragonflies. The ant lion is a cunning hunter. It digs a small funnel-shaped pit in the sand, then buries itself in the bottom, and lies in wait. When a victim, such as an ant, falls into the pit, the ant lion pounces, and grabs its prey in its powerful jaws.

Ant lion

What is the fastest animal in the world?

Cheetahs live in dry grasslands in Africa. These sleek, lithe cats can race along at speeds of up to 62 mph (100 kph) to outrun fast prey such as gazelles.

Cheetah

What makes the kangaroo rat jump?

KANGAROO RATS LEAP HIGH IN THE AIR TO AVOID ENEMIES, SUCH AS SNAKES and foxes. Their darting leaps confuse the predator, and they may also kick sand in its face, before racing away.

What jams itself in a crack?

Chuckwalla lizards live in deserts, in the western United States. If danger threatens, the lizard speeds into a crack in the rock, then fills its body with air so it swells up. It jams itself into the crevice so a predator, such as a kit fox, cannot pull it out.

What is the domino beetle's secret weapon?

The domino ground beetle has a secret weapon. It can produce a jet of burning chemicals from its abdomen (rear end), which it squirts in the face of enemies, to ward off attack.

When does an owl sound like a snake?

Burrowing owls of American deserts are talented mimics. They can make a hissing, rattling noise that sounds like an angry rattlesnake. The noise frightens away most predators trying to enter the owl's burrow.

What loses its tail to save its life?

A web-footed gecko's tail helps it to balance when running, but it is not vital to the creature's survival. If a hunting bird seizes the tail, it breaks off at a special point, and the gecko escapes. Its muscles contract to stop the bleeding. In time, a new tail grows from the stump.

Desert hedgehog

What wears armour in the desert?

The desert tortoise moves far too slowly to outrun its enemies. Instead, it has an armor-plated shell, made up of many bony plates fused together. When it is threatened, the reptile pulls its head and limbs inside the shell so a hunter cannot reach the soft parts of its body.

Desert tortoise

The tortoise's shell stops it from drying out.

A fox attempting to attack a desert hedgehog will end up with a mouthful of prickles.

Which snake pretends to be dead?

Hognose snakes are non-venomous snakes from the western United States and Mexico. The snake hisses loudly to frighten away attackers. If this does not work the hognose plays dead, rolling on to its back and lying still, with its mouth open and its tongue lolling out. Many predators will not touch dead prey, so the snake's plan often works well.

What puts up its hood and spits poison?

The red cobra is a poisonous snake that lurks by waterholes in East Africa. When danger threatens, the cobra raises the skin round its neck to make a threatening hood. If an intruder, such as a person, does not back away, the snake spits poison into its victim's eyes. Humans, who've been attacked, can go blind if their eyes are not treated quickly.

Why might a fox get a mouthful of prickles?

Desert hedgehogs live in North Africa and Arabia. If a predator, such as a fennec fox, attacks, the hedgehog curls up into a ball. Tough spines protect its back, and the fox cannot reach its head and soft belly.

How did the domino beetle get its name?
The domino beetle is so-called because the white spots on its black body make it look like a domino. This coloration also acts as a warning signal, showing that the beetle is armed with poisonous chemicals. Predators that have been sprayed with poison once will avoid these beetles in future.

Vibrant markings, like those on the desert beetle, show that a creature is poisonous.

Desert beetle

Predators looking at the "two heads" of the shingleback lizard don't know which end might bite back.

Shingleback lizard

Why does the sand cat seem invisible?

THE SAND CAT'S FUR IS BROWNY-YELLOW IN COLOR, WITH DARK markings on its head, legs, and tail. These subtle colors and patterns, known as camouflage, blend in with its surroundings, so the cat can hunt without being seen. It stalks prey, such as jerboas, by approaching stealthily with its body flattened against the rocks, until it is close enough to pounce. The sand cat lives in African and Asian deserts.

Which creature seems to have two heads?
The Australian shingleback lizard has a short, plump tail that acts as a fat store. The tail also provides good camouflage, to confuse predators. It looks very like the lizard's stumpy head, so enemies don't know which end to attack.

170

When does a squirrel look like an antelope?

Antelope squirrels, of American deserts, use camouflage to hide from their enemies. The squirrel has mainly brown fur, with a white stripe, like an antelope's, running down its body. The stripe helps to break up its outline, making it hard for enemies to spot. If danger threatens, the squirrel freezes and becomes almost invisible against the rocks and sand.

Which snake waits in the sand for its dinner?

The sand viper, of North African and Arabian deserts, is light brown in color. The snake hunts by lying in wait for passing lizards, and other small creatures. It chooses a spot where it can wriggle down into the loose sand. More sand blows over its body and soon only the head and watchful eyes can be seen. The viper's perfect disguise has an added advantage: it is also cooler under the desert sand.

When is a gerbil relieved to lose its tail?

Gerbils are mainly sandy-colored, so they blend in well with the Mongolian desert. But the rodent has a tuft of dark hair on its tail. If a predator, such as a fox, spots the creature moving, it will attack the dark tail end, which is easier to see than the head. If the fox manages to grab the gerbil's tail it can break off, giving the animal a chance to escape, though its tail will not grow again.

Why would a lizard put up an umbrella?

The Australian frilled lizard has a loose flap of skin around its neck. This frill is supported by stiff rods like those in an umbrella. When the lizard is threatened it can raise its ruff to look like a fierce and much larger creature. If this trick doesn't work, the lizard may charge and bite.

Why is the king snake orange and black?

THE KING SNAKE OF AMERICAN DESERTS IS NOT POISONOUS. BUT ITS ORANGE- and-black stripes mimic the colors of the deadly coral snake, of the same region. Enemies are fooled by its disguise and will not go near it, thinking it is a coral snake.

What colors warn that the gila monster is poisonous?

The poisonous gila monster lizard has orange-and-black stripes on its scaly skin. These colors are common to poisonous creatures all over the world, so they act as a warning sign that the creature is dangerous. Other animals recognize the colors and know to avoid the lizard.

Which insects do desert people fear the most?

Locusts are large grasshoppers found in African and Asian deserts. When their plant food is plentiful, they breed quickly, and gather in huge groups called swarms. A locust swarm may contain many millions of insects; as it flies off in search of food, it turns the sky black. Farmers fear these insects, because a giant swarm can destroy many acres of carefully tended crops in minutes, causing whole villages to go hungry.

Why is there safety in numbers?

Oryx are large antelope that live in herds in African and Arabian deserts. The herd provides safety in numbers because a hunter, such as a big cat, will find it difficult to target a single victim in a great herd. The oryx usually canter off to escape from danger, but if these beasts are cornered, they defend themselves with their horns.

How do harvester ants work together?

Harvester ants nest in a large colony with a single queen. Most of the group are workers, with different jobs to do. Scout ants search out new sources of seeds, the colony's food. Other workers carry the seeds back to the nest, where soldier ants, with huge jaws, crack them open. The juicy nut kernels are carried inside the nest, and stored in special chambers, leaving a huge pile of husks outside.

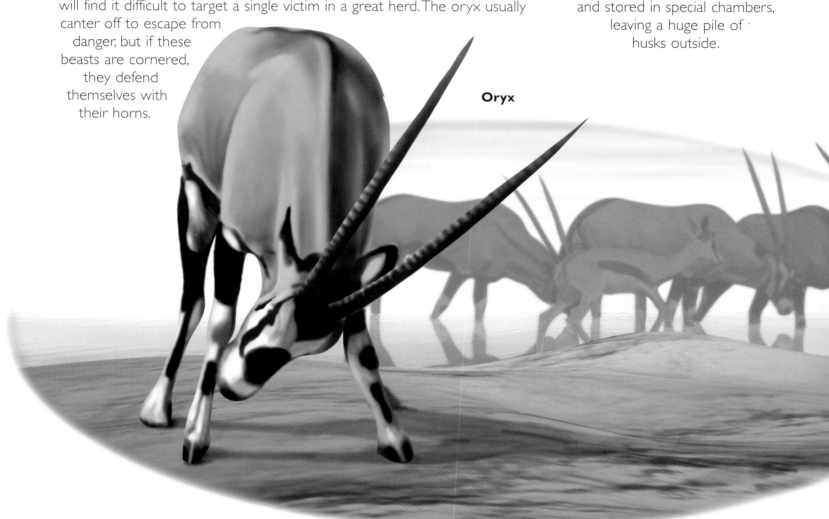

Oryx

An oryx lowers its head and threatens its attackers with its curved horns.

What birds run after clouds?

EMUS LIVE IN FLOCKS IN DRY PARTS OF AUSTRALIA. THESE GIANT BIRDS FEED on plants, fruit, insects, and lizards. They cannot fly, but roam the land on foot looking for food. Farmers build long stretches of tall fences, to prevent emus from destroying their crops. In times of drought, emus watch for rain clouds and run after them, in search of places where rain has fallen.

Which creature gives instructions in scent?

Naked mole rats are strange, blind mammals that live in underground burrows in Africa. The colony is ruled by a female, called the queen, who alone gives birth to young. She communicates with the other mole rats by giving off special scent signals, known as pheromones, which tell the group what to do.

172

Which desert birds are nomads?
Budgerigars live in flocks in the Australian outback. They have no fixed home, but fly on continually in search of areas where rain has fallen, and plants are producing seeds, their favourite food. When seeds are plentiful, the budgies take their chance to settle temporarily, make nests, and rear their young.

The budgerigar is a member of the parakeet family.

Budgerigar

Meerkat guards bark to warn the rest of the colony if an enemy approaches.

Why does a meerkat stand on its hind legs?

Many different desert animals live in groups. Meerkats are furry mammals that live in a network of underground tunnels called a colony. These animals co-operate so they can feed safely above ground. One meerkat stands up on its hind legs and keeps a sharp eye out for enemies, such as snakes and hawks, while the rest feed. If the sentry spots a predator, it gives a warning bark and the group quickly disappears.

Meerkat group

Where do gerbils store their food?
When the gerbil finds a good food source, its stuffs the pouches in its cheeks with seeds. Then it returns to the safety of its burrow, to feast in peace.,

Which desert mammal is a speedy mover?
Jack rabbits of North American deserts are champion racers. They can speed along at up to 35 mph (55 kph), to outdistance predators, such as foxes.

How does the kit fox find its food?
The kit fox feeds on insects, lizards, mice and rabbits. At night, when it goes hunting, its vision is little help to track down food, but its large ears pick up the tiniest noises that betray the presence of scurrying prey. The kit fox is also known as the swift fox, because it can run very fast.

How do echidnas eat their meals?
The echidna, or spiny anteater, is an unusual mammal found in the Australian outback. It feeds on insects and termites, which it slurps up with its long, sticky tongue.

What makes its nest in a cactus bush?

PACK RATS BUILD THEIR NESTS IN CACTUS BUSHES IN NORTH American deserts. They pile more cacti up around the nest to deter predators, such as foxes, and leave only a tiny entrance hole so the fox cannot get in. The nest contains several cool, comfy chambers, where the pack rats sleep by day.

Gerbil

What desert beast is known for its bad temper?

Camels are well known for their bad temper and unpredictable behavior. They may savagely bite, or kick anyone, who annoys them, or spit foul-smelling liquid. At night, their owners have to hobble them (tie their legs together) to stop them escaping back to the wild.

What is a camel's hump made of?

A camel's hump does not contain water, as some people think. In fact, it is a store of fat, which the animal can live off when food is scarce. An Arabian camel's hump shrinks, as the fat inside is used up in hard times. A bactrian camel's humps flop over.

Camels

The two-humped bactrian and one-humped dromedary camel.

How many humps do camels have?

There are two different types of camel. Arabian camels (dromedaries) have a single hump. They are found in North Africa as well as Arabia. Bactrian camels come from the Gobi Desert and other dry parts of Asia. These hairy beasts have not one hump, but two.

Why is the camel called the ship of the desert?

Camels are strong, hardy beasts that have been domesticated (tamed) for thousands of years. Before the days of trucks and planes, they were used to ferry heavy loads across the desert, where the huge sand dunes often look like waves. Camels are also used as riding animals, but their rolling walk gives a bumpy ride, rather like a boat in a choppy sea. It makes some riders "seasick"!

Gerbils are desert rodents that feed mainly on seeds.

Why don't camels get sand up their noses and in their eyes?

Windy deserts are no problem for camels. Their nostrils close between breaths to keep the sand out, and long eyelashes protect their eyes from blowing sand. In sandstorms they shut their eyes, but can see well enough through their thin eyelids to keep moving, if necessary.

175

Gila
woodpecker

**Which bird makes a hole in a cactus
to nest in?**

Woodpeckers normally nest in trees, but
there are few trees in the desert. The gila
woodpecker, of American deserts nests in
the tall saguaro cactus instead. It drills
out its nest hole with its strong, sharp
beak. In time, the juicy flesh, inside the
hole, dries out to make a cool, safe
place for the bird to raise
its chicks.

Gila woodpeckers chisel out their
home with their powerful beaks.

Which bird lives in a burrow?

THE BURROWING OWL MAKES ITS
HOME UNDERGROUND. IT CAN
dig out its own nest burrow with its sharp beak and claws,
but the bird is naturally lazy: it prefers to take over an
abandoned ground squirrel burrow, if it can.

**What desert bird has a
secondhand home?**

The elf owl takes over the nest
hole drilled by gila woodpeckers,
once the woodpeckers have left. It
rests in its secondhand home by
day, and goes out at night to hunt
insects, spiders, and small lizards.

Why don't vultures get thirsty?

VULTURES ARE SCAVENGERS: THEY FEED ON THE CARCASSES OF DEAD creatures. These large birds get all the liquid they need, from the blood and flesh of the beasts on which they feed. In deserts, they soar high in the air to keep cool.

Which American bird is a speedy runner?

The roadrunner, from the west of North American West races along the ground at speeds of up to 40 mph (67 kph). The bird puts on a burst of speed to overtake its prey. It uses its short wings to balance, and its long tail as a rudder, to help it swerve and steer.

Roadrunner

How do roadrunners kill their prey?

The roadrunner feeds on insects, rodents, birds, and even fierce lizards and snakes. It kills its prey with one peck of its vicious beak, or crushes its victim with its powerful feet.

Which bird builds a nest on top of a cactus?

The cactus wren nests in the saguaro cactus. It builds a large domed nest high on the cactus, where the rows of sharp spines put off any hunters, that might prey on the nestlings. The wren's tough feathers and scaly legs protect it from the spines.

How did roadrunners get their name?

In the days of the American pioneers, roadrunners were named for their habit of running along desert tracks, behind the wagon trains. The birds followed the wagons to catch insects, disturbed by the cartwheels and the horses' hooves.

How did the mourning dove get its name?

The mourning dove lives in the deserts and plains of North America. It is named for the sad, cooing sound it makes. This dove can survive in the hottest parts of the desert, but must drink regularly. It will fly up to 60 miles (100 km) each day to find water.

Roadrunners are weak fliers but fast runners.

**Honeypot
ants**

In Australia, Aborigines eat
honeypot ants like sweets.

How
do
honey
pot ants get
their name?

**Why do honeypot ants take
other insects prisoner?**
Honeypots ants live in a colony.
Most kinds feed on nectar from
flowers, but some get their food in
an amazing way. They capture
aphids, or cochineal insects, and
keep them captive in their nest.
The ants stroke their prisoners
with their antennae (feelers), to
make the insects produce
honeydew, a sweet liquid, for the
colony to drink.

HONEYPOT ANTS THAT FEED ON FLOWER
NECTAR RUN LOW ON FOOD IN THE
long dry season. But they have a clever way of storing food.
When flowers are plentiful, they feed the nectar to special
ants called repletes. The bodies of these ants swell up so
they become living honey stores (or honeypots). The
repletes feed the other ants, when food is scarce.

Why does a scorpion have hairy legs?

Scorpions have poor eyesight, but a keen sense of touch and smell. Their legs are covered with tiny sensitive bristles. The little hairs can detect vibrations caused by other creatures' movements. The scorpion can tell the size of its prey from the signals it receives.

How do scorpions eat mice and lizards?

Scorpions catch quite large prey, such as mice and lizards, but they only have tiny mouths. They smother their prey in digestive juices. Their powerful pincers help pull the animal apart, and crush it to a crunchy mush, which the scorpion sucks into its mouth.

How does the jewel wasp feed its young?

WHEN THE JEWEL WASP IS READY TO LAY ITS EGGS, IT DIGS A BURROW and then goes hunting. It catches a cockroach and paralyzes it with its sting. Then it drags its victim back to the burrow, and lays an egg on it. When the wasp larva hatches out, it enjoys live cockroach meat.

How does the jewel wasp get its name?

The jewel wasp, of western America, is named for the bright metallic colors on its body case, which make it look like a gleaming jewel.

A female jewel wasp drags a victim back to her nest. Her young are legless, because they do not need to move to find their food.

Jewel wasp

How do trapdoor spiders get their name?

The trapdoor spider, which lives in western America, sets a clever trap for its prey. It digs a burrow and lines it with silk, from its abdomen. Then it fashions a little lid from earth and silk, and attaches it to the top with a silken hinge. It lurks just inside its burrow. When an insect passes, the spider flips its lid and leaps out to grab its meal.

What insects do people like to eat?

Young insects called wichetty grubs are a favorite food of Australian Aborigines. These grubs live underground on tree roots. Aborigines dig them up and eat them raw or cooked. In African deserts, people also eat grasshoppers and other insects.

Which spider eats until it drops?

Camel spiders of African deserts are greedy hunters. They can eat as many as 100 insects in a day, and sometimes get so full they can hardly walk. The camel spider hunts at night, and before it has eaten it can move very quickly. Its front legs have special suckers, so it can run straight up smooth walls, to grab lizards and even small birds in its powerful jaws.

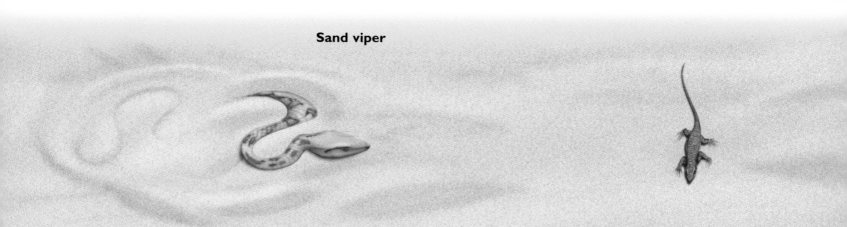

The sand viper takes many days to digest a large meal.

What uses its eyeballs to help it swallow?

THE GREEN TOAD CATCHES INSECTS AND OTHER MINIBEASTS WITH ITS long, sticky tongue. As it has no teeth, the toad can't chew, and must swallow its prey whole. As it swallows, its eyeballs sink down into its mouth, to help force the food down its throat.

How do snakes swallow creatures bigger than themselves?

Desert snakes hunt largish prey, such as rats and ground squirrels. They do not chew their food, but swallow it whole. Their jaws are very flexible with a double hinge, so the reptile can open its mouth very wide, and swallow prey larger than its own head.

The green toad has an effective green camouflage.

Green toad

How can you tell a rattlesnake's age?

A rattlesnake's rattle is made up of loose rings of hard scales. A new ring is added to the rattle each time the snake sheds its skin, so the oldest snakes often have the loudest rattles.

Which invisible creature hunts with its tongue?

The chameleon is a true camouflage expert. This lizard can change the color of its skin, to match its surroundings, and so sneak up on insect prey. When the chameleon gets close, it shoots out its long, sticky-tipped tongue to catch its victim.

What lizard spends most of its life asleep?

The chuckwalla lizard is up and about in spring and early summer, when the desert flowers are blooming. It spends its waking days feeding on flowers, but sleeps for seven months of the year when the weather is harsh, and there is little food to eat.

What beats off enemies with its tail?

The spiny-tailed agama is a lizard, from the Sahara Desert, with a fat, scaly tail. If an enemy approaches, the agama runs into its burrow head-first, but leaves its tail sticking out. The armored tail swishes furiously from side to side, to ward off attack.

Do desert tortoises eat fast food?

No! The tortoise is too slow to catch active prey, but it is an all-round feeder. It eats green plants, flowers, and also dung and dead animals — in fact, most things that can't run away!

As it slithers sideways, only a small part of the sidewinder's body touches the burning sand.

What smells with its tongue?

SNAKES CAN'T HEAR OR SEE WELL ENOUGH TO HUNT THEIR PREY, but they can sense vibrations in the ground, and they have an excellent sense of smell. Tiny scent particles in the air are collected by the snake's flickering tongue. They are transferred to a special scent-detecting organ, called the Jacobson's organ, found in the roof of the snake's mouth.

Which snake moves sideways?

Sidewinder snakes, of North America, are so-called because they move by looping their body and slithering sideways. Scales on the underside of the snake's body grip the sand. As it passes, the sidewinder leaves a line of parallel tracks across the desert.

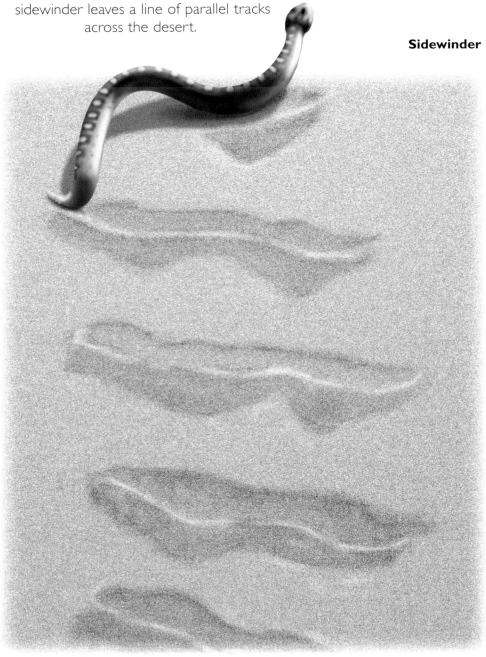

Sidewinder

What desert bird is always faithful?

Galahs are from Australia, with pink breast feathers. These pretty birds pair up for life, and return, each year, to the same nest hole in a tree. They feed their chicks on seeds, and change their breeding habits according to desert conditions. If rain has fallen, and there is plenty of food, they raise up to five chicks. In times of drought, they raise only one chick, or none at all.

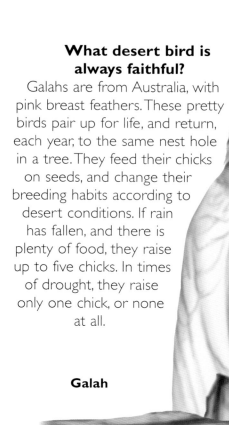

Galah

Galahs are members of the cockatoo family.

How do dung beetles get their name?

THE FEMALE DUNG BEETLE GOES TO A LOT of trouble to feed her babies. She finds a pile of animal dung, and molds some into a ball. Then she rolls her ball to a good spot, lays an egg in it, and buries it in the ground. When the young insect hatches out, it feeds on the dung.

How do green toads croak?

After a rainstorm, male green toads croak to attract their partners. The male produces the sound, by pumping air through vocal cords in his throat. The croaks are amplified (made louder) as they pass through air sacs in the toad's throat, which blow up like balloons.

How do great bustards dress to impress?

Great bustards are large birds of Asian deserts. In the breeding season, the male puts on a spectacular display to win a mate. He fluffs out his neck feathers, raises his tail to reveal white underfeathers, and spreads his wings to make two dazzling white fans. Then he struts about proudly. If the female is impressed, she will mate with him.

What has a tooth on its snout?

After mating, the female tortoise digs a hole in the sand, and buries her eggs there. When the young are fully developed, they break out of the shells, using a hard "tooth" on their snouts. Young tortoises have many enemies, including hawks and falcons. Most do not survive to reach adulthood.

Which male gazelle has a harem of females?

Dorcas gazelles are small, delicate deer from North African and Arabian deserts. The male has a small herd of females called a harem. He locks horns with rival males, and fights off challenges, for the right to mate with the females. After mating, the female gazelles often give birth to twins.

What gets eaten if it doesn't dance well?

Before mating, scorpions court by performing a jerky "dance" together. They clasp their front pincers, and hop up and down on the desert floor. Females may kill and eat their partners after mating, if the males don't dance well.

How do locusts make music?

The male locust makes a loud chirping sound to attract a female. He rubs a row of pegs, on each hind leg, against stiff veins on his wings, to produce the grating sound. After mating, the female locust lays her eggs in the sand.

Which desert mammal lays eggs?

The echidna, or spiny anteater, has very unusual breeding habits. It is one of only two kinds of mammals, in the world, that lay eggs. The other is the duck-billed platypus.

The female echidna keeps her eggs in a special pouch in her body.

Echidna

What do budgies feed their young?

ONLY MAMMALS PRODUCE REAL MILK FOR THEIR BABIES, BUT BUDGIES FEED their chicks on a pale fluid known as "budgie milk." The females make this nutritious liquid in their throats, and feed it to their babies with their beaks. After about a month, the young budgies are strong enough to fly, and leave the nest.

Which creature hatches in two days and grows up in two weeks?

Spadefoot toads spend most of the year buried in the mud. When rain falls, they emerge and breed quickly, before the pool dries up again. The females lay their eggs in the water, and the tadpoles hatch after only two days. Most tadpoles take months to grow up, but spadefoot tadpoles become adults in just two weeks. As the pool dries out and turns to mud, the young toads bury themselves, to wait for the next shower of rain.

Emus

An emu chick sheltering from the sun beneath its father's large body.

What large birds make caring fathers?

Female emus lay their eggs in the male birds' nests, and the father sits on the eggs to incubate them. When the chicks hatch out, they follow their father for 18 months.

Which desert beast rears its young in a pouch?

Marsupials are a group of mammals that rear their young in a pouch. Marsupial moles live underground in Australian deserts. The mother's pouch opens backward, towards the tail, so sand does not smother the baby as she burrows along.

Marsupial mole

Marsupial moles spend most of their lives underground, and have very poor vision.

Which chick drinks from its father's feathers?

Sandgrouse are birds of South African deserts. They fly a long way to drink water daily. The male bird also visits the waterhole to bring water to his thirsty chicks. He wades in and soaks up water with his fluffy breast feathers. When he flies back to the nest, the chicks drink from his soggy feathers.

What happens to ant lions when they grow up?

Ant lions are young, wingless insects with fat bodies. The adult insects are long, delicate winged creatures like dragonflies. When the ant lion is fully grown it changes into a pupa (chrysalis). As it rests inside the hard pupa case, its body is transformed. Eventually, the case splits open and a beautiful winged insect climbs out.

Which insect sheds many skins?

Like other insects, hoppers have a hard outer skin. This tough layer provides good protection, but there is no space inside to grow. The young insect must molt (shed its skin) many times as it grows bigger, until it gradually reaches its adult form.

Which animal mothers employ a nanny?

Young meerkats are born in the safety of the underground colony. Like all mammals, they feed on their mother's milk. Female meerkats, known as "nannies," look after the babies when their mothers go off to feed.

How do scorpions look after their young?

MOST MINIBEASTS TAKE LITTLE CARE OF THEIR YOUNG, BUT FEMALE SCORPIONS are protective mothers. The young ride round on their mother's back, safe beneath her sting. After three weeks they are strong enough to drop off and fend for themselves.

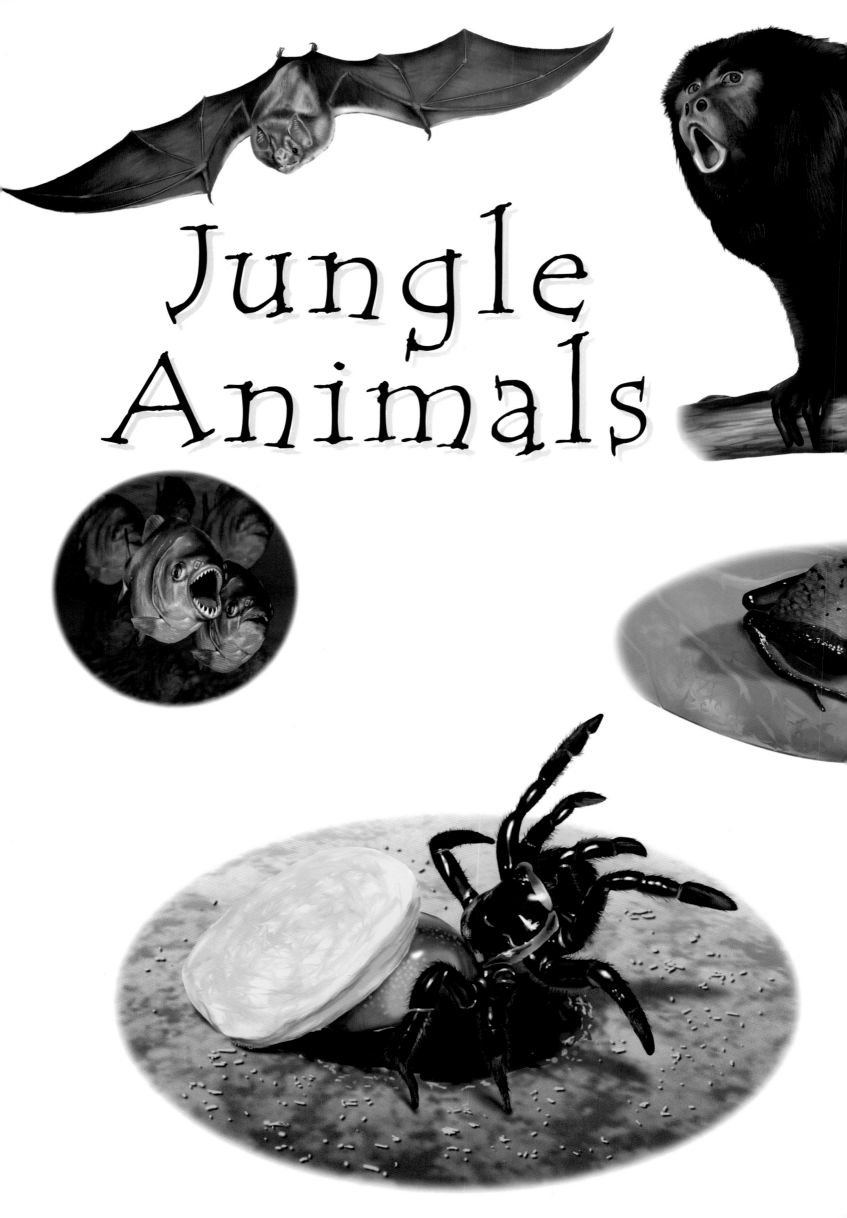

Jungle
Animals

How many animals live in the rainforests?

ALTHOUGH RAINFORESTS COVER ONLY ABOUT A TENTH OF THE EARTH'S surface, they are home to at least half of the world's species of animals and plants – that's thousands of insects alone. About 1.5 million people also live in the rainforests.

What is being done to save them?

All over the world, conservation groups are working hard to save the rainforests. If the destruction is not stopped, the forests will disappear in 50 years time. We will then lose millions of animals, plants, and precious resources like rainforest plants, that could be used to make medicine.

The jaguars like to live close to water, where they can fish for food.

Where do rainforests grow?

Rainforests grow along the Equator in the areas called the tropics, which are hot, sticky and steamy all year round. The biggest forests grow in South and Central America and South-east Asia. There are also smaller forests in China, Australia, India, Madagascar, Papua New Guinea and on some of the islands in the Caribbean. Many other countries can claim to have tiny scraps of rainforest.

Where is the biggest rainforest?

The world's biggest rainforest grows in South America, along the banks of the River Amazon. It is bigger than all the other rainforests put together. At 3,862 miles (6,437 km), the River Amazon is the world's second longest river, next to Egypt's River Nile.

Where do most rainforest animals live?

Most rainforest animals, from large, sleepy sloths to tiny insects, live in the thick layer of trees that makes up the canopy. This is the layer that gets most sun and rain. Here the trees produce plenty of fruit, seeds, leaves and flowers – a feast for the animals.

Jaguar

Why are they called rainforests?

Because of where they grow, rainforests are hot and wet all year round. There are no real seasons – just hot and wet, and even hotter and wetter. On the wettest days, up to 10 in (250 mm) of rain can fall, and there are thunderstorms in the afternoons.

Are rainforests the same as jungles?

You often hear rainforests called jungles, and the two words mean much the same thing. The word jungle comes from an old Indian word for a thick tangle of plants and trees. Jungle is a more poetic word, rainforest a more scientific word.

Why are rainforests being cut down?

Rainforests were once twice the size they are today, and they are disappearing fast. To clear land for farming and cattle ranching, the forests are being cut down and burned at the rate of 60 soccer pitches worth every single minute.

The rainforest canopy

Little sunlight reaches the forest floor, which is dark, gloomy and thick with rotting leaves.

How do rainforests grow?

Rainforests grow in layers, depending on the height of the trees. At the very top is the emergent layer, where the tallest trees poke out above the rest. Beneath is a thick layer of treetops called the canopy, growing like a leafy, green umbrella over the rainforest. Below that is the understory, made up of smaller trees and saplings.

Are there more animals to be discovered?

Yes, there are! scientists believe that there may be many more animals, especially insects, that they have never seen, or identified. Every so often, they discover a new one. Part of the problem is that many rainforest animals are nocturnal – they only come out at night. Others rarely venture down from their treetop homes.

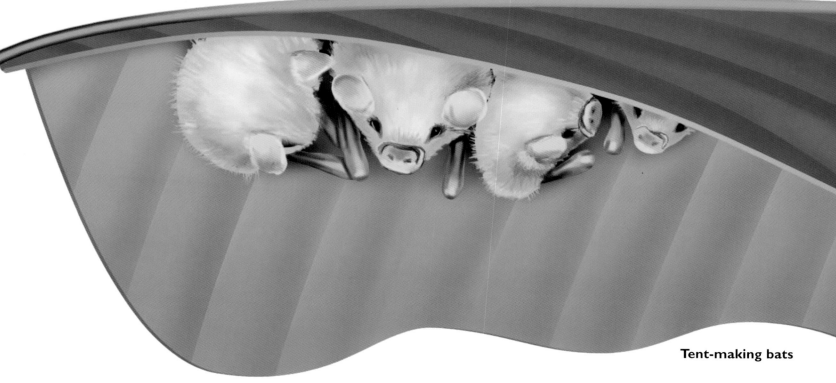

These bats are white. But when the sun shines through their green tent walls, the bats take on a greenish tinge, which hides them from enemies.

Which bats make tents?

ONE TYPE OF SOUTH AMERICAN BAT, THE TENT-MAKING BAT

(*Ectophylla alba*), makes a tent-like shelter from a large leaf, with the leaf still attached to its tree. The bats chew away along either side of the leaf's mid-rib so that the leaf hangs down on either side – just like a tent! Then they spend the day roosting underneath, clinging on to the mid-rib with their claws.

Which insects live in a tower?

Termites are tiny creatures, no bigger than grains of rice. They live in the rainforests of Africa, Asia and South America, in huge groups, many millions strong. Some termites build tower-like nests on the forest floor, made of chewed-up wood, glued together with spit. Others build their nests in trees.

Who lives in a tree ant's nest?

Tree ants, of course! But when the tree ants move out, birds, called trogons, move in. These brightly colored rainforest birds from Africa, Asia, Central and South America do not build their own nests. Instead, they dig holes in abandoned tree ants' nests and lay their eggs inside.

Which birds hang their nests from trees?

In the rainforests of South America, oropendola birds build nests hanging from tree branches. One tree may be home to hundreds of birds. The nests look a bit like saggy string bags, over 3 feet (1 m) long. The birds like to share their tree with bees, because the bees keep harmful flies away from their chicks.

Which kangaroo lives in trees?

Most kangaroos are adapted for hopping about on the ground. But not all! In Papua New Guinea, several types live up in the forest canopy. To help them climb, they have strong front arms, for gripping the trees, and wide feet with non-slip soles.

Who lives in a treehouse and eats monkeys?

Giant eagles, such as the monkey-eating eagle of the Philippines and the South American harpy eagle, live high up in the tops of the emergent trees. They swoop through the canopy on the look-out for monkeys to eat. The eagles build huge twig platforms in the treetops, where they lay their eggs. They use the same nest year after year.

Where do gorillas sleep?

AT NIGHT, A GORILLA WILL FIND A SAFE PLACE TO SLEEP ON THE ground, or in the trees. Then it builds itself a cosy bed from branches and leaves. This takes about five minutes. Then the gorilla snuggles down for a rest, pressing the bed into shape with its body. Gorillas live in tiny patches of rainforest in Africa.

Orangutans are endangered because their forest homes are being chopped down.

Orangutan

What do orangutans use as umbrellas?

It rains almost every day in the rainforest. Some animals don't mind the rain, but orangutans try to avoid a soaking. If they are caught in a shower, they pick a large leaf for an umbrella and shelter beneath it until the rain stops. orangutans live in the rainforests of Borneo and Sumatra, in South-east Asia.

What is a bushmaster?

A BUSHMASTER IS A HUGE AND DEADLY POISONOUS VIPER from Central and South America. It lies curled up on the forest floor, waiting for a juicy rat or small animal to pass by. The snake's brown markings keep it perfectly hidden, among the dead leaves on the ground. Its prey does not see it until it is too late. Humans should watch out too. Its poison could kill you within a few hours!

Which bird uses its head like a battering ram?

Cassowaries are huge birds that live in the rainforests of Australia and Papua New Guinea. They crash through the undergrowth, using the big, bony growths on their heads like battering rams to push aside plants and rummage for food.

What is slimy and moldy?

Slime molds are very strange life-forms that live on the rainforest floor in South America. They slither over fallen tree trunks, like a slimy animal, in search of food. But they scatter spores, like plants, which grow into new slime molds. Weird! They're actually half fungus, and half bacteria.

Which creepy-crawly lives under a trapdoor?

Trapdoor spiders dig a burrow in the forest floor, and cover it with an earth trapdoor. The spider lurks in its burrow, the door half-open, until something tasty to eat walks by. Then it pounces, drags the prey underground, and slams the trapdoor shut.

Trapdoor spider

Trapdoor spiders come from Central America.

What's flat and slithers along the forest floor?

During a downpour, long, colorful flatworms ooze along the forest floor in rainforests all over the world. They can measure up to 6 in (15 cm) long. Flatworms are fierce hunters, able to gobble up snails more than twice their size. Their striking orange, black and yellow colors warn enemies to stay well away.

Tapirs are very good swimmers. They are threatened with extinction.

Malayan tapir

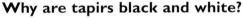

Why are tapirs black and white?

You might think that a Malayan tapir's black and white stripes would make it stick out like a sore thumb! But the opposite is true. The stripy pattern actually helps the tapir to hide among the patches of light and shade on the rainforest floor. Baby tapirs are born with a pattern of spots and stripes for even better camouflage. They lose these markings when they are eight months old.

How did the elephant shrew get its name?

From its long, trunk-like nose! These little creatures are about the size of rats with long, twitchy noses, like miniature elephants' trunks. They use their trunks to gather food on the forest floor, in Africa, and to sniff out termites and other insects.

Which frog looks like a leaf?

IS IT A LEAF? IS IT A FROG? WITH THE HORNED FROG, IT'S HARD TO tell. Its brown markings, combined with the small spiky horns on its head, which give it its name, make the perfect disguise. Hiding on the forest floor, in the Amazon rainforest, it looks just like a wrinkled dead leaf.

Why do tenrecs spit?

A TENREC IS A PRICKLY, HEDGEHOG-LIKE ANIMAL FROM MADAGASCAR. It sets out its territory by spitting on the spot it wants to mark, then rubbing its own strong body smell on to the wet spot. Other tenrecs recognize the smell and stay away.

Which animal burps a lot?

Male orangutans of South-east Asia burp loudly to warn other males to keep out of their territory. They fill the saggy pouches of skin around their throats with air, then let out a long call, that starts off as a loud roar and ends with bubbling burps and groans.

Which is the quietest rainforest animal?

The tapirs of South America and Asia are very shy, secretive animals. They make hardly any noise at all, for fear of being heard by hungry enemies, such as jaguars and other big cats. Often the only sign that a tapir has been about is a line of its three-toed tracks.

Why does the mouse deer stamp its feet?

Mouse deer live in Asia. They are about the size of hares, with short, thin legs. They stamp their tiny feet to signal to each other. Mouse deer are extremely nervous. When they are startled, they freeze, then run away in a zig-zag through the forest.

Which animals use their tails like flags?

When ring-tailed lemurs go for a walk through the forests of Madagascar to patrol their territory, each lemur keeps its stripy tail raised high in the air. This is a signal to the other lemurs, like someone waving a flag. It shows them where each lemur is, and helps to keep the group together. The lemurs mark the trees in their territory with a smelly scent, to warn other ring-tails to keep out.

Why do tarsiers have such big eyes?

Tarsiers are tiny, monkey-like animals from South-east Asia. They come out to feed at night. They use their enormous eyes and sensitive ears to help them locate their prey of insects, lizards, and birds in the dark. Then they leap through the branches, grab their prey in both hands and gobble it down, head first.

Mouse deer have two teeth that stick out from their top jaw.

Mouse deer

Black howler monkey

Which bird sounds like a bell?
To attract a mate, the male bellbird of Central and South America opens its mouth wide and makes a call that sounds like a large, clanging bell. The bellbird has the loudest voice of any bird, so loud it can be heard a mile or more away.

Which monkey turns red with rage?
Many monkeys have brightly colored skin or hair to signal to others. The odd-looking uakari lives in the rainforests of South America. Its face goes red, if it is angry or excited. Uakaris also go bright red in the sun.

The howler monkey has a special voice box that allows it to howl loudly.

Which rainforest animal shouts loudest?

O F ALL THE ANIMALS IN THE RAINFOREST, THE HOWLER monkey has the loudest voice. It lives high up in the forests of South America. Every morning and evening, groups of howler monkeys wail and roar, in an ear-splitting chorus. They do this to defend their own special patch of forest and their own particular food trees. You can't miss their call. Their voices are so loud that they can be heard some 5 miles (8 km) away.

Which animal uses semaphore?
It can be difficult to be heard in the noisy rainforests of South America. So many animals turn to color to attract attention. Frogs usually communicate by croaking, but if it's too noisy, they wave their brightly colored legs at each other, in a type of froggy semaphore.

Which animals squeeze their prey to death?

Snakes called boas kill their prey by squeezing. The gray tree boa, for example, lives in the understory, of the African rainforest, and preys on small mammals and birds. It head butts its prey to stun it, wraps its coils around it, until it suffocates, then swallows it whole.

Why do macaws eat soil?

M ACAWS USUALLY EAT FRUIT AND SEEDS FROM RAINFOREST TREES, where they live in South America. But occasionally they gather along the river bank to peck away at the earth. This provides them with vital minerals, lacking in their normal diet.

Which vines eat frogs?

Vine snakes hang down head-first from the trees in rainforests all over the world, looking just like harmless vines or creepers. But when an unsuspecting frog or lizard goes by, the vine darts out, catches it, and gobbles it up!

Lemurs are closely related to monkeys and live in trees.

Aye-aye

Which spiders spin the biggest webs?

The biggest, strongest spider webs are built by golden orb-weaver spiders of Papua New Guinea. Their gigantic wheel-shaped webs can measure 5 feet (1.5 m) across. The "guy-ropes" that support the webs are even longer, measuring an astonishing 19 feet (6 m) in length.

Which is the fiercest rainforest hunter?

The jaguar is king of the South American rainforest. A fierce hunter, it patrols the forest on the look-out for tapirs, deer, and wild pigs to eat. Sometimes it drops down on its prey from a tree. It is also a fast swimmer, chasing after fish and even alligators.

Which animal uses its fingers like forks?

The aye-aye is a very rare lemur, from Madagascar. It uses its long, spindly middle fingers like forks, to dig out juicy grubs from under tree bark. To locate the grubs, it knocks on the bark and listens for signs of movement.

What makes the orchid bee drunk?

The orchid bees, of South America, carry pollen from one gongora orchid to another to fertilize the plants. The orchid has a cunning way of enticing the bee into its flower. It produces a chemical that makes the bee drunk. It then tumbles into the flower, and drops its load of pollen.

What can strip the meat off a cow in minutes?

Piranhas are small, snappy fish with a terrible reputation. The deadliest of all freshwater fish, they live in the rivers of South America. They usually prey on other fish, but may attack larger animals that fall into the water or come there to drink, such as tapirs, horses, and cows. Not all piranhas eat meat. Some are harmless vegetarians, living on a diet of fruit!

Piranhas

With their razor-sharp teeth, a shoal of hungry piranhas can strip an animal to the bone, in a matter of minutes.

Vampire bat

Bats' wings have long finger and arm bones that suport it as it flies.

Which rainforest bats drink blood?

FORGET HORROR FILMS AND COUNT DRACULA! REAL VAMPIRES LIVE IN the rainforests of Central and South America. Vampire bats live on a diet of blood, from horses, cows, goats, and, occasionally, humans. They hunt at night, attacking animals as they sleep. A bat lands on its prey and takes a bite with its sharp, pointed teeth. Then it laps up the blood with its tongue. Its saliva contains a substance that stops blood clotting, so it keeps flowing freely from the wound.

How does the fishing bat catch its supper?

The fishing bat, of South America, hunts for its food using sound. It make a series of high clicking noises that hit ripples in the water. By listening out for the echoes, the bat can tell not only where the ripples are, but also locate the fish that made them.

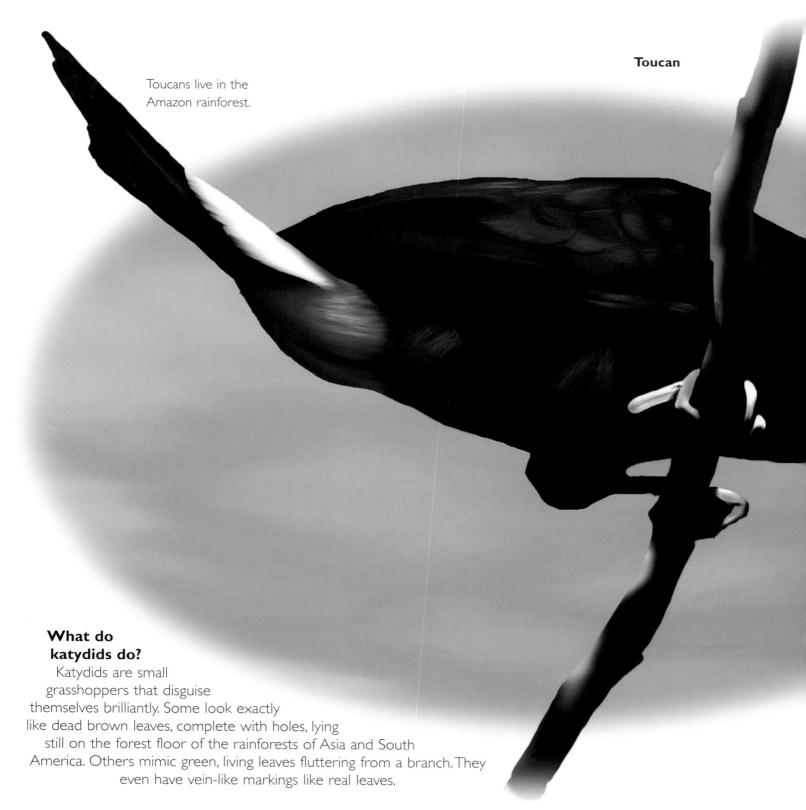

Toucans live in the
Amazon rainforest.

Toucan

What do katydids do?

Katydids are small
grasshoppers that disguise
themselves brilliantly. Some look exactly
like dead brown leaves, complete with holes, lying
still on the forest floor of the rainforests of Asia and South
America. Others mimic green, living leaves fluttering from a branch. They
even have vein-like markings like real leaves.

Why do sloths have green fur?

SLOTHS ARE SO SLOW-MOVING THAT
TINY GREEN PLANTS, CALLED
algae, grow on their coats. This helps to camouflage the
sloth among the trees of the rainforests, of Central and
South America. The algae provides food for the moth
caterpillars, that also live happily on the sloth's fur.

Which rainforest insect looks like a flower?

In the rainforest, things aren't
always what they seem. Many
animals are cleverly disguised as
twigs, leaves, bark, and even
flowers. This hides them from
hungry enemies, and allows them
to sneak up on prey unawares. The
exquisite orchid mantis, of
Malaysia, looks just like a beautiful
flower, right down to its delicate
petals. The mantis lurks on a twig,
ready to shoot out its arms and
grab interested insects, such as flies
and butterflies.

Which butterflies keep vanishing?

As a *Morpho* butterfly flies through the rainforest trees of South America, it seems to vanish, then reappear. This is because its wings are brilliant electric-blue on top, and brown underneath. Each beat of its wings produces a flash, like a strobe light.

Why do tigers have stripes?

A TIGER'S STRIPES HELP TO HIDE IT AMONG THE UNDERGROWTH

as it stalks, or lies in wait, for its prey. Its black and gold stripes break up the outline of its body, making it more difficult to see. Today, tigers are very rare. Only a few still live in the rainforests of Asia.

Which animal can change color?

Chameleons are masters of disguise. Their skin is usually green or brown, but they can change color to blend in with their background, or show that they are angry or frightened. They do this by enlarging, or shrinking, special color cells in their skin. Chameleons live in the rainforests of Asia and Africa.

Why do toucans have such colorful beaks?

Toucans are famous for their striking beaks, which can grow longer than their bodies. They use their beaks for reaching over and plucking fruit from branches. The bright colors may help the toucans to recognize each other, and to scare off other birds.

What disguises itself as a bird dropping?

The crab spider! To take their insect prey by surprise, some crab spiders are disguised as bird droppings sitting on a leaf. Even at close range, it's difficult to tell the difference. Crab spiders live in rainforests all over the world. They get their name from the way they scuttle about, like tiny crabs.

Geckos often stick out their big, red tongues to scare attackers away!

Gecko

What makes a leaf-tailed gecko invisible?

The leaf-tailed gecko, of Madagascar, spends the day head-down on a tree trunk. You might think that this would make it an easy target for enemies – but you'd be wrong! The gecko is superbly camouflaged. Its dappled green-brown skin matches the color of the bark perfectly. Its large, flat tail, and ragged frill of skin make it look just like a woody bump.

Pangolin

Which animal looks like a pine cone?
A pangolin is like a type of anteater covered in hard, sharp scales that overlap, like the shingles on a roof. This provides the pangolin with a tough, armor-plated coat. When danger threatens, the pangolin curls up into a tight ball, like a large pine cone, to protect its soft belly. They eat ants and termites, which they lap up with their long, thin tongues.

Pangolins live in Asia and Africa.

What makes a cockroach hiss?
In the rainforests of Madagascar, big brown cockroaches come out at night, to forage for fungi and fallen leaves, especially after rainfall. Some grow up to 4 in (10 cm) long! To scare away attackers and warn off rivals, the cockroaches make a loud hissing sound, by pushing air out through two holes in their sides. Males also hiss more gently, to attract a female cockroach for mating.

Which butterfly has two heads?

IT'S DIFFICULT TO TELL ONE END OF A HAIRSTREAK BUTTERFLY FROM the other. This butterfly, from South America, has a dummy head on its back wings, complete with false antennae. This tricks birds into attacking the wrong end of the butterfly, and leaving its real head alone.

Which spiders throw sticks?

FROM THEIR RESTING PLACE IN THE TREETOPS, SPIDER MONKEYS, OF Central and South America, sometimes throw twigs and small branches at intruders, to scare them away from their home territory. So if things start landing on your head on a rainforest walk, you know who to blame!

How sharp are a wild boar's tusks?

Very sharp indeed! Wild boars live in some parts of Asia. They use their tusks as weapons, for fighting off rivals for a mate, and for defending themselves against enemies. The tusks are actually overgrown canine teeth, growing upward from the boar's lower jaws.

Which caterpillar acts like a snake?

Caterpillars make tasty meals for rainforest birds. To scare off hungry predators, the hawk moth caterpillar waves its body to look like a miniature snake. It also flashes the big false eyes on its underside, to make it look more threatening. Hawkmoths live in rainforests all over the world.

Electric eel

Which animal blows up like a balloon?

The huge rococo toad, from South America, protects itself from hungry enemies by oozing out poison, from behind its head. It also gulps in air, to blow itself up to the size of a small balloon. This makes it almost impossible to swallow.

Why do some moths have four eyes?

When it is resting on the forest floor, in South America, the wild silkmoth is perfectly camouflaged to look like a leaf. But if a lizard or bird tries to have a closer look, the moth flashes the huge, staring eyespots on its back wings, to frighten it away.

Which fish could give you a nasty shock?

Electric eels live in slow, sluggish streams in the Amazon rainforest. They use electricity, made in their muscles, to stun their prey and make it easier to swallow, and to warn off would-be attackers. They can also give humans a nasty shock.

The electric eel has special organs in its body that produce electricity.

Fer-de-lance snake

There are 2700 types of snake, but only 400 are poisonous.

Which snake was once used as a weapon?

The fer-de-lance is a deadly poisonous snake that grows up to 8 feet (2.5 m) long. It is said that local people, in South America, used to slip these snakes into tubes and use them as lethal weapons to fire at their enemies.

How do arrow-poison frogs get their name?

THE BRIGHTLY COLORED SKIN OF A SOUTH AMERICAN arrow-poison frog is a signal to would-be attackers. It warns them that the frog is very nasty indeed to eat. The frog's slimy skin is deadly poisonous. Forest people extract the poison, and use it to tip their hunting arrows. This is how arrow-poison frogs get their name.

Which animal has a sting in its tail?

If you're out and about in rainforests all over the world, particularly at night, watch out for scorpions. They have a sting in their tails, loaded with deadly poison. A scorpion uses its tail mainly in self-defence, and holds it curled above its body, ready to strike.

What would happen if you trod on a stingray?

You'd get a painful shock! Stingrays are usually quite harmless, unless you go and step on one. Sharp poisonous spines grow near the end of their long thin tails. If disturbed, a stingray whips its tail round, and stabs the spine into its attacker. Stingrays live in the Amazon River in South America.

Arrow poison frog

Which animal shoots boiling poison at its enemies?

Bombardier beetles have a very unusual and unpleasant way of warning off enemies. When provoked, the beetle swivels the tip of its abdomen round, and shoots a spray of boiling hot, poisonous chemicals at its attacker. The spray is made inside the beetle's body, from two otherwise quite harmless chemicals. They react together with an explosive sound loud enough for you to hear. There's no escape – the beetle has a very accurate aim!

How do people get poison from arrow-poison frogs?

To extract poison from arrow-poison frogs, South American hunters roast the frogs over a fire, so that the poison oozes out. The poison is so deadly that the hunters have to wrap their hands in leaves for protection.

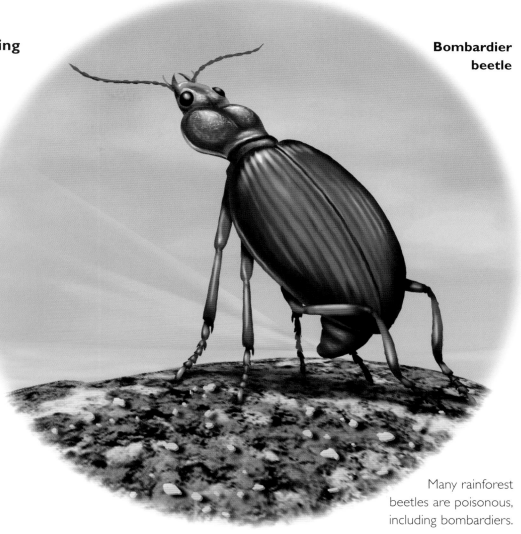

Bombardier beetle

Many rainforest beetles are poisonous, including bombardiers.

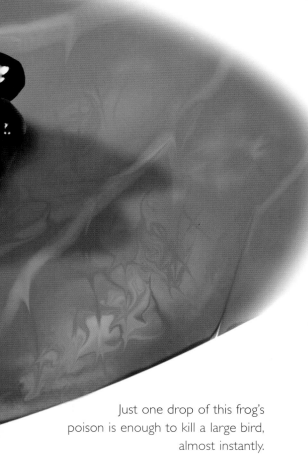

Just one drop of this frog's poison is enough to kill a large bird, almost instantly.

Do centipedes have a poisonous bite?

Centipedes are fierce hunters, and their first pair of legs is modified into fangs. These are used to inject poison into prey. Most centipedes are small and harmless to people. But large centipedes can pack an agonizingly painful bite. Centipedes live in rainforests all over the world.

Which snake pretends to be poisonous?

For some rainforest animals, pretending to be poisonous is the next best thing to being poisonous. In South America, harmless false coral snakes mimic the bright colors of extremely poisonous true coral snakes to trick their enemies into leaving them alone.

Are any birds poisonous?

Until recently, scientists did not think so. Then, in 1992, it was found that the feathers and skin of the pitohui bird, of Papua New Guinea, contained a poison strong enough to kill mice and frogs. In people, it can cause numbness, burning, and sneezing.

203

Spider monkey

Many rainforest snakes are excellent climbers. Their long, muscular bodies are good for slithering along the branches, and they have rough scales on their bellies to help them grip. Then they loop their coils over a branch and lie in wait for prey.

How do gibbons swing so fast?
Gibbons have arms that are longer than their bodies. This helps them to swing very fast through the trees. With its huge armspan, a gibbon can swing about 32 feet (10 metres), from one branch to another in one go, gripping the branches with its long fingers. Gibbons live in the rainforests of South-east Asia.

Spider monkeys live in Central and South America.

How many legs does a spider monkey have?

THE ANSWER IS FOUR, LIKE ANY OTHER MONKEY! BUT SPIDER MONKEYS also use their long tails as an extra arm or leg for gripping on to branches. In fact, their tails are so strong that the monkeys can swing by their tails alone.

Are there dragons in the rainforest?
Yes, there are — flying dragons! These are a type of lizard. They have flaps of skin stretched between their front and back legs, on either side of their bodies. They use these like wings, to glide through the air from tree to tree, in some of the Asian rainforests.

What bird is like a helicopter?

Hummingbirds feed on nectar, found deep inside rainforest flowers in South America. To reach its food, a hummingbird hovers in front of a flower, like a tiny helicopter. It has to beat its wings up to 20 times a second, so quickly that they make a humming sound. Then the bird probes into the flower with its long, thin bill and laps up the nectar, with its tube-like tongue. A hummingbird can also fly forward and backward, and up and down.

Which animals bounce across the ground?

Sifakas are lemurs from Madagascar. They can't run on all fours because their legs are much longer than their arms. Instead they bounce along the ground, hopping from one foot to the other, holding their arms up in the air.

Can snakes fly?

SNAKES CAN'T REALLY FLY BECAUSE THEY DON'T HAVE WINGS. BUT

some have a go. The paradise flying snake lives high up in the rainforest trees in Borneo. To set off in search of lizards to eat, it launches itself from a branch and flattens its body, so that it can glide through the trees. These snakes are also excellent climbers, with sharp ridges on their bellies for grip. If they land in a tree with plenty of lizards to eat, they may not move off it for months on end.

Why do frogs have suckers on their feet?

Many rainforest frogs live high up in the trees to avoid hungry predators on the ground. They have to be good at climbing. To help them, they have pads of sticky hairs, like suckers, on their fingers and toes, and loose, sticky skin on their bellies.

Which creature performs a miracle?

The basilisk lizard of South America has an amazing ability. It walks on water! It literally runs across the surface of a pond or pool, without sinking. It is thought that its sheer speed keeps it afloat, while its long tail helps it to balance.

Basilisk lizard

The basilisk lizard uses its water-walking skills to escape from enemies.

Why do glow-worms glow?

AT NIGHT, SOME RAINFOREST TREES ARE FILLED WITH TINY FLASHING lights. These are made by glow-worms, or fireflies. They produce their yellow-green lights through chemical reactions inside their bodies. Glow-worms flash their lights in the dark to attract a mate. Each species has its own pattern of flashes, which other members of its species can recognize. Despite the name, glow-worms are actually a type of beetle.

Which baby bird has claws on its wings?
Hoatzins live in South America. They build their nests in trees that overhang rainforest rivers and streams. If danger threatens, hoatzin chicks simply dive headfirst into the river. When it is safe, the chicks climb slowly back up, using tiny claws on their wings to help them grip.

Hoatzin adult and chick

This hoatzin chick makes a dive for safety as its parent looks on.

Which bird imprisons itself in a tree?

In Africa, a female hornbill lays her eggs in a hole in a tree. Then, helped by her mate, she seals herself in, covering the entrance with droppings and mud. Only a tiny slit is left, through which the male delivers food. This keeps the nest safe from snakes until the chicks are old enough to leave the nest, and learn how to fly.

Which tadpoles learn to swim in a plant?

Bromeliads are rainforest plants related to pineapples. They grow high up on tree branches in South America. Rainwater collects in tiny pools formed by their overlapping leaves. These pools are used as nurseries, for arrow-poison frog tadpoles.

What wasp lays its eggs in the body of a live insect?

In many rainforests, female ichneumon wasps lay their eggs in the body of another insect, while it is still alive. When the eggs hatch, the wasp grubs feed on the insect. They leave its vital parts until last, to keep it alive and fresh for longer. Scary!

Which minibeast carries its babies on its back?

A female scorpion carries her babies on her back, to keep them safe from enemies. The babies cling on with their sharp pincers. If one falls off, their mother stops and waits for it to climb back on again. After a few days, they are ready to fend for themselves. Scorpions are found in rainforests all over the world.

Birds of paradise live in Australia and Papua New Guinea.

Blue bird of paradise

Which bird hangs upside down to show off?

The dazzling feathers of male birds of paradise give the birds their names. People thought that these birds were so stunning they could only come from paradise. The males use their feathers to attract a mate. The Count Raggi's bird of paradise, puts on a special courtship display. He hangs upside down from a branch, to show off his magnificent orange feathers. After mating, he loses his feathers, and has to grow them again the following year.

Which insect sings to its mate?

THE CICADA IS THE LOUDEST INSECT IN THE RAINFOREST. TO ATTRACT A mate, the male cicada clicks small plates of skin on its sides, at a rate of more than 1,000 times a second. Meanwhile, it listens for a female to reply, with a flick of her wings. Cicadas live in rainforests all over the world.

Which caterpillars live in a tent?

The tent-caterpillar moth of South America gets its name from the way its caterpillars live. They build fine, silk nests among the rainforest trees. The adult moths are superbly camouflaged, to blend in with the lichens growing on a tree trunk.

The bright yellow body of Queen Alexandra's birdwing shows that it is poisonous.

Which butterfly is as big as a bird?

THE QUEEN ALEXANDRA'S BIRDWING IS THE BIGGEST BUTTERFLY IN THE rainforest and in the world. It lives in Papua New Guinea, flitting among the tops of the rainforest trees. Female butterflies may have a wingspan of over 11 in (28 cm) – twice the width of your outstretched hand! Males are much smaller. Sadly, these beautiful creatures are now very rare because of overtrapping by collectors and the destruction of their forest home.

Are ants good at needlework?

Some are! Tailor ants make their nests from living leaves, still attached to the tree. Instead of needles and thread, they use a type of silk, made in the mouths of their own grubs. The grubs are passed to and fro between the leaves, to sew them together. These smart creatures live in the rainforests of Asia.

Why are grasshoppers flashy?

At rest, many rainforest grasshoppers are well camouflaged among the green leaves. But if they are disturbed, they fly away, flashing brightly colored back wings. Then they land again, and seem to disappear to confuse their attacker.

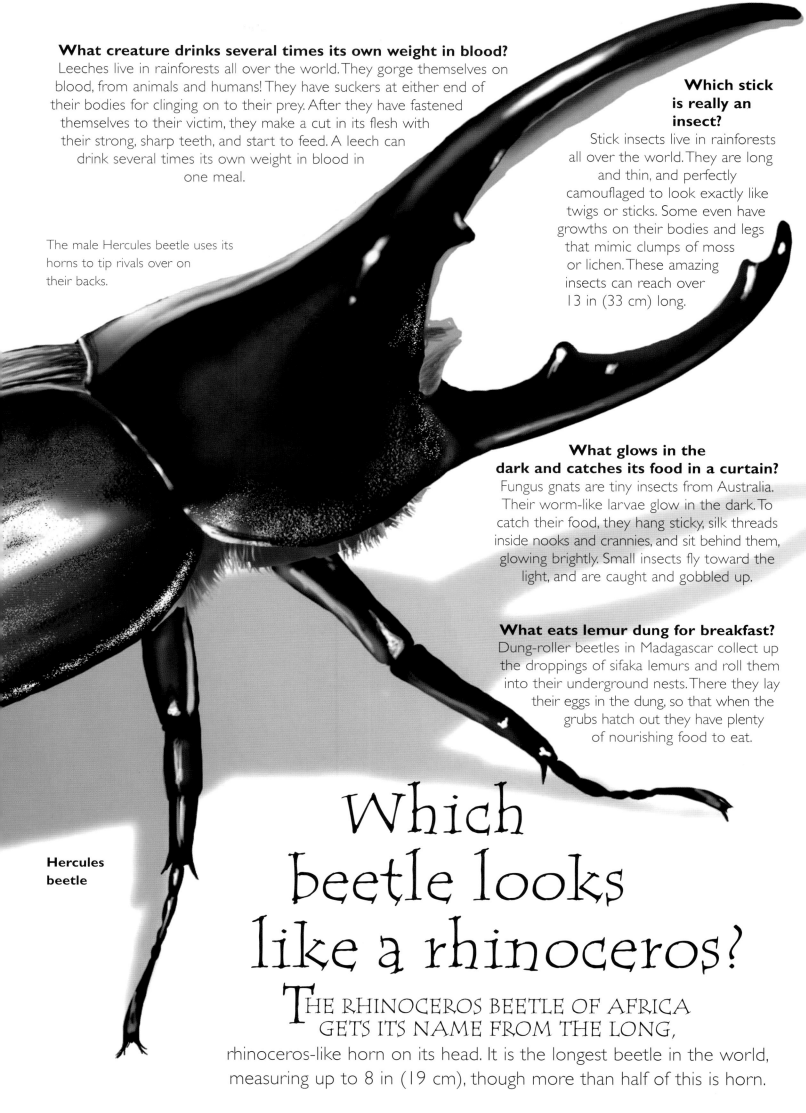

What creature drinks several times its own weight in blood?
Leeches live in rainforests all over the world. They gorge themselves on blood, from animals and humans! They have suckers at either end of their bodies for clinging on to their prey. After they have fastened themselves to their victim, they make a cut in its flesh with their strong, sharp teeth, and start to feed. A leech can drink several times its own weight in blood in one meal.

The male Hercules beetle uses its horns to tip rivals over on their backs.

Which stick is really an insect?
Stick insects live in rainforests all over the world. They are long and thin, and perfectly camouflaged to look exactly like twigs or sticks. Some even have growths on their bodies and legs that mimic clumps of moss or lichen. These amazing insects can reach over 13 in (33 cm) long.

What glows in the dark and catches its food in a curtain?
Fungus gnats are tiny insects from Australia. Their worm-like larvae glow in the dark. To catch their food, they hang sticky, silk threads inside nooks and crannies, and sit behind them, glowing brightly. Small insects fly toward the light, and are caught and gobbled up.

What eats lemur dung for breakfast?
Dung-roller beetles in Madagascar collect up the droppings of sifaka lemurs and roll them into their underground nests. There they lay their eggs in the dung, so that when the grubs hatch out they have plenty of nourishing food to eat.

Hercules beetle

Which beetle looks like a rhinoceros?

THE RHINOCEROS BEETLE OF AFRICA GETS ITS NAME FROM THE LONG, rhinoceros-like horn on its head. It is the longest beetle in the world, measuring up to 8 in (19 cm), though more than half of this is horn.

Which rainforest bird helps people find honey?

The honeyguide is a small bird that lives in Africa and Asia. Like many rainforest birds, it feeds on insects, but its favorite food is beeswax. In Africa, honeyguides and local people help each other. The bird leads them to a bees' nest, flying and calling, to show the way. Then men climb the tree and break the nest open. They take the honey and leave the beeswax, for the bird to feast on.

Hyacinth macaw

It is thought that only 3,000 macaws are left in the wild.

When can a hyacinth fly?

The spectacular hyacinth macaw of South America is one of the rarest birds in the rainforest. It is also the world's largest parrot. Unfortunately, so much of its rainforest home has been destroyed, and so many macaws have been captured, for zoos and the pet trade that this beautiful bird is now facing extinction.

Which birds have the longest tails?

The male argus pheasant of Asia has the longest feathers of any flying birds. Its tail feathers often reach 6 feet (1.7 m) in length. Its long wing feathers are covered in "eyes." The male fans out these feathers to attract a mate.

How do sunbirds slurp up their food?

Like hummingbirds, sunbirds from Asia and Africa feed on nectar from rainforest flowers. They have long, thin beaks for reaching deep inside the flowers, and long, tubular tongues for sucking up nectar, as if through a straw.

What sleeps like a bunch of leaves?

HANGING PARROTS SLEEP HANGING UPSIDE DOWN FROM TREE branches. From a distance, the parrots look just like bunches of leaves, which makes them very tricky for enemies to spot. Hanging parrots live in the rainforests of Asia.

Which bird sniffs out its food?

Cock-of-the-rocks

P~ITTAS ARE BRIGHTLY COLORED~
BIRDS THAT LIVE IN SOUTH-EAST
Asia. They forage for food on the rainforest
floor. They mainly eat insects, worms, and
snails. They use their superb sense of smell
to sniff out their prey, from among the
leaf litter and under the ground.

Which bird was worshipped as a god?
Quetzals are glittering green and
crimson birds from Central
America. In Aztec times, the
quetzal was worshiped as
the god of the air. Its
trailing tail feathers, which
can grow 2 ft (60 cm)
long, were highly
prized for making
into costumes and
head-dresses.

Why do cock-of-the-rocks like dancing?
Male cock-of-the-rocks are
brilliant orange and black birds. To
attract mates, the males clear a
space on the forest floor, and
perform a type of dance. This
includes spreading out their
beautiful feathers, to show off to
females in the nearby trees.

How do antbirds avoid getting stung?
Antbirds follow armies of ants, as
they swarm through the South
American rainforests. They don't
eat the ants themselves, but feed
on other insects disturbed by the
ants. A thick ruff of feathers
around the birds' face stops it
from getting painfully stung
by the ants!

Cock-of-the-rocks
live in Central and
South America.

Giraffe-necked weevil

Which beetle looks like a giraffe?

The bizarre giraffe-necked weevil, from Madagascar, is one of the oddest-looking insects in the rainforest. Males have very long heads – about half the length of their bodies.

How does a turtle keep its nostrils dry?

The matamata turtle uses its long neck as a snorkel to hold its nostrils up out of the water. This means that it can breathe without moving and frightening away the fish on which it feeds. The turtle lives in muddy rivers in South America.

No one knows why this weevil has such a strange head.

Which flies' eyes pop out on stalks?

Diopsid flies live in many rainforests. They have eyes on the end of long stalks. No one is quite sure why. One idea is that the stalks look like wasps' antennae. Predators mistake the flies for wasps, which might sting if they get any closer.

Which bug has a lantern head?

THE LANTERN BUG, FROM SOUTH AMERICA, GOT its name because people once thought that its odd-shaped head glowed in the dark. In fact, its large head looks a bit like a miniature crocodile. It may be useful for scaring off enemies and stopping the bug from being eaten.

Which is the shyest rainforest animal?

The shyest animal in the rainforest is probably the okapi. These timid creatures are related to giraffes, and look like a cross between a short-necked giraffe and a zebra. They live only in the rainforests of Zaire, Africa. Okapis are so secretive and solitary that, apart from local people, no one knew they even existed until 1901.

Okapis are endangered because their forest homes are being destroyed and they are poached for their meat.

Okapi

Which is the rarest rainforest animal?

So much of their forest home has been cleared to make space for coffee, rubber, and banana plantations that there may be fewer than 250 golden lion tamarins left in the wild. The last remaining tamarins live in a few patches of rainforest, along the Atlantic coast of Brazil. Efforts are being made to save the tamarins. If these fail, they could be extinct within just a few years.

Golden lion tamarin

Golden lion tamarins are illegally captured for the pet trade and zoos.

How many mountain gorillas are there?

THERE ARE THREE SEPARATE GROUPS OF MOUNTAIN GORILLAS, ALL IN THE rainforests of Central Africa. All three are endangered because of forest clearance, and poaching for their meat. Scientists estimate that there may be fewer than 40,000 left in the wild.

What keeps its baby in a watertight pouch?

The yapok is a marsupial from Central and South America that is adapted for life in water. It has webbed back feet to help it swim after its prey of fish, frogs, and crustaceans. Its pouch opens backwards so that it stays watertight when the yapok dives into the water.

What is white and pink and keeps its baby in its pocket?

A cuscus is a marsupial from Papua New Guinea. It has a pouch on its front where its young grow and develop. The cuscus has a thick white coat and a long tail, with a bare pink tip. It uses its tail to help it climb through the trees.

Which spider is as big as a plate?

Including its eight hairy legs, a bird-eating spider, or tarantula, can grow as big as a plate. It's the biggest spider in the world, and lives in South America. Bird-eating spiders hunt at night, on the rainforest floor. Despite their name, they very rarely catch birds.

Which rodent breaks records?

The world's biggest rodent is the capybara, from South America. (Rodents are animals such as mice and rats.) It's about the size of a pig, and lives around lakes, rivers, and marshes. Its arch enemy is the jaguar, the fiercest hunter in the rainforest.

Three-toed sloth

Are big animals the most dangerous?

No, THEY'RE NOT! THE MOST DANGEROUS ANIMALS

are small insects – mosquitoes. They spread malaria, a disease that kills millions of people each year. Symptoms include a raging fever. Mosquitoes can also pass on yellow fever and elephantiasis. They live in rainforests all over the world.

The three-toed sloth even eats its food hanging upside down.

Which is the laziest rainforest animal?

The laziest animal in the rainforest has to be the three-toed sloth, from South America. This idle animal spends about 18 hours a day hanging upside down from a tree branch, fast asleep. It spends the rest of the time looking for food. Unusually, its shaggy hair also grows upside down, from its belly towards its back. This is so that the rain runs off it more easily, and the sleepy sloth does not get waterlogged!

Which bird builds the smallest nests?

The vervain hummingbird of South America builds a nest from plants and cobwebs, that's only about the size of half a walnut shell. There it lays the smallest eggs of any bird, barely the size of peas. The bee hummingbird's nest is also tiny, about the size of a thimble.

Anaconda

Anacondas like to live in trees as well as in water.

Which is the biggest rainforest snake?

THE GIGANTIC ANACONDA OF SOUTH AMERICA IS THE WORLD'S BIGGEST snake. The heaviest on record was 27 feet (8.45 m) long, more than 3 feet (1 m) round its middle and weighed almost a quarter of a ton. Anacondas lurk in the water at the river's edge, with just their eyes and nostrils showing, waiting for their prey. They can kill prey as large as deer, goats, and alligators, crushing them to death with their huge coils.

How big is the biggest moth in the rainforest?

The Hercules atlas moth, from Australia and Papua New Guinea, has a wingspan of up to 11 in (28 cm), and it may grow even bigger. The moth has long, feathery antennae for smelling, touching, and telling how hard the wind is blowing.

Which animal has the biggest appetite?

You might think that the answer would be a jaguar, or an alligator. In fact, it's the larva of the polyphemus moth, which lives in Central America. It eats a staggering 86,000 times its own birth weight, in food, in the first two days of its life!

Which bird is smaller than a butterfly?

The bee hummingbird of South America is the world's smallest bird. It measures just over 2 in (5.7 cm) in length, nearly half of which is its bill and tail. This tiny creature is smaller than many of the butterflies and moths in its rainforest home.

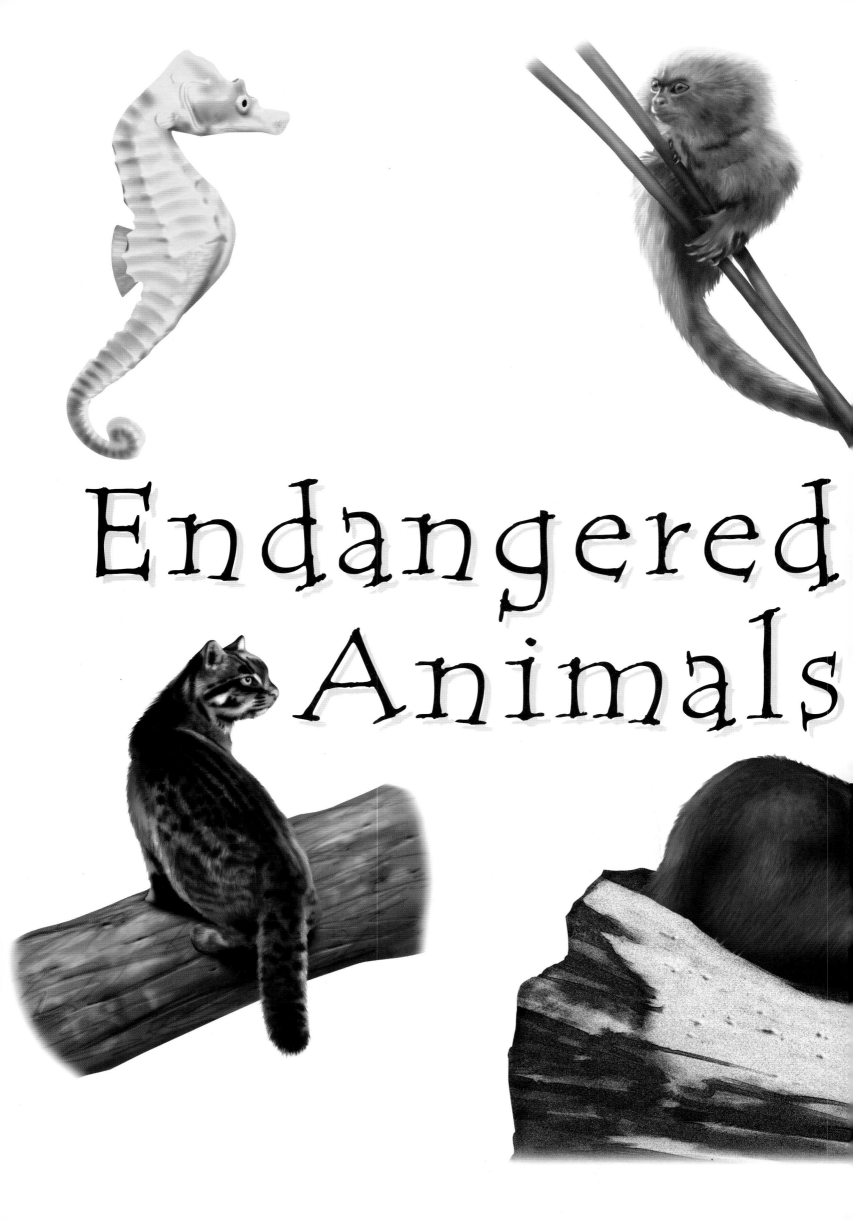

Endangered Animals

How tall is a gorilla?

A FEMALE GORILLA STANDS AT ABOUT 4 FEET (1.2 metres) on her hind legs. A silverback male can reach up to 7 feet (2.1 metres), although the average height of a male is 5 feet 6 in (1.7 metres). Males are called "silverbacks" when hair on their backs turns silver in mature adulthood.

Silverback gorilla

Gorillas are the most intelligent animals next to human beings.

What do gorillas need from their habitat?

Shelter and a good supply of food. If the climate is favorable, both mountain and lowland habitats can provide a gorilla family with all the food and nutrients they need. Mountain gorillas are severely endangered. Gorillas are mainly vegetarian and their habitats are rich in lush vegetation, as well as plentiful insects.

How do gorillas communicate?

They use body signals and noises – perhaps the most famous of these is the male's habit of standing on his hind legs and beating his chest when angry. They play together, which teaches their young vital skills for survival.

What happens to gorillas in wartime?

Gorillas are often innocent victims of fierce fighting. Occasionally, they get caught in the crossfire. Hungry troops may also track down a gorilla and kill it for food. As there are very few gorillas left in the world, killing even one could contribute to the extinction of the species.

Are we related to gorillas?

Yes. Gorillas and humans have a common ancestor. This creature lived on earth many millions of years ago. The descendants of our common ancestor started two separate families, or evolutionary lines. One became human, the other became the ancestor of gorillas. Like humans, gorillas are a member of the Primate order. Within this order, both humans, and gorillas are members of a scientific family called *Hominoidea*.

Why are gorillas hunted?

Tragically, one of the most common reasons they are hunted is as 'trophies' – so hunters can show off their skills. Gorillas' skulls, hands, and feet are sold as souvenirs, just as elephant feet were in the 19th century. Gorillas have also been hunted for their meat, particularly during the famine that gripped Rwanda in the 1980s and 1990s.

What is life like in the gorilla group?

Gorilla society is run by male gorillas – it is called a patriarchal society, from the Latin word for father. The leader of the group is always a silverback (a mature male). Males often fight to show who is the boss, and the loser must leave the group, or be killed. Those that leave will often set up a new group of females and young.

Can people see gorillas in the wild?

Yes, small groups of people are taken to the gorillas' habitat. There are strict rules and people have to be extremely careful not to disturb the gorillas. Visitors are kept at a respectful distance and instructed how to behave. Human illnesses – even the common cold – can be caught by gorillas and could prove fatal, because they have no resistance to our diseases. So people should not attempt the trip if they feel at all unwell.

Who tried to save the gorillas?

Dr Dian Fossey was the gorillas' most famous helper. She spent much of her life trying to stop gorillas being captured or killed for trade. Sadly she was murdered in 1985. Since Dian Fossey's death, many action groups have continued her work. The story of her life was made into a film, *Gorillas In The Mist*.

Why are gorillas endangered?

Gorillas live in Africa – in Zaire, Rwanda, and Uganda – in mountainous areas, and in the lowland rainforests. In 1925, their mountain home was made the first national park in Africa. Sadly, Zaire, Rwanda, and Uganda have suffered severely over the last few decades, experiencing terrifying wars, droughts, and famines. This has caused terrible devastation to the gorilla population, as well as to the human world. All gorilla species are endangered.

Mountain gorilla

The mountain gorilla is the most endangered of the gorillas.

219

Most colobus monkeys have a shortened – or missing – thumb.

Colobus monkey

Which species of monkey are in danger?

THE MOST ENDANGERED SPECIES IS THE gorilla. Orangutans are also at risk from poachers, but more at risk is Africa's colobus monkey, which is often killed for its luxuriant black-and-white coat. India's lion-tailed macaque is also at risk from poachers and from erosion of its habitat.

Where do monkeys come from?
Monkeys can be found in Asia, Africa, and Central and South America. They prefer warm climates, although a few species live in cold areas, such as the Himalayas. Most types of monkey live in areas where trees are plentiful, although some African monkeys live in the savannah (grassland) with few trees.

How many types of monkey are there?
There are around 133 different species of monkey in the world. Monkeys are primates – a type of mammal. Other primates include humans, bushbabies, lemurs and marmosets. Many marmosets are endangered. A collective term for monkeys is anthropoids. This word means that they share similarities with human beings.

How do baby monkeys climb trees?
Baby monkeys cling on to their mother's fur and swing through the trees with her. Some species carry their young on their backs, some underneath their bellies, like a kangaroo – only without a protective pouch. Baby monkeys have to cling on with the tightest grip imaginable to survive the rigorous journeys.

Which religion has a monkey god?
Hinduism. The monkey god's name is Hanuman and his mischievous sense of humour often gets him into trouble. He plays an important part in one of Hinduism's scriptures, the Ramayana. In one story he helps Rama rescue his kidnapped wife, Sita. At holy festivals, Hindu men sometimes dress up as Hanuman.

Can monkeys talk?
Monkeys don't talk like humans do, but they do have their own highly developed languages. Howler monkeys shout very loudly to one another. When monkeys talk together in a group they sound very excited, and the noise is often referred to as chattering. People who study the way monkeys communicate believe they can discuss plans for moving to new feeding grounds.

What do monkeys eat?
Monkeys eat fruit, leaves, nuts, plants, insects and small animals. They will also drink water, although as their diet is rich in moisture, they often don't need to drink as well as eat. Most monkeys spend much of their life in trees, which is where they find their food.

How big is a monkey?
Monkeys range vastly in size. The smallest is the tiny pygmy marmoset, which weighs approximately 5 oz (150 g); the largest is the mountain gorilla – males can stand up to 7 feet (2.1 metres) tall and weigh over 500 lb (225 kg). There are monkeys of all sizes in between these extremes.

Pygmy marmoset
The pygmy marmoset likes to gnaw holes in trees and feed on the gum that oozes out.

Have any species become extinct?

NOT IN RECENT CENTURIES. CHINA'S YUNNAN SNUB-NOSED MONKEY was believed to be extinct because it had not been spotted for 70 years. But recently it was rediscovered – the population numbers around 1,000. Brazil's golden lion tamarins were on the brink of extinction. But thanks to the work of conservation groups such as WWF, their numbers are now increasing.

Which red wolf may not be around much longer?

The red wolf in the USA has been cross-bred with so many other species that it is now endangered.

Are there wolves in Australia?

Yes, but maybe not for long. The Tasmanian wolf used to live happily in Australia, but conservationists haven't spotted one for well over ten years, so they are beginning to become concerned that it has been hunted to extinction.

Are pet dogs endangered?

No! The ancestors of all domestic dogs were once wild animals. They were tamed by people who found them useful for hunting and as guards for their property. Today, after many centuries of domestication, most pet dogs are totally different from their wild ancestors – and not endangered at all.

What bones are used in folk medicine?

CONSERVATIONISTS ARE TRYING TO STOP canines being killed for their fur, and for parts of their bodies used in traditional medicines. In Africa, the simien jackal is hunted for its beautiful coat, and in South America the maned wolf is hunted for its bones. When powdered, the bones are believed to cure a variety of ills.

Does a fox cub make a good pet?

No wild animal should be kept as a pet. It takes many generations of breeding to completely tame any species. A fox cub may seem very playful and friendly, but its wild instincts would soon take over. No other pets, such as cats or rabbits, would be safe from it, and it could also attack humans, even those it knew well, through fear.

Jackals like to feed on fruit, small mammals and even the bodies of larger animals that have died.

Simien jackal

Are werewolves extinct?

No! They never existed. A werewolf is an imaginary beast – supposedly a human who can change into a wolf and attack other humans and animals. In folklore, this change takes place at the full moon – when people believe there is more crime and madness. Werewolves remain an important part of traditional storytelling, particularly in Eastern Europe, where there are many people who still believe werewolves exist.

Coyote

A coyote's howl can be heard several miles away.

Which is the smallest wild dog?

The smallest alive today is the fennec fox, which lives in parts of Africa and the Middle East. The fennec fox is under threat from predators and habitat erosion. When born, a fennec cub weighs only 2 lb (0.8 kg); as an adult it will weigh about 3 lb (1.5 kg). The largest wild dog of all is the gray wolf – an adult can weigh up to 176 lb (80 kg).

When did wolves become extinct in Britain?

Once Britain was almost covered in dense forest. When people began cutting it down, they destroyed the wolves' habitat and source of food – making wolves hungry and dangerous. The last wolf killed in Britain was in Scotland, in 1743. Ireland's last wolf perished about 50 years before, and in England, wolves were extinct by 1500.

In what countries do wolves, foxes, and wild dogs live?

In every continent. There are wolves in eastern Europe and Asia, jackals in Africa, coyotes in America, and dingoes in Australia. From the black-backed jackal in Africa to the gray wolf in Europe, many wolves are under threat. The wolves hunt in packs and kill their own prey as well as scavenging on dead animals. All wolves are disliked by farmers!

This moth is now a protected species.

Spanish moon moth

Which insects have become extinct?

Today, arthropods (insects and arachnids) make up 80 per cent of all animal species on earth. And because fossillized remains have been found, we know that many hundreds of species have also become extinct in the past. More recently, the Duke of Burgundy butterfly, from Europe, and the American burying beetle. from the USA, are just two of many insects that have become extinct. The Spanish moon moth and giant weta cricket are at risk and are now protected species. Scientists think that there are many more living arthropods still to be discovered, and probably more extinct species, too.

Which mate-eating creature is under threat?
The female praying mantis. After mating, she kills and eats the male! The praying mantis gets its name because it often has its front pair of legs raised – which makes it look as though it is praying. Mantis' are at risk from habitat erosion and pesticides.

Are arthropods poisonous to each other?
Yes they are. For instance, when a spider traps a fly, it gives it a venomous bite to paralyze it. Once the fly stops moving, the spider can eat it without a struggle. Being poisonous also protects an insect from being eaten itself.

How can you tell an arachnid from an insect?

The most obvious difference is in the number of legs. An insect (for example, an ant) has six legs, and an arachnid (for example, a scorpion) has eight. Both insects and arachnids are members of a large group called arthropods. This group also includes crustaceans (such as crabs), centipedes, and millipedes. Many arthropods are endangered by human activities.

Why are people scared of spiders?

Many people are frightened of spiders because of the unusual way they move. A fear of spiders (called arachnophobia, from the Latin words for spiders and fear) is one of the most common phobias in the world. Really, spiders should be afraid of humans because many of them, such as the bone cave harvestman, and the spruce-fir moss spider from the USA, are endangered.

Which insects and arachnids are poisonous?

MORE THAN YOU MIGHT THINK! SCORPIONS AND REDBACK SPIDERS are well known to be poisonous. But in fact most insects are poisonous to a greater or lesser degree. A wasp sting is poisonous, and hurts, but in large doses (or to those who are allergic) it can be fatal. Most spider venom would be poisonous to humans – but very few spiders are able to bite through human skin. If they can, most inject only a small dose of venom.

What creature could survive a nuclear war?

There are many endangered arthropods, such as the painted rocksnail from the USA. Many live in the rainforests. Their habitat is being destroyed at an alarming rate, making countless arthropod species extinct each year. However, they are also extremely hardy – scientists believe cockroaches would be the only creatures to survive a nuclear war!

Which beach-dwelling arthropods are at risk?

Many arthropods live in beach or ocean habitats. They are under threat from pollution, which makes the beach and water uninhabitable. Many crab, shrimp, and crayfish species are at risk, such as the longhorn fairy shrimp and the common cave crayfish, both from the USA. Arthropods are also killed in huge numbers by pesticides, and many are lost when their wild habitat is destroyed for building.

Giant weta cricket

Fossilized weta crickets have been found that date back more than 180 million years ago.

Which snail was eaten to extinction?

All seven species of land snail were once found in Moorea, in French Polynesia. When French settlers imported their own French snails to farm for eating, these larger foreign visitors ate the local snails and they no longer exist!

225

The red panda eats bamboo, roots and some small animals.

Red panda

How many types of panda are there?

THE GIANT PANDA HAS ONE OTHER

Where do giant pandas live?
In bamboo forests in China. Once they were seen all over this vast country, but sadly today they can be found in only three small provinces in western China.
Red pandas are more adaptable to changes in habitat, and can be found in China and other parts of Asia, including the Himalayas.

Which animal is all thumbs?
Giant pandas have an extra "finger" on their front paws. It is where a human's little finger would be, and works like a thumb. This gives the panda the power of two thumbs, so it can grip its food while eating.

panda relation – the red panda. Red pandas are much smaller, and used to be thought of as not a panda at all, but a type of raccoon. They live in trees, have long, striped tails and thin, cat-like faces with pointed ears. Their red fur has paler markings. Red pandas are often hunted, and some are captured alive, to be sold as pets.

Are pandas vegetarian?

Like all bears, pandas are omnivorous, which means they eat meat or vegetation. But giant pandas seldom eat meat, for the simple reason that they find it difficult to catch! If they come across a dead or wounded animal they will eat it, but they usually eat vegetation, and almost always this is bamboo.

How many giant pandas are left in the world?

There are believed to be fewer than 1,000 giant pandas left in the wild. Since 1974 their bamboo forests have died out at an alarming rate: in just 14 years half the forests died. Since then conservationists have been working tirelessly to preserve the pandas' habitat.

How long does a panda take to eat lunch?

Almost all its waking hours! Giant pandas spend around 14 hours every day eating. An adult panda will eat up to 66 lb (30 kg) of bamboo in a day – this is one third of its body weight! The reason they need to eat so much is because bamboo has very little nutritional value.

How often do giant pandas have babies?

Their cubs are born only every two years, at the most. This is another reason why giant pandas are endangered, especially as many cubs die shortly after birth. Cubs are born blind, and without teeth, making them entirely dependent on their mothers.

The giant panda has special cheek teeth for crushing and slicing plant food.

What is threatening the Giant Panda?

THE SHORTAGE OF BAMBOO, WHICH IS THE PANDA'S FOOD. BAMBOO FORESTS ARE very delicate. Bamboo does not keep growing like other forest plants. When it flowers, it dies. If the bamboo in one forest is all of the same age, the whole forest will die at the same time. All the pandas living in that forest will then starve. Humans are the pandas' biggest enemies, because they have taken their land and hunted them. It is now illegal in China to harm a panda in any way, and traders risk the death penalty.

How much do giant pandas weigh?

Around 19 stone (120 kg). They have heavy bones and thick fur. It is this beautiful fur that has led to many giant pandas being slaughtered by hunters.

Giant panda

Bears have bad eyesight, so tend to hunt their prey by smell.

Do bears really like honey?
Yes they do. Many bears are expert climbers, and with their excellent sense of smell, finding a bee's nest is easy for them. Bears are omnivorous, which means they eat both meat and vegetation. They like eating other mammals, insects (even wasps, bees and termites, whose stings seem not to bother them), plants, nuts, fish, eggs, fruit, and people's picnics – if they can find them. They will also eat carrion (rotting meat) if necessary.

Spectacled bear

When is a brown bear blue?

NOT COUNTING PANDAS, THERE ARE SEVEN SPECIES OF BEAR: THE American black bear, Asian black bear, brown bear, polar bear, sloth bear, spectacled bear, and sun bear. These names are very misleading. For instance, a brown bear's coat can range in color from cream to very dark brown, and it can also look gray-blue! Black bears can also be brown and, to most people who aren't experts, two bears of the same species can look very different from one another.

Are polar bears endangered?
Polar bears live in the Arctic, the area around the North Pole. The other species of bear are found all over North and South America, parts of Europe, and Asia. They live in the mountains and lowland, in areas where food is plentiful, but they are endangered by hunters, who are after polar bear skin and meat.

Why should a bear follow its nose?
Bears often have bad eyesight, which is made up for by an excellent sense of smell. This sense is vital to the survival of the species. It warns them of danger, in the form of humans, or other predatory animals, and tells them where to find water and food.

Why are bears hunted?

For their bones, bile, and gall bladders, which are made into traditional medicines, and for their fur. Bear meat is also eaten, in particular their paws. And there are still people who hunt bears as "trophies" for sport. Most cruelly, bears are trapped to be used as dancing bears or for bear baiting.

Why do bears hibernate?

They sleep all winter because food is scarce. In summer a bear will eat continually, storing up fat to use for energy during the winter. Females need to store up very large fat reserves as their cubs are born during hibernation, and need to be fed with rich milk.

Why is a grizzly bear grizzly?

A grizzly is actually one of the many different types of brown bear. The word grizzly comes from the french word *gris*, meaning gray. When the sun catches a grizzly bear's fur, the tips of the hairs look as if they are tinged with gray.

Grizzlies are solitary animals, apart from the springtime, when males search for females to mate with.

The kodiak bear is a type of grizzly bear.

Kodiak bear

Do bears like fish?

Yes, fish makes up a large part of their diet in parts of the world where rivers are plentiful. In North America, Alaska, and Canada bears can often be seen skilfully catching enormous salmon.

Which is the biggest bear?

THE BIGGEST BEAR IN THE WORLD IS THE ENDANGERED KODIAK BEAR, a member of the brown bear species. It lives in Alaska and stands up to 10 feet (3 m) tall. It can weigh up to 704 lb (320 kg).

Grizzly bear

Which bears are most endangered?

The most endangered bear in the world is the giant panda, although all species of brown bear, the polar bear, and black bears are killed for their fur, and are under threat from fur hunters.

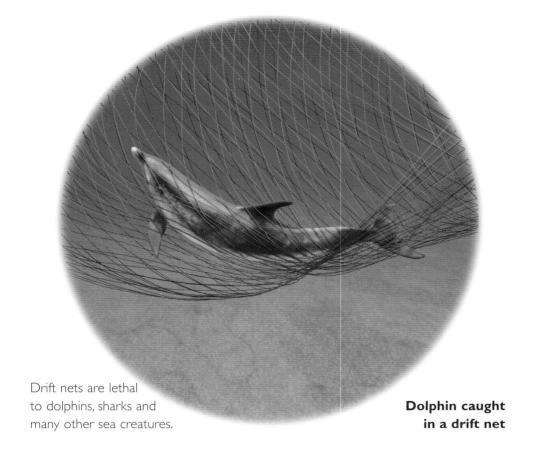

Drift nets are lethal to dolphins, sharks and many other sea creatures.

Dolphin caught in a drift net

What is a cetacean?

Cetacean is the word for all species of whale, dolphin, and porpoise. There are about 80 different species of cetacean and many, including the Indus and Ganges river dolphins, the southern right whale, and the beluga whale, are endangered. The first cetaceans lived on land, around 60 million years ago. Today they live in seas, oceans, and some rivers all over the world – but they are mammals, not fish.

What is the difference between a dolphin and a porpoise?

They are quite hard to tell apart without examining their teeth! Dolphins have teeth shaped like cones, but porpoise's teeth are spade-shaped. Porpoises are usually smaller than dolphins, and have more rounded bellies. The two groups often swim together and are extremely playful. There are endangered species within both groups, such as the vaquita porpoise and the Yangtze river dolphin.

How do drift nets kill dolphins and sharks?

Drift nets are enormous nets used for commercial fishing. They cover huge areas, often reaching right down to the sea-bed. The nets trap and kill many other sea creatures, as well as fish – especially dolphins, porpoises, sharks, and turtles. Drift nets have been banned in most countries, but are still used illegally.

Why must we save the whales?

The ecosystem of the seas is very delicate. Breaking one link in the food chain, that goes all the way from the smallest microscopic creature to the biggest whale, would have devastating effects. In 1986, the International Whaling Commission (IWC) announced a worldwide ban on whaling. Today it allows a small number of whales to be taken every year "for scientific reasons." Peoples, like the Inuit, who have always depended on whaling, are allowed to continue whaling using traditional methods.

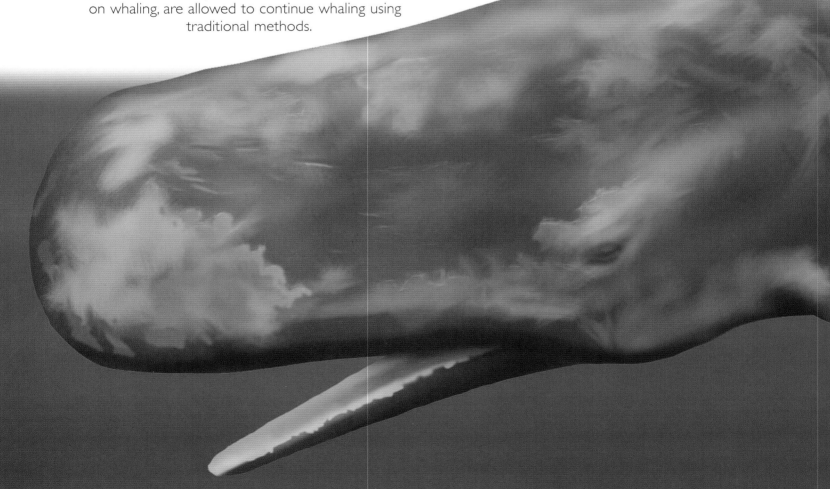

Are killer whales killers?

No. A killer whale, or orca, is unlikely to eat a person.

They prefer to eat fish, other cetaceans, and seals. In fact they are in more danger from humans than vice versa. In New Zealand an orca once tried to eat a man diving near a colony of seals. The man was wearing a shiny black wetsuit and must have looked like a sleek, tasty sea lion. When the orca realized its mistake it spat the man out and he survived!

How big is the biggest whale?

The biggest whale is the blue whale which is now officially protected to prevent its extinction. It is the largest-known mammal ever to have lived. The average length of a female is 87 feet (26.2 m); males are shorter at about 80 feet (24.1 m). The biggest recorded blue whale measured 110 feet (33 m) and weighed 160 tons.

What happens to cetaceans when people catch too many fish?

If there are not enough fish, cetaceans will starve. The more fish that are caught, the more cetaceans die. Fishermen also sometimes kill cetaceans, to stop them "stealing" their catch. Of course, overfishing is not good for fish either. It affects how the ones that are left behind reproduce and where they breed.

If too many fish are caught, the world's fish stocks could slowly die out. Cetaceans would die with them.

Which whale has a horn like a unicorn?

The narwhal, which lives in waters around the Arctic, is almost extinct. The male narwhal has a horn or tusk, which is actually a very long tooth, made of ivory. Very occasionally a narwhal has two tusks. The myth of unicorns probably began when an explorer returned to Europe with a narwhal's tusk.

A sperm whale can swim over half a mile (1 km) below the surface of the sea and hold its breath for around one hour.

Sperm whale

How do whales eat?

All dolphins and porpoises, and some whales,

have teeth. Other whales, such as the almost extinct blue whale, have baleen – this is a huge sieve, made up of hundreds of stiff blades of keratin, a type of protein like fingernails. Baleen whales sieve the microscopic shrimp-like creatures, called krill, with these tools. Toothed cetaceans, such as the endangered sperm whale, eat fish and sea creatures, such as seals, squid, and smaller cetaceans.

What sea cow is about to die out?

Sea cow is the name for both manatees and dugongs, the two remaining members of the order *Sirenia*. They were nicknamed sea cows because they graze plants that grow on the sea-bed, just as cows graze in fields. Both of these animals are so badly endangered that they are expected to be extinct by around 2020.

Are sharks related to whales?

No, a shark is a fish, and a whale is a mammal – fish are cold-blooded, and mammals are warm-blooded. The best way to tell if you are looking at a whale or a shark is that the point of a shark's tail sticks up out of the water, but a whale's tail lies flat against the surface. Whales need air to breathe, which they do through blowholes on the top of their heads, but sharks do not need air to breathe, and have gills. Hammerhead sharks, great white sharks, and the Ganges shark are just three of the long list of endangered sharks.

Did mermaids become extinct?

No! They never existed. Unlikely as it may sound, the myth of mermaids came from delirious sailors seeing sea cows! Manatees and dugongs sing in a rasping, grunting way, and sometimes sailors, suffering from a lack of food and water, mistook them for beautiful women singing with harmonious voices.

Are sea snakes poisonous?

Yes, a bite from a sea snake can kill a healthy adult in five minutes. However, unlike land snakes, sea snakes cannot dislocate their jaws, which means they usually can't open their mouths wide enough to bite you. Sea snakes are at risk of extinction, where there is pollution, and where coral reefs are breaking down due to habitat erosion.

What sea creatures are in danger?

ENDANGERED SEA CREATURES INCLUDE MANATEES, dugongs, and some turtles, seals, sharks, cetaceans, and coral (which is an animal and not a plant, as is often believed). Many creatures that live in the Mediterranean Sea, such as the green sea turtle and monk seal, are also endangered because it is the most polluted sea on earth.

Manatees like to rest on the bottom of the ocean on their backs – as if they were sunbathing!

Is the sea-horse really a horse?

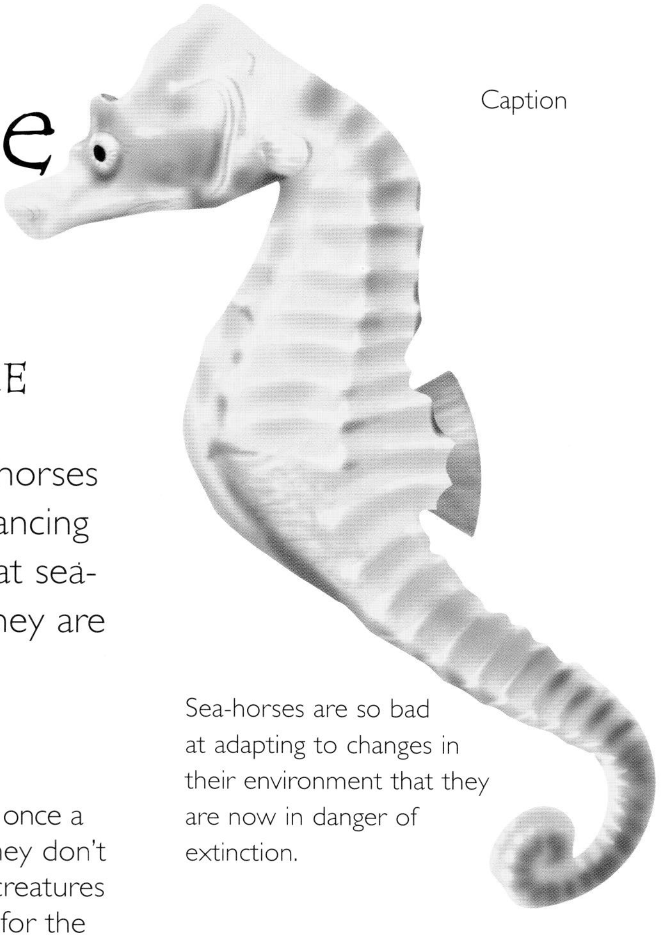

No, a sea-horse is a fish. Its name comes from its long, curved neck and head, which are shaped like a horse's. Sea-horses also swim upright, like herds of miniature horses prancing on their hind legs. Centuries ago people believed that sea-horses could grow as big as real horses, but in fact they are small, fragile creatures.

Caption

Sea-horses are so bad at adapting to changes in their environment that they are now in danger of extinction.

Why is the monk seal dying out?

The monk seal, a gray seal that lives around the Mediterranean, was once a common sight, but no longer. Fishermen kill these seals because they don't like them eating "their" fish. Many other sea creatures have become endangered for the same reason.

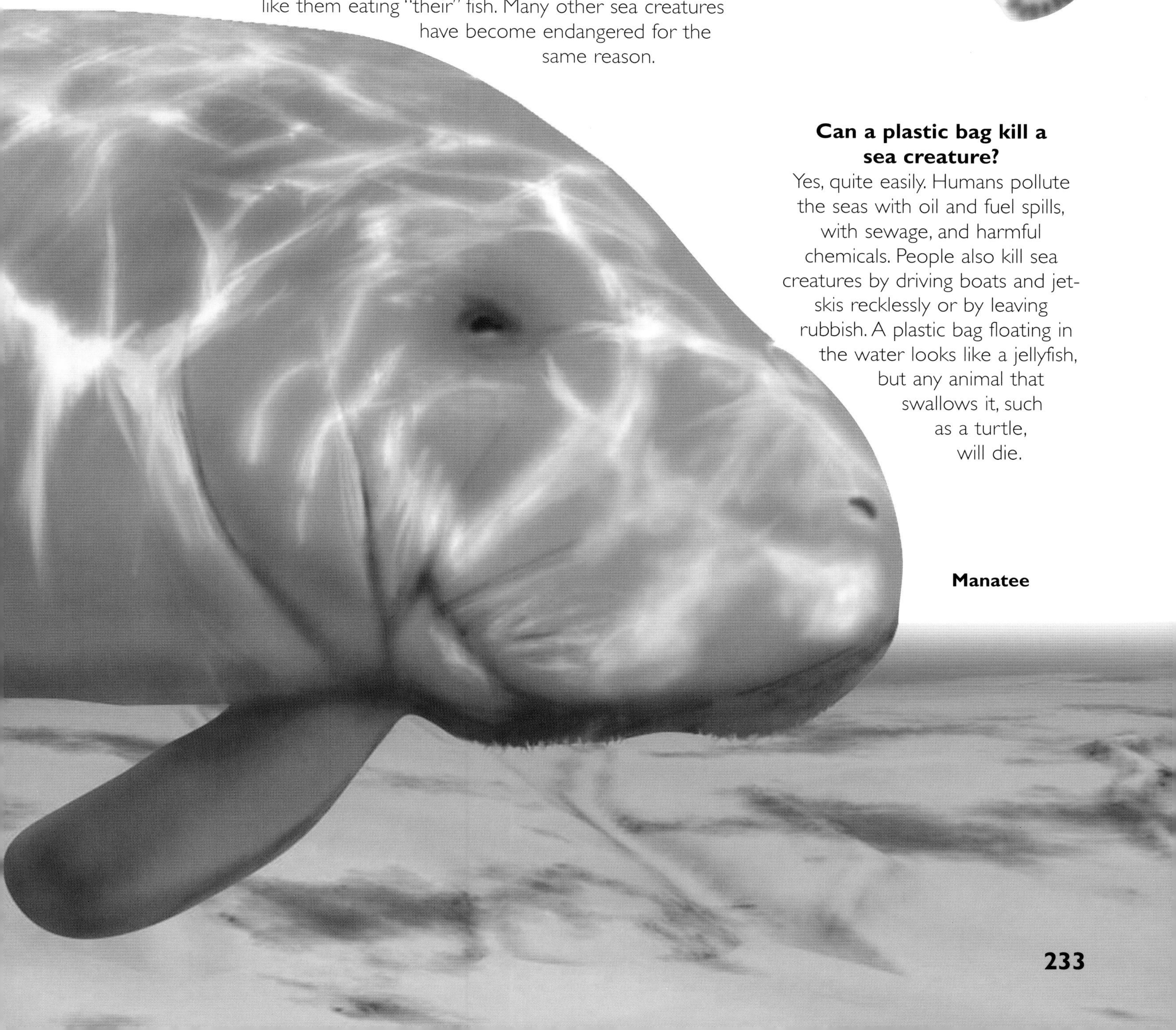

Can a plastic bag kill a sea creature?

Yes, quite easily. Humans pollute the seas with oil and fuel spills, with sewage, and harmful chemicals. People also kill sea creatures by driving boats and jet-skis recklessly or by leaving rubbish. A plastic bag floating in the water looks like a jellyfish, but any animal that swallows it, such as a turtle, will die.

Manatee

Javan rhinoceros

Rhinos have a very good sense of smell and good hearing.

Why are rhinos in danger of extinction?

Because there are so few rhinos left in the world, that just a few more years of hunting could wipe them out. An added danger is the sinister fact that, when something is in short supply, it always becomes more valuable – some poachers want to kill all rhinos just to make the rhino horn they own even more valuable.

Where does the rhinoceros get its name?

Rhino means nose, and ceros means horn – the dinosaur *Triceratops* was so-named because it had three horns. A rhinoceros's horn is a useful weapon in a fight, and scares off many predators. Horns are made of a protein called keratin (like human hair and nails), which is very hard.

Why are rhinos killed?

Unfortunately, rhinos are hunted for their horns, which many peoples believe have magical or medicinal powers. Traditional herbalists give powdered rhino horn to people suffering from fever and for use in love potions. In North Yemen rhino horns are carved to make dagger handles.

Where do rhinos live?

White and black rhinos live all over Africa. The Javan, Sumatran, and Indian rhinos, as their names suggest, live in Java, Sumatra, and India, all countries in Asia. Rhinos are also kept in zoos and safari parks all over the world. Many wildlife sanctuaries have set up rhinoceros breeding programmes, hoping to help save the species from extinction.

How many rhinos are there left in the world?

There are less than 8,500 white rhinos still living. Almost all of these are southern whites, so the northern white rhinos are extremely endangered. There are around 2,600 black rhinos; 2,050 Indian rhinos; about 400 Sumatran rhinos; and – most endangered of all – only around 70 Javan rhinos left.

What is the rhino's biggest enemy?

Big cats prey on rhinos, but they kill only a few. Humans are the reason rhinos are endangered. As well as poachers wanting their horn, farmers often shoot rhinos to stop them eating or trampling their crops. Previously, rhinos were also shot as "trophies" by big-game hunters.

Black rhinoceros

What is being done to help rhinos?

Where rhinos are found there are also specially trained guards. Obviously they can't be with the animals all the time, but they track them and make sure they know where the groups are. In many parts of the world, conservationists tranquilize rhinos and saw off their horns. This is not painful – it is like us cutting our hair or nails. Conservationists hope that if a rhino has no horn, the poachers will not kill it.

Does the rhino have any extinct relations?

THERE ARE FIVE SPECIES OF RHINO: WHITE, BLACK, SUMATRAN, JAVAN, and Indian and they are all endangered. Thousands and thousands of years ago the rhino had a great many more relations – there was even a woolly rhino, with a similar coat to the woolly mammoth – but these are all now extinct.

The black rhinoceros has no hair on its body and a very thick skin or hide.

What is happening to the rhinos' habitat?

Many Asian rhinos are endangered because their habitat – the rainforest – has been cut down for timber. This is a worldwide problem, as most rainforest countries are also poor countries, that need to sell their resources. In Africa, the savannah (grassland), where the rhinos live, is often under threat of drought.

Where do elephants live?

As their names suggest, African elephants live in Africa – in countries such as Kenya, Zimbabwe, South Africa, and Tanzania. Asian elephants live, of course, in Asia – in Nepal, India, Sri Lanka, and Thailand. Both species are able to survive, in either tropical forests, or savannah (grassland) areas.

African elephants are larger than Asian elephants.

African elephant

Which elephant ancestor became extinct 11,000 years ago?
In the past there were many species of elephant and their relatives. One was the woolly mammoth, which died out about 11,000 years ago. Its coat was so warm, it lived as far north as Britain. Today the elephants' closest relation is a small mammal, the hyrax, which is the size of a little dog!

How do elephants communicate?
To warn of danger – perhaps hunters after ivory – elephants make a trumpeting sound. They are very affectionate creatures and often walk along with their trunks touching another member of the group – mothers and their babies especially.

What happens to elephants in captivity?
Male elephants can become very aggressive, which is how they react in the wild, if threatened. Wild elephants cover enormous distances in a single day's walking, so keeping them in an enclosure – even one that seems big to us – can make an elephant extremely unhappy. The stress they suffer can shorten their lifespan and affect breeding.

How heavy is a baby elephant?
At birth, baby Asian elephants weigh about 440 lb (200 kg); baby African elephants are heavier, at around 581 lb (264 kg). This may seem very heavy, but the babies have a long way to go to reach the average adult weight of 4 tons.

Can elephants cry?
Many people, who know elephants well, are sure that they do cry. Zoologists often say that elephants' tears have nothing to do with sadness, but people have often seen elephants cry when they find a dead elephant. Others report that circus elephants cry when they are cruelly treated.

Why do people kill elephants?

Some people kill them because they threaten their homes and crops; but more often they are killed for their tusks, which are made of ivory. Ivory was used in the past for making white chess pieces, carved ornaments, piano keys, and even false teeth! Today it is against international law to sell ivory, but many traders still manage to make a fortune from selling it illegally.

Asian elephant

Asian elephants are often dressed in colourful materials to take part in Indian ceremonies.

What can be done to save the elephants?

The ban on selling ivory needs to be enforced, so that poachers and traders can be caught and punished. The elephants' habitat also needs to be protected. In recent years, conservationists have begun to study new ways of coping with elephants as neighbors. And electronic tracking devices have been fixed to high-risk elephants, so that rangers can monitor them.

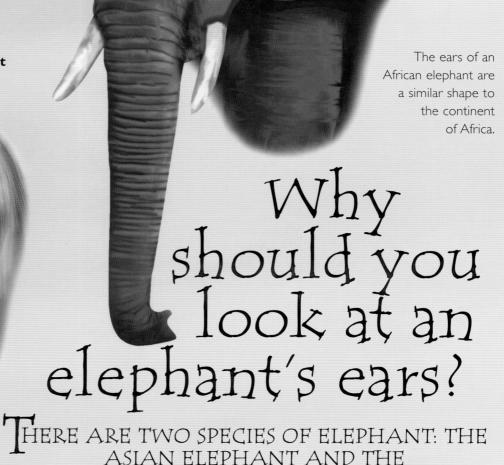

African elephant

The ears of an African elephant are a similar shape to the continent of Africa.

Why should you look at an elephant's ears?

THERE ARE TWO SPECIES OF ELEPHANT: THE ASIAN ELEPHANT AND THE African elephant, and both are endangered. The easiest way to tell them apart is by their ears – those of an Asian elephant are smaller. It is sometimes said that the ears of an African elephant are a similar shape to the continent of Africa. Another difference between the two is their tusks: both male and female African elephants have tusks; whereas only male Asian elephants have them (and these are sometimes very small).

What is the elephant's worst enemy?

People. Healthy elephants have no natural predators, apart from humans – their weight, strength, and habit of living in large herds protect them from packs of hunting animals. The herd will usually stay with a wounded elephant, keeping away scavengers such as big cats. Baby elephants are equally fiercely protected.

The iriomote looks very similar to a domestic cat.

Iriomote cat

Which big cats are endangered?

MANY BIG CATS ARE ENDANGERED BY HUNTERS, BECAUSE OF THE BEAUTY of their skin. Hunters can get rich selling the pelts (skins) of slaughtered big cats (such as the ocelot), to people who make fur coats. Some hunters still kill big cats for sport. Many big cats, such as the mountain lion, are also threatened with the loss of their habitat, which is destroyed by developers, or by wars. The most endangered big cats are: mountain lion, tiger, snow leopard (also called an ounce), jaguar, ocelot, clouded leopard, iriomote, and cheetah.

Are big cats related to domestic cats?

Yes, they are. All cats are of the order *Carnivora* (meat-eaters) and the family *Felidae* (felines). The domestic cat has much in common with the tiger, and its large relations. They hunt in similar ways and they all eat meat, but unlike their relations, they are not endangered.

What is big and lazy?

The male lion is the biggest of the cat family, weighing about 528 lb (240 kg). Despite his size, he does little work, leaving the hunting and killing of his food, and the raising of cubs, to the lioness. Lions can sleep for up to 20 hours a day. All lions are on the list of endangered animals.

Do lions climb trees to escape danger?

No. They often climb trees to look out over the surrounding land, to search for prey and to sleep, protected from the sun. Lions will not climb trees after a big meal, as they eat so much at one time that they need several hours to digest their prey.

Tiger

Tigers are unusual cats because they like water.

Do big cats mate for life?

No. A male cat may have more than one mate at a time, and females may mate with a different male, from one season to the next. Males live alone or with one or more females. They can't live together, as they fight over territory and females.

Snow leopard

Leopards often live close to towns and villages.

Are white tigers and Siberian tigers extinct?

Nearly. The Siberian tiger is paler than most other tigers, but still orange-brown in color. Truly white tigers are extremely rare. They are not a distinct species of tiger, as any species can produce a white cub.

Which speedy animal is endangered?

The cheetah. It can run up to 62 mph (100 kph). It can't keep up its speed over a long distance, but runs this fast in short bursts. Both the African and Indian cheetah are endangered.

Where do big cats live?

Mostly in Africa, but also in Asia and the Americas. Both African and Asian lions are at risk. There are even some medium-sized cats in Europe – one is the European lynx, which is at risk from habitat erosion and hunting.

When did the first cats live?

The first known cats lived 35 million years ago. They were the ancestors of two feline families. One produced all today's cats (big and small), the other was the sabre-toothed family. The last sabre-toothed tiger died out several thousand years ago.

Which cats are the big cats?

LIONS, TIGERS, CHEETAHS, LEOPARDS (INCLUDING PANTHERS), COUGARS (also called pumas), and jaguars are all big cats and animals from each group are endangered. There are also medium-sized cats, such as ocelots and lynxes, that are endangered. These are too big to be counted as wild cats, but too small to be called big cats. Both the Texas ocelot and the Spanish lynx are endangered.

How small is the smallest bat?

The smallest bat is the pipistrelle. They weigh between just 0.15 and 0.25 oz (4–7 g). From head to tail, they measure 1–2 in (35–45 mm), and their wingspan measures 7–11 in (190–260 mm). The Myanmar pipistrelle is on the "critical" list of endangered animals.

Are bats really blind?

No, they aren't. However, their hearing is more highly developed than their sight, as they rely mainly on sound for catching their food. As bats are mainly nocturnal (active at night), hearing is more important to them than seeing.

How many species of bat are there?

There are 951 species of bat, divided into 19 scientific families, and all of them are in danger of extinction. All these make up one scientific order, *Chiroptera*.

Where do bats live?

Bats can be found all over the world, in Asia, Australasia, the Americas, Africa, and Europe. The only places bats would not be found are at the Poles. They live in a variety of habitats, such as buildings, caves, and forests. They often spend the nights in towns, searching for food, but will usually return to their roost before dawn. Loss of habitat is one of the main reasons why so many bat species, such as the Seychelles seath-tailed bat, and the cusp-toothed flying fox from the Solomon Islands, are endangered.

When is a fox not a fox?

A FLYING FOX IS ACTUALLY A FRUIT BAT, A VEGETARIAN BAT THAT FEEDS mainly on fruit. Many fruit bats, such as Bulmer's fruit bat from Papua New Guinea, are endangered. One of these species, the colugo bat, is also known as the Philippine flying lemur. The largest flying fox's wingspan can measure up to 3 feet (1 m). Fruit bats live in warm parts of the world, such as Australia, Africa, the Pacific islands and Asia.

Flying fox

Is a bat really a bird?

No, unlike birds, bats are mammals, which means they have hair, or fur, and give birth to live young, rather than laying eggs. They also suckle their young, whereas baby birds are weaned from the moment they hatch. Bats are unique animals because they are the only mammals that can really fly.

How do bats find their way in the dark?

By using echolocation. This means that they make high-pitched sounds that echo from their surroundings. By listening to the echo, the bat can work out the shape and density of its surroundings and find food. Echolocation is also used by dolphins, porpoises, and whales.

Do vampires really exist?

Vampire bats are the only real vampires. There are three species of vampire bat, all of which live in South and Central America. These species feed on the blood of livestock, such as cattle, sheep, or pigs. Vampire bats are quite small and, although their bites leave distinctive marks, they don't usually kill the animals they feed on. But if the bat is carrying a disease, such as rabies, its bite can be fatal. Vampire bats are endangered because people are afraid of them, and tend to kill them as pests.

Horseshoe bat

The horseshoe bat has a horseshoe-shaped flap on its nose.

The flying fox is so-called because it has a fox-like face.

Why are bats endangered?

LIKE MANY OTHER CREATURES BATS, SUCH AS THE HORSESHOE BAT, ARE threatened by developers and farmers who destroy their habitat. They are also in danger from the growing number of people who enjoy caving and potholing, and the common practice of cutting down old trees. Bats that live on fruit or insects, such as the Philippines tube-nosed fruit bat, are endangered by the use of pesticides.

How can people help bats?

Many people are frightened of bats. They feature in horror stories, because they are night creatures, and fly in a jagged way that can seem spooky. The best way of helping bats is to explain to people that they are harmless. Bats are very clean and do not attack people. People who realize that bats need friends sometimes put up bat boxes for them to nest in. These are like bird nesting boxes and they allow bats to roost and hibernate in peace.

Gray squirrel

Are rats related to squirrels?

Yes, they are both mammals, called rodents. The rodent family (scientific name *Rodentia*) includes rats, mice, dormice, beavers, porcupines, and squirrels. Many of them, such as the lesser-toothed small rat and the common fieldmouse, are endangered. They all have strong front teeth (incisors), which they use to slice through vegetation, such as strong grasses and tree bark – and beavers even saw through tree trunks. Like other mammals, rodents are warm-blooded and give birth to live young, which they feed with mother's milk.

How do beavers build dams?

Beavers can cut down trees by biting through the trunk. Then they gnaw them into pieces and drag the logs to the water to build a dam. They lay the logs across each other and stop up any gaps with stones and mud. Beavers are severely endangered due to logging in Canada and North America.

Most squirrels only live for one to two years.

Did gray squirrels kill off red squirrels ?

Squirrels have very strong front paws for gripping their food.

No. THE RED SQUIRREL WAS THE ONLY SQUIRREL LIVING IN THE UK UNTIL the gray squirrel was brought in from the USA. When red squirrels started to disappear, many people thought gray squirrels were killing them. But now scientists believe that the red squirrel was endangered by other predators, such as stoats, foxes and eagles. A highly contagious disease also killed vast numbers of red squirrels, in the first half of the 20th century. Gray squirrels are larger and more hardy than red squirrels, so have survived better.

Are badgers related to weasels?

Yes! Badgers are a member of the weasel family, and so are stoats. They are all mammals, but weasels and stoats are carnivorous, which means they eat only meat, whereas badgers are omnivorous, which means they eat plant food as well as meat. Badgers are protected by law because they were in danger of extinction in the mid-20th century, from badger baiting (where dogs are used to kill badgers for sport).

How sleepy are dormice?

Dormice are said to be very sleepy creatures, but in fact they don't sleep for long periods every day. Like many mammals (including squirrels and bears) they hibernate in winter. They go to sleep in October and wake up in April. They wake up from time to time in winter, to eat food that they have stored up during the summer months. Dormice are endangered by pollution and pesticides as well as development.

Which small mammals are endangered?

Many small mammals, such as beavers in the USA and the red squirrel in Europe, are endangered because their habitat is being destroyed by humans developing land for building and farming. Others, such as weasels, are poisoned by dangerous chemicals used in industry and farming.

Otter

Otters bark and chirp to communicate.

Red squirrel

Where do otters live?

IN EUROPE, ASIA, AND THE AMERICAS. OTTERS NEED UNPOLLUTED WATER and they live wherever the water is pure — in streams, canals, and lakes, in mountainous regions as well as in valleys. Many otters are endangered because habitat destruction has caused them to starve, or because they cannot find unpolluted water.

Are rabbits or hares endangered?

Most species of rabbits and hares breed, well, like rabbits, and are not endangered! But a few species, such as the omilteme cottontail rabbit from Mexico and the Sumatran short-eared rabbit from Asia, are endangered because people are destroying their habitat. In many countries, such as Australia, rabbits are killed as pests.

Are any small mammals already extinct?

Yes. Scientists have found fossilized remains of several small mammals that died out many centuries ago, such as the macaca (monkey-like) and the leithia (a dormouse-like animal). Unfortunately many more small mammals may die out because of the destruction of their habitat — particularly animals that live in the rainforests, which are being destroyed by large-scale farming.

What is the world's rarest bird?

BRAZIL'S SPIX MACAW. THERE IS ONLY ONE MALE LEFT IN THE WILD. Almost as rare is New Zealand's kakapo, of which there are only a few pairs left. Endangered birds include several birds of prey, shot as pests by farmers, and exotic birds, such as the flightless notornis, hunted by traders.

Why are people the birds' worst enemies?
People destroy birds' habitat by cutting down forests and draining marshland. A bird can die if it swallows a fishing hook, or fishing line, or rubbish that could injure or choke it. People sometimes steal birds' eggs, but if they disturb or look in nests, parent birds will leave their chicks to die. Exotic birds, such as parrots, pheasants, hummingbirds, eagles, and birds of paradise, are trapped to be sold as pets and often die while being transported. They are also killed for their beautiful feathers, or to be stuffed.

Kakapo

How can we count the birds?
We can't! There are birds in every continent of the world, and it is impossible to say definitely how many species exist. Even today, scientists are constantly discovering new species.

Where do budgies come from?
Budgies, or budgerigars, are native to Australia, where flocks of them can be seen flying wild. Their name comes from an aboriginal word meaning colored bird. They are a member of the parakeet family – which also includes parrots, cockatiels, cockatoos and lorikeets. Most wild budgerigars are green and yellow and they are at risk from hunters who shoot them as pests, or capture them to sell to the pet trade.

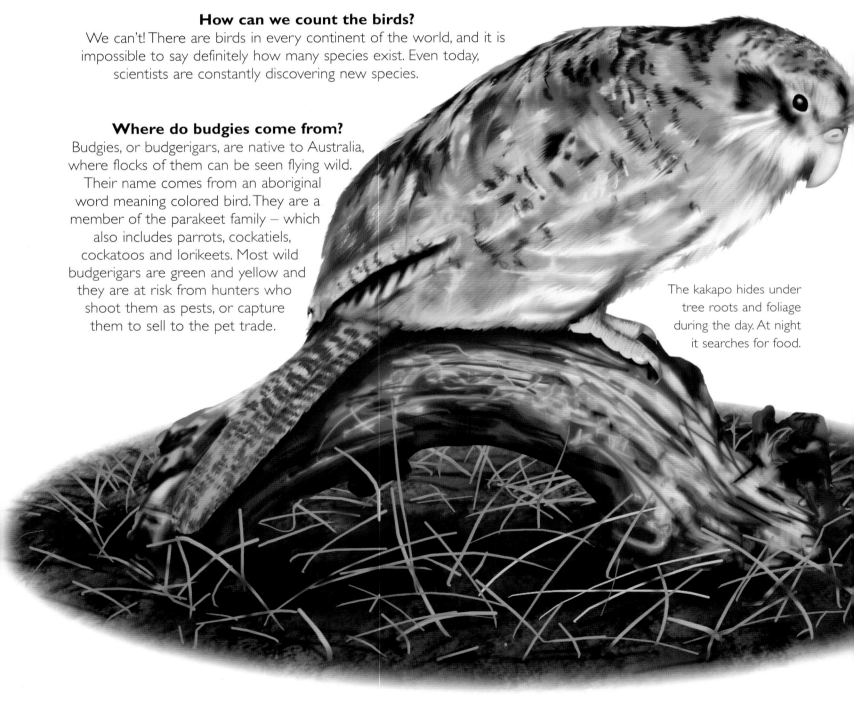

The kakapo hides under tree roots and foliage during the day. At night it searches for food.

Do crop pesticides harm birds?
Yes. Birds that eat sprayed crops, such as budgerigars and lapwings, can die from poisoning. Farm chemicals also pollute rivers and marshes and destroy water birds, such as the Jamaica petrel and the crested ibis from Africa, and their habitat.

Which are the biggest and smallest birds of prey?
The Andean condor is the largest bird of prey, with a wingspan of more than 10 feet (3 m). The smallest birds of prey are pygmy falcons. Some are only 6 in (15 cm) long. Both of these birds are endangered by loss of habitat.

Californian condors

The Californian condor only lays one egg when it breeds and it doesn't breed until it is six years old.

Are any birds extinct?
Yes. Some – such as the *Archaeopteryx* – died out with the dinosaurs. Others have been hunted to extinction more recently. Perhaps the most famous extinct bird is the dodo, which lived on the island of Mauritius and was finally killed off by hungry sailors.

Which endangered bird has the largest wingspan?
The wedge-tailed eagle, which can be found in Australasia, has a wingspan of up to 6 feet (1.8 m). From head to foot, the wedge-tailed eagle can reach a height of just over 3 feet (1 m).

What is a bird of prey?
THIS GROUP OF BIRDS INCLUDES EAGLES, FALCONS, HAWKS, AND OWLS. WHERE as most birds exist on a diet of small insects, nuts, and seeds, a bird of prey eats other birds and animals. Birds of prey have sharp, flexible talons (claws), used for grabbing their prey and for killing it. They also have hooked beaks for tearing and ripping at flesh. Because they are such beautiful creatures they are often hunted, to be kept and trained as pets. The Californian condor is one huge bird of prey that is endangered.

Quiz questions

SEA CREATURES

1. Whereabouts does the carpet shark live in the sea?

2. Which long, thin fish hides in seaweed?

3. Which fish lives in swamps and muddy areas?

4. What does the torpedo ray use to kill its prey?

5. Which crab doesn't have a shell of its own?

6. Which fish can change its color to match its surroundings?

7. How often does a crab usually shed its shell?

8. Is coral a plant or an animal?

9. Which fish lashes out with a sharp tail?

10. Which Australian jellyfish is deadly poisonous?

11. Can crocodiles ever live in the sea?

12. What is the largest animal on earth?

POLAR ANIMALS

1. Which gray bear hibernates in winter?

2. What large mammals do polar bears like to eat?

3. Which butterfly can survive the polar weather?

4. Which fish has nearly see-through skin?

5. Which whale looks like a unicorn?

6. Which sea creature's bones were used to make brushes and umbrellas?

7. Which duck's feathers are popular for filling quilts?

8. What do crabeater seals eat?

9. What do snowy owls like to feed on?

10. How many chicks does an albatross raise in one year?

11. How deep can a penguin dive?

BIRDS

1. What do birds use to navigate on long-distance flights?

2. Which bird was worshipped by the ancient Aztecs?

3. Why do some birds have an egg tooth?

4. Which birds leave their young in other birds' nests?

5. What do male peacocks use their colorful tail feathers for?

6. Which bird eats the chicks of other birds?

7. Which vitamin is found in the oil on birds' feathers?

8. Why do birds use echolocation?

9. Which is the fastest bird on earth?

10. Which Mauritian bird is now extinct?

11. Who was the Egyptian bird-god of wisdom?

12. Which birds were trained to hunt other birds?

Quiz answers

SEA CREATURES
1. On the sea-bed
2. The pipefish
3. The mudskipper
4. Electricity
5. The hermit crab
6. The plaice
7. Once a year
8. An animal
9. The surgeon fish
10. The sea wasp jellyfish
11. Yes
12. The blue whale

POLAR ANIMALS
1. The grizzly bear
2. Ringed seals
3. The Arctic clouded yellow butterfly
4. The icefish
5. The narwhal
6. Whales
7. Eider ducks
8. Krill
9. Lemmings
10. Two
11. 850 feet (260 metres)

REPTILES
1. The saltwater crocodile
2. St. Patrick
3. Flies
4. Two years
5. Baby reptiles use them to break out of their egg when they hatch
6. 65 million years ago
7. Scales on a crocodile's body
8. No
9. At least 2,500
10. The anaconda
11. No

BIRDS
1. The position of the sun, stars and recognizable landmarks
2. The quetzal
3. To break out of the egg when they hatch
4. Cuckoos
5. To attract mates and defend their territory
6. The jay
7. Vitamin D
8. To avoid flying into things in the dark
9. The ostrich
10. The dodo
11. Thoth
12. Falcons

REPTILES

1. **What is the world's heaviest reptile?**

2. **Which saint sent all the snakes away from Ireland?**

3. **What is the gecko's favorite food?**

4. **What is the longest a snake can go without food?**

5. **What are egg caruncles for?**

6. **When did the dinosaurs die out?**

7. **What are osteoderms?**

8. **Do lizards live in the Antarctic?**

9. **How many different kinds of lizard are there?**

10. **Which is the heaviest snake?**

11. **Do snakes have ears?**

Quiz questions

CREEPY CRAWLIES

1. Which spider's bite can cause heart failure and breathing problems?

2. Where does the dust mite like to live?

3. How long is the largest centipede?

4. What is the aardvark's favorite food?

5. Would ants attack humans?

6. How do bees know where to find good pollen sources?

7. How big did dragonflies grow 280 million years ago?

8. Where are a cricket's ears?

9. Which is the most common flea today?

10. When do ladybirds bleed from their legs?

11. What is the name of the 'skin' that covers the snail's body in its shell?

DESERT ANIMALS

1. Which desert foxes use their large ears to keep cool?

2. When are deserts cold?

3. Which American desert cactus is poisonous?

4. What protects the sand cat's feet from the hot desert sand?

5. What method does the king snake use to kill its prey?

6. How fast can a cheetah run?

7. Which snake can blind a human with its spit?

8. Where does the shingleback lizard live?

9. What do budgerigars eat?

10. What is special about a camel's eyelids?

11. How does a scorpion detect movement?

12. Is the echidna (spiny anteater) a mammal or a reptile?

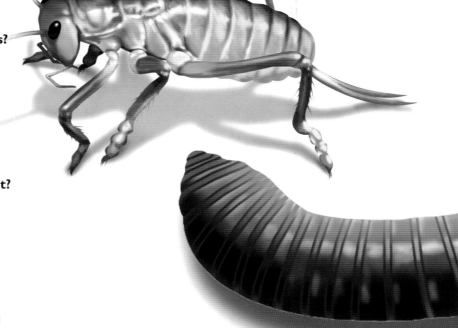

Quiz answers

CREEPY CRAWLIES
1. The Australian Sydney funnel-web spider
2. In beds and mattresses
3. 13 inches (33 cm)
4. Termites
5. Yes
6. Other bees show them by their movements in a special dance
7. About the size of a small dog
8. On its legs
9. The cat flea
10. When they are attacked
11. The mantle

DESERT ANIMALS
1. The fennec fox and the kit fox
2. Deserts are often very cold at night
3. The saguaro cactus
4. Hair
5. Suffocation
6. 62 mph (100 kph)
7. The red cobra
8. Australia
9. Seeds
10. They are thin enough to see through if the camel shuts its eyes
11. By feeling vibrations which are picked up by hair on its legs
12. Mammal

JUNGLE ANIMALS
1. Nocturnal
2. Spit
3. Termites and other insects
4. To scare other males away from their territory
5. As big as 5 feet (1.5 m) across
6. A woody bump
7. They are actually overgrown canine teeth
8. Around 400
9. The rapid beating of its wings as it hovers
10. The cicada
11. To stop them from being stung by ants
12. There are said to be under 40,000

ENDANGERED ANIMALS
1. Silverbacks
2. Anthropoids
3. The pygmy marmoset
4. Arachnophobia
5. Dolphins
6. The Mediterranean
7. Asian
8. No, they give birth to live young
9. Warm-blooded
10. If something is omnivorous it eats both meat and plants

JUNGLE ANIMALS

1. What is the word used to describe creatures that only come out at night?

2. What do termites use to glue their wooden towers together?

3. What do elephant shrews like to eat?

4. Why do orangutans burp?

5. How big are the webs of the orb-weaver spiders?

6. What does a leaf-tailed gecko try to look like?

7. What is unusual about a wild boar's tusks?

8. How many types of poisonous snake are there?

9. What is it that makes the humming sound of a hummingbird?

10. What is the loudest insect in the rainforest?

11. Why do antbirds have feather ruffs around their heads?

12. How many mountain gorillas are left in the wild?

ENDANGERED ANIMALS

1. What are male gorillas called?

2. What is the term used to describe animals who share similarities with humans?

3. Which is the smallest monkey?

4. What is the fear of spiders called?

5. Which are bigger: porpoises or dolphins?

6. Which is the most polluted sea on earth?

7. Do African or Asian elephants have the biggest ears?

8. Do bats lay eggs?

9. Are rodents cold-blooded or warm-blooded?

10. What does omnivorous mean?

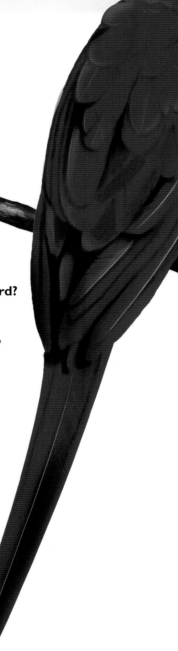

Index

A

acacia ants 134
addax antelopes 161, 163
adders 100, 108, 124
Adelie penguins 90, 91
aestivation 159
African fish eagles 50
African hornbills 49
African weavers 44, 45
albatrosses 38, 40, 41, 88, 89, 94
algae 13
alligator snapping turtles 112
alligators 98, 101, 108, 114, 196, 215
ammonites 79
anacondas 121, 215
angelfish 8
anglerfish 12, 13, 21, 32
anole lizards 107
ant lions 167, 185
Antarctica
        birds 86—7
        camouflage 70
        keeping warm 69
        minibeasts 76
        penguins 90, 95
        seas 78, 79
antbirds 211
antelope squirrels 171
antelopes 104, 161, 163, 166
ants 116, 120, 132, 133, 134—5, 172, 190, 200, 208
aphids 135, 141, 146
arachnids 224, 225
Archaeopteryx 52
archerfish 13
Arctic
        birds 84—7, 92, 94
        camouflage 70, 71
        keeping warm 68, 69
        minibeasts 76, 77
        seas 78, 79
Arctic foxes 68, 69, 74, 84
Arctic Ocean 71, 72
Arctic terns 43, 87
argus pheasants 210
armor 107, 112, 115
arrow-poison frogs 202, 203, 207
assassin bugs 140
auks 56
avocets 65
aye-ayes 196

B

baby reptiles 108
bactrian camels 159, 175
badgers 242
bald eagles 39, 44, 64
bandicoots 56
barn owls 45, 53, 58
barracudas 12
basilisk lizards 119, 205
basking crocodiles 115
basking sharks 28
bats 190, 197, 240—41
beaded lizards 116
beaked sea snakes 122
bears 227, 228—9, 243
beavers 242, 243
bed-bugs 141
bee hummingbirds 41, 45
bees 124, 136, 137, 139, 146, 190, 196, 228
beetles 118, 139, 148—9, 160, 168, 170, 182, 203, 209, 212
bellbirds 195
beluga whales 80, 240
big-headed turtles 113
bird-eating spiders 128, 214
birds 69, 84—9, 115, 158, 163, 165, 166, 167, 172, 173, 176, 177, 182, 184, 185, 186, 190, 192, 194, 195, 201, 203, 205, 206, 207, 210, 214, 244—5
birds of paradise 49, 207, 244
birds of prey 245
black bears 228, 229
black garden ants 135
black howler monkeys 195
black rhinoceroses 234, 235
black spitting cobras 122
black storks 47
black swallowers 21
black widow spiders 129
black-backed jackals 223
blackbirds 43
blind snakes 120
blowflies 147
blubber 69, 80, 91
blue whales 24, 34, 80, 81, 231
blue-ringed octopuses 22
bluebottles 146
bluetits 40, 62
boa constrictors 121
boars 201
body fat 86
body temperatures 101
bolas spiders 129
boll weevils 149
bombardier beetles 149, 203

bone cave harvestmen 225
boobies 41
bower birds 48
bowhead whales 80
box jellyfish 23
box turtles 113
Brachiosaurus 110
brain power 99
Brant geese 94
brimstone butterflies 150
brown bears 228, 229
bubble-netting 31
budgerigars 173, 184, 235, 244
bugs 141
bumblebees 136, 137, 146
burrow-dwellers 158, 159, 160, 163, 166, 168, 176
burrowing owls 168
burying beetles 224
bushbabies 220
bushmasters 192
butterfish 17
butterflies 77, 113, 150, 151, 198, 199, 200, 208, 215, 224

C

cacti 104, 105
cactus wrens 177
caimans 114
camel spiders 179
camels 159, 160, 163, 175
camouflage 9, 19, 20, 33, 70—71, 98, 106, 118
Canada 87
capercaillies 49
capybaras 214
caracals 165, 166
caribou 69, 70, 71, 72, 74, 75, 76, 92, 94
carpet beetles 148
carpet sharks 9
cassowaries 56, 57, 192
caterpillars 201
catfish 34, 35
cats 113, 165, 166, 170, 238—9
cattle egrets 62
cave swiftlets 45, 54
centipedes 131, 203
cetaceans 230, 231, 232
chaffinches 43, 47
chameleons 104, 118, 181, 199
cheetahs 167, 238, 239
chimeras 26
chinstrap penguins 90, 91
chuckwalla lizards 117, 168, 181
cicadas 140, 207
cinnabar moths 151
clams 19, 25

U

V

W

XYZ